METHODOLOGICAL PRAGMATISM

METHODOLOGICAL PRAGMATISM

A Systems–Theoretic Approach
to the Theory of Knowledge

NICHOLAS RESCHER

New York · New York University Press · 1977

Published in the USA by New York University Press

Library of Congress Catalog Card Number: 76-54605

ISBN: 0-8147-7371-0

Printed in Great Britain

For four philosophical colleagues
With whose views I sometimes disagree
But from whose writings I have drawn much profit
And whose workmanship I always admire
  Lewis White Beck
  Roderick Chisholm
  Max Fisch
  Stephan Körner

CONTENTS

PREFACE

This book revolves about the problem of the *legitimation* of factual knowledge regarding what goes on in the world. It addresses itself to the question: What sort of legitimative backing does our "knowledge" in this area have—how can we tell that what we *claim* to know about the world is actually *genuine* knowledge? This issue is not the definitional one (What is "knowledge"?), not the historical one (How did we come by the knowledge we have?), and not the evidential one (On what sort of evidence does this or that type of knowledge-claim rest?). Rather, it is the issue of *rational warrant*: What sort of rationale is at work to entitle our claims to *knowledge* to this proud title? It is, in short, the central question of the mainstream of Western epistemological tradition, that of cognitive rationality.

The aspirations of the book are ambitious. It seeks a fundamentally new way of exploiting the basic ideas of pragmatism in the interests of epistemology. Whether—and to what extent—these ambitions are realized is a question on which the reader must make up his own mind. There are no doubt many slips between the cup of achievement and the lip of aspiration.

This book is the third and final member of my "Pragmatic Idealism" trilogy, its companions in this triad being *Conceptual Idealism* (Oxford: Basil Blackwell, 1973) and *The Primacy of Practice* (Oxford: Basil Blackwell, 1973). Though I myself view the book less as a culmination than as a basis for further work—because it has brought me to the threshhold of various further problems—still, it does represent a completion in one direction. For it develops in considerable amplitude the pragmatic approach that underlies and links the idealist metaphysic of *Conceptual Idealism* with the coherentist epistemology of *The Coherence Theory of Truth* (Oxford: The Clarendon Press, 1973). The present discussion thus rounds off the exposition of the cognitive pragmatism that was initially adumbrated in my sect. 8 of Pt. III of my *Scientific Explanation* (New York: The Free Press, 1970), and developed in the opening chapters of *The Primacy of Practice*.

The book accordingly brings to a stage of at least rough-hewn completeness the project of expounding in fuller and more persuasive detail the specifically *methodological* pragmatism mooted in these earlier works, a pragmatism whose guiding idea is a specifically method-oriented conception of the linkage between affective/behavioral and cognitive/theoretical rationality.

A word about the tendency of a *pragmatic* idealism is in order. The difference between a *pure* idealism and its contraries turns on the question of whether the truth about the world is accessible to an inquiring intelligence proceeding wholly through its *own* resources, or whether the content of such knowledge is constrained by an external and independent reality wholly outside the cognitive domain and (for the most part) indifferent to it. On this issue, a *pragmatic* idealism is not pure: it recognizes the shaping of our knowledge as subject to mind-external constraints, but takes these constraints to manifest themselves wholly or predominantly on the side of *praxis*. It is this sort of an idealism that I have tried to expound in the trilogy completed in this volume.

A large-scale effort in philosophy is pretty much bound to see itself as representing in some degree an outgrowth of the work of certain preceding thinkers—precursors on whose shoulders one must stand in this as in any other field of inquiry. But rather strange bedfellows come together in the book: the Academic Sceptics as regards their rejection of immediate knowledge, Hegel and the neo-Hegelians in regard to the centrality of system and coherence, Peirce, James and their congeners in regard to pragmatism, Kant as regards a "Copernican Inversion" with respect to truth, Darwin and the whole tribe of neo-Darwinian cognitivists in regard to evolutionary epistemology, C. I. Lewis and W. V. Quine as regards latter-day pragmatic tendencies of thought. This list could be prolonged, but it suffices for the main point. Like most ventures in philosophy, the present work endeavors to pour new wine into old bottles.

One of the inevitable drawbacks of producing a systematic work in philosophy that runs through different books each of which aims at a reasonable measure of self-sufficiency and self-containment—rather than publishing a single great monster—is that one cannot avoid letting each book overlap to some extent with some others. (After all, it is important in the nature of a *system* that its several parts put forth hooks to link them to the rest.) Thus roughly one-seventh of the present book is redundant with earlier publications. I state this by way of information rather than apology, because there is, in the very nature of things, no way of avoiding this circumstance: remove such overlaps and one removes a crucial part of what makes the argument of the book a cohesive whole.

Work on the final chapters of the volume was aided by a grant from the National Science Foundation for 1974–1975 (Grant No. GS–43160). And the coherentist ideas of Chapter VII were worked out in the course of another NSF-supported research project during 1973–1974 (Grant No. GS–37883). I am grateful to the Foundation for this support. William C. House served as my research assistant while I was working on this material, and offered comments and *corrigenda* for which I thank him. During the Fall Term of 1974 I gave at the University of Pittsburgh a series of public lectures based on a draft version of this book. I am indebted to the participants in this series for helpful discussions—especially to Professors William C. Harper and John Haugeland. I also wish to thank Mrs. Kathleen Reznik for the competence and patience with which she steered the typescript through the seemingly endless sequence of its revisions, and to thank Ms. Barbara Hill for her help with the proofreading.

PITTSBURGH
December 1974

Chapter I

THE GENERAL STRUCTURE OF INSTRUMENTAL JUSTIFICATION

1. AIMS AND OBJECTIVES

This book seeks to exploit the fundamental ideas of the pragmatic theory of truth in giving a systems-theoretic treatment of the rationale of knowledge. It proposes to view the pursuit of knowledge in *methodological* terms: as a specific instance of the generic idea of a procedure or *process* aimed at the development of a result or *product*. The theory of knowledge will thus be approached from the direction of epistemological methodology, that is, from the angle of the methods, processes, techniques, procedures, and instrumentalities used in the "production of knowledge." This strategy makes it possible to bring the generic and universal facts about methodology-in-general to bear on the particular issue of knowledge-generating methods, with the prospect that controversial issues of epistemology can profitably be illuminated—and some of them even resolved—by applying the general theory of method to the special case of *cognitive* methodology.

It is desirable to become clear at the very outset regarding the nature of the enterprise on which we are about to embark, and to state clearly the questions which we shall endeavor to answer. The pivotal issue is this: What is the appropriate rational justification or legitimation of claims to knowledge? But while this formula has the merit of simplicity and compactness, it has the defect of obscurity: it cries out for commentary and explanation. To begin with a negative point, we shall not be concerned with questions of the form "How do you know that *P*?" (that copper conducts electricity, that *p* entails *p*-or-*q*, that 2+2=4). Detailed problems of this sort about what is or is not the case are to be resolved with reference simply to the particular procedures appropriate to the specific issues with which they deal. One answers such questions with reference to the pertinent criteriology, in terms of the teachings of physics or biology or arithmetic. But behind this level of consideration there lies a deeper level at which one can raise such questions as: What is it that qualifies the procedures of physics (or biology or logic or arithmetic) as the proper and appropriate devices for answering such questions? Admitting that we standardly use such-and-such norms or standards or procedures in supporting the knowledge-claims we make, what sorts of considerations establish the legitimacy or appropriateness of these in their turn as an adequate and appropriate basis for the sort of thing we call *knowledge*? This higher-level issue of rational justification or legitimation will remain at the focus of present concern. Consider the exchange: Q: "You claim that (say) *P*, but how do you know this is so; on what basis does your claim rest?" A: "I claim *P* to be so because . . . (i.e., for such-and-such reasons)." Q: "But what is it about *these* reasons (or whatever other reasons you might have given) that establishes them as a probatively proper and appropriate basis for the claim on whose behalf they are adduced?" The deliberations of the book will move at this subsequent, philosophically deeper level at which issues of the legitimation of knowledge can arise. Its central issue is thus that of the rationalization of cognitive methods.

2. ASPECTS OF METHODOLOGY: TELEOLOGY

It is advisable to begin with some abstract considerations regarding the theory of methodology-in-general. Regrettably, the discussion must thus unfold in a way that makes its beginning at a substantial remove from its principal topic, the theory of knowledge, and the reader must be asked to bear with these indispensable preliminaries. This chapter is accordingly devoted to an as yet virtually unborn discipline, that of *metamethodology*—what the French might call *méthodologie générale* or the Germans *Methodenlehre*. The mission of such a discipline is to study the general theory of methods in its various aspects: comparative methodology, methods for devising methods, the methodology for evaluating, refining, and improving methods, etc. The literature of this subject is almost nonexistent, apart from studies of the methodology of particular areas of knowledge (natural science, philosophy, mathematics, etc.) and articles under the relevant rubrics in dictionaries and encyclopedias.[1] Within this general range, we shall focus on the evaluation of methods or—regarding the same issue from another perspective—that of their justification or validation.

To be justified *instrumentally* is to be justified in the way inherently appropriate to an instrumentality, tool, method, procedure, *modus operandi*, technique, or the like. The fundamental idea in this area is that of *agency* at the generic levels of ways of acting or of doing things. By their very nature, instrumentalities (techniques, methods, and the rest) are *means for doing things of a certain sort*. Accordingly, an *instrumental* justification is one given in a manner appropriate to *means* as such, one that is naturally "fitting and proper" with regard to instrumentalities. This leads straightaway to a consideration of the purposive dimension of the matter.

Just how in general is a "means for doing things of a certain sort" to be justified or legitimated? Clearly this will have to be done in a purposive or *teleological* manner. A method is never a method pure and simple, but always a method-for-the-realization-of-some-end, so that the inevitably teleological question of its *effectiveness* in the realization of its purposes becomes altogether central to the issue of justification. A *method*, after all, is something intrinsically purpose-relative.

It is thus clear that, with particular regard to *methodology* at any rate, the pragmatists were surely right: there can be no better or more natural way of justifying a *method* than by establishing that "it works" with respect to the specific appointed tasks that are in view for it. The proper test for the correctness or appropriateness of anything methodological in nature is plainly and obviously posed by the paradigmatically pragmatic questions: Does it *work?* Does it attain its intended purposes? Does it—to put it crassly—deliver the goods? Instrumentalities (methods, etc.) are invariably *purposive:* they are means for the realization of certain ends. Accordingly, anything methodological, be it a tool, procedure, instrumentality, program or policy of action,

---

[1] One of the better instances of the latter is the article "Methode" by Friederich Rapp in H. Krings, H. M. Baumgartner, and C. Wild (eds), *Handbuch philosophischer Grundbegriffe* (Munich, 1973), Vol. IV, pp. 913–29.

etc., is properly validated in terms of its ability to achieve the purposes at issue—its success at accomplishing its appropriate task.

It follows from such considerations that *the natural standard for the rational evaluation of methods is that of success*. The proper test of a method lies in its capacity to realize effectively and efficiently the sort of product that constitutes its teleological *raison d'être*. The justificatory rationale of a method thus turns on the pivotal issue of its *serviceability*, and the "justification" of a method resides in an *instrumental* analysis that determines its suitability to the task in hand. The pivotal issue is the "pragmatic" one of assessing whether the method actually works in practice. The test that is appropriate here lies in the area of quality-control, in determining whether the *results of using* the method in fact realize the purposes for which it was instituted. In sum, the rational legitimation of a method is not at all a question of *theoretical* considerations turning on matters of abstract principle, but is essentially *practical* in its orientation. Its *success in application*, its capacity to do its intended work, in short, its usefulness, is the decisive consideration when the validation of a method is at issue.

The over-all process of instrumental justification natural to a method (procedure, *modus operandi*, etc.) thus has the structure indicated in Figure 1.

Figure 1

STRUCTURE OF THE INSTRUMENTAL JUSTIFICATION
OF A METHOD

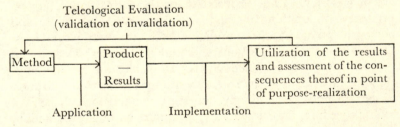

This process represents what might be characterized as a systems-model of instrumental justification. It proceeds in terms of the key concepts of systems-analysis, viz., *input* (the use of a method), *output* (the results of applying the method), and *quality-control* (the assessment of purpose-realization).

3. ASPECTS OF METHODOLOGY: GENERALITY

The instrumental justification of a method is inevitably general and, as it were, statistical in its bearing; it is a procedure of inherent open-endedness. Suppose one applies a method just once, and meets with "success"—i.e., arrives at a result that fully answers to the hoped-for purposes. This would clearly cut but little ice. The "success" might have come our way gratuitously —by accident or luck or thanks to some unrecognized special feature of the particular case at hand. One swallow does not make a summer, and one success does not validate a method. A method is a generic device capable of repetitive application; indeed there can be no such thing as an inherently one-time method (though, of course, occasion for the use of an inherently general method might conceivably arise but once). Something that is by its very nature a way of producing one specific result on one specific occasion could not be dignified by the name of "method": anything that deserves this name must be a means of producing a certain type of result on any suitable occasion. And the working of a method (unlike a talent) is impersonal—it does not work just for X or Y, but for anybody. Methodological efficacy is a matter of how things go "across the board" generally and in the long run.[2] Thus "working" on one occasion does not have sufficiently general import, and "failing" on one occasion is not necessarily invalidating. Accordingly, the instrumental justification is only to be sought at this generic and systematic plane.[3]

[2] Thus when we turn to specifically *cognitive* methods of inquiry we shall be led to an essentially Peircean perspective in coordinating cognitive rationality with the concerns of the human community in its "at large" distribution over space and time.

[3] The importance for inductive considerations of the inherent generality of methods was clearly perceived by Peirce, who held that "synthetic inferences are founded upon the classification of facts, not according to their characters, but *according to the manner of obtaining them.*" (Quoted in Ernest Nagel, "Principles of the Theory of Probability," International Encyclopedia of Unified Science, Vol. I [Chicago, 1955], pp. 343–422 [see p. 414].)

4. THE CRITICAL EVALUATION OF METHODS AND THE DYNAMICS OF METHODOLOGICAL PROGRESS

The preceding discussion has concerned itself with the issue of the instrumental justification in the case of one particular method or procedure (etc.). But particular interest attaches to the question of the comparative appraisal of competing or *alternative* methods for realizing the same set of specified purposes. Clearly, once we are in a position to examine the matter of the extent to which a single method is justified, we shall also be in a position to assess the relative justification of rival methods. Exactly the same issue —namely the comparative analysis of the various degrees of success—is the crucial factor for both sorts of problems.

This train of thought moves with special impetus in the direction of the dynamic process of refining or improving a method, a process whose structure is represented in Figure 2:

Figure 2

THE PROCESS OF METHOD-REFINEMENT

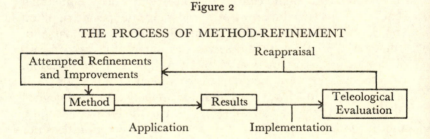

Here the cyclically iterative nature of the procedure clearly manifests itself in a feed-back recycling into early stages of the circuit. The over-all procedure manifests a feed-back mechanism of producing at later stages materials for re-entry in later iterations into previous stages of the process.[4] The structure of such a mechanism clearly exhibits the form of a dialectic process of sequential stages:

---

[4] This latter-day idea of a cyclic feed-back renders obsolete in suitable circumstances the proscription of an earlier day against what Hugo Dingler condemned as a *methodological or pragmatic circle*, namely "a step [in a procedure] that requires performing another step that becomes possible through it." (*Die Methode der Physik* [Munich, 1938], p. 71.)

i-th stage:
    method M_i ———————————⟶ proposed refinement M'_i
$i +$ 1st stage:
    method $M_{i+1} = M_i{}^{*}$ ⟵———⟶ proposed refinement M'_{i+1}
        winner of i-th
        comparison of
        M_i and M'_i

The systematic pattern of the feed-back cycle at issue in this dialectical process is represented in Figure 3.

Figure 3

THE CYCLE OF METHOD-REVISION

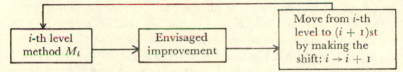

A rational person would obviously only recognize a revision in a method as affording an *actual* (rather than merely *putative*) improvement of it when there is good reason to think that it is indeed superior on the basis of the teleological evaluation of results. Superior performance is the key to progress in methodology, and the role of considerations regarding efficiency and effectiveness in realizing the purposive *raison d'être* of the method is clearly central here.

The *dynamic* aspect of historical replacement or revision assimilates this approach to methods to the general situation of performance-monitoring systems that proceed in terms of the cyclic sequence set out in Figure 4.

Figure 4

THE DYNAMICS OF PERFORMANCE-MONITORING

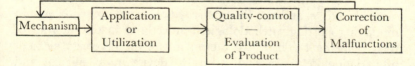

Of course, in our present case the process is not wholly *self*-adjusting, because the issue of *finding* the refinements needed to correct malfunctions is certainly not automatic nor even indeed is it always determinable through simple trial-and-error variation. In general, it requires something exogenous to the whole process as described—the intervention of creative ingenuity.

5. THE DARWINIAN DIMENSION

The system-process envisaged above provides a model for methodological comparison and improvement in both the static/probative and the dynamic/historical dimensions. Basically, it provides the mechanism for elaborating a rationale of theoretical justification, and so proceeds on the plane of theory. But it has a signficant historical dimension. For the historical phenomena can be described in just these same terms—as for example when one envisages a temporal sequence of attempts to improve on various methods by trial and error. Under suitable circumstances (pre-eminently including the rationality of the method-users at issue) the systematic course of theoretical justification and the historical course of evolutionary development both represent different versions of the same basic pattern. On the one hand it can describe the *essentially static process of theoretical justification* that characterizes their warranting rationale, on the other hand it can be used to account for their *dynamic process of historical development* in the course of time—but both of them conform to the same underlying model for the teleological critique of methods.

The essential ingredients of any evolutionary model are but two: *variation* and *selection*. To apprehend their mode of operation in the present case we must begin by noting certain relevant features of the historical community of persons that provides the setting within which methods are adopted and employed.

As regards *variation*, two factors are crucial: (i) the *constancy of purpose* which serves to assure that, throughout the historical process, the methods at issue address themselves to essentially the same objectives, and also (ii) *creative operational innovativeness* in modifying existing methodological procedures in the interests of their refinement. These two factors assure the necessary element of variation in a continual effort to devise more efficient and effective methods for the realization of ongoing purposive goals.

As regards *selection*, the crucial factor is that of *critical rationality* in adopting, from among competing alternatives, that method which proves in the course of applications to be more successful in point of goal-realization—and correspondingly in abandoning those methods that have shown themselves less successful. Thus in our methodological case, where overtly purposive instrumentalities rather than biological organisms are at issue, the operative factor in the developmental process is not that of *natural selection*, but that of *rational selection* in the light of explicitly purpose-oriented considerations. This, of course, is a significant point of difference from evolution in its classical Darwinian form where survival alone, rather than any other more elaborately rational purpose is the operative factor. In the present case, where methods are overtly purpose-correlative, an explicitly rational teleology is called for. This point of difference is, however, quite irrelevant to the basic evolutionary pattern of the present model of the historical process. It has the classic form of an evolutionary pattern based on variation and selection. (This Darwinian aspect of methodological progress will preoccupy us at greater length later on.)

The interaction between the historical and the justificatory dimensions of our developmental model is a phenomenon of particular interest. For subject to certain relatively plausible assumptions about the rationality of the relevant community (which render it plausible to suppose that they tend only to adopt changes in a method or procedure when these reflect superior performance), one can take an essentially Hegelian view of the matter, so that historical survival also represents justificatory superiority, with the upshot that the course of evolutionary development can be seen at the same time as reflecting a process of rational justification. On this approach, the process of historical development comes to represent a progressive advance to new methods that have demonstrated their superiority over their earlier congeners in terms of improved performance.

From the standpoint of such a methodological Darwinism, the pivotal aspect of human history is an ever-quickening pace in the development of its methodological repertoire in the co-ordinate spheres of action and cognition: locomotion by walking (a timespan of an order of magnitude (OM) of 10^6 years ago), the introduction of manipulable tools (OM 10^5 years), the invention of writing (OM 10^4 years), the development of mathematics and astronomy (OM 10^3 years), the launching of natural science (OM 10^2 years), and the harnessing of atomic power (OM 10^1 years).

If certain preconditions are satisfied within the setting of a method-using community—specifically the factors we have characterized as constancy of purpose, operational innovativeness, and critical rationality—then the historical course of this community's methodological proceedings will parallel an essentially justificatory course. Under the indicated circumstances, the historical ontogenesis of methods will replicate a probatively ordered line of rational justification: the course of historical evolution reflects the unfolding of a dynamic rationale of warrant. One fundamentally isomorphic process-structure underlies *both* the static rational order of justification *and*—in its dynamic dimension—the historical course of evolutionary development.

It is also of interest to contemplate the prospect of a developing final stabilization as the evolutionary process of methodological development ultimately attains an essentially constant condition (a "steady state"). The attainment of an evolutionary niche of this sort is of special interest and merits closer attention. Methodological stability over the long run—in appropriate circumstances—provides an effective mark of adequacy, furnishing a sign that shows that we are in fact doing as well (on the methodological side) as the operative circumstances of the case admit of. Stability and long-run survival can serve as an indicator of theoretical justification of the methodological instrumentalities in hand—in much the manner envisaged by Charles S. Peirce.[5]

In these conditions, history represents an evaluative tribunal for methods along lines reminiscent of Hegel's notorious dictum. And specifically, the *survival* of a method over a long and varied

---

[5] This idea of the validating force of considerations of stability traces back to Peirce, but with certain crucial differences: (1) Peirce was concerned specifically with the *cognitive* case (rather than that of methodology in general as with the present discussion). (2) The cognitive stability that concerned him here related to the acceptance of *theses* rather than to the use of *methods*. The subsequent discussion will, however, narrow these gaps in various ways.

historical course of applications thus comes to be seen as a factor on which the warrant of its rational claims to acceptance can appropriately be based. Methodological survival is—under appropriate circumstances—indicative of probatively rational justification, *and evolutionary development replicates rational substantiation.* But, of course, this evolutionary and progressivistic aspect characterizes only *instrumentalities* (methods, etc.). Since even superior methods can on occasion produce inferior results (and can certainly do so when in the hands of inferior workmen), there is no decisive reason for joining to a progressivistic view of *methods* a correlatively optimistic view of the associated *products.*

6. PROSPECT

To this point, the discussion has dealt with the generic process of the instrumental (i.e., teleological or purpose-oriented) assessment of methods in abstract generality—both in its static, justificatory and in its dynamic and evolutionary aspect. In the ensuing chapters these general considerations will be brought to bear in detail upon the special case of *cognitive* methodology—i.e., those epistemological methods used for the "production of knowledge." It will (hopefully) emerge that some of the traditional issues of the theory of knowledge can helpfully be clarified from this perspective.

Chapter II

THE PRAGMATIC ROOTS OF
FACTUAL KNOWLEDGE

I. THE ACCEPTANCE MODEL OF KNOWLEDGE

To have *information* about what goes on in the world calls for espousing—and rightly espousing—various theses about it. Accordingly, if one is to hold of either scientific or of common-life inquiry that they yield information about the world, one is constrained to the view that they entitle us to *accept* certain factual theses—with "acceptance," of course, to be understood as acceptance-*as-true*.[1] Any view of scientific or of everyday-life claims as *information*-providing proceeds on an acceptance-model of rational inquiry into "the truth" of things. Our present concern is thus with the truth of claims about the world—not, to be sure, with its nature (i.e., with what truth is) but with its *criteriology* (i.e., how one tests for it to determine whether it is reasonable to claim one has found it). We may, of course, not actually succeed in finding "the real truth", but unless we are prepared to take a committal stance towards what we do find—unless we are prepared at any rate to *claim* that our findings represent what is actually the case, and so to accept them (at least provisionally) as

---

[1] Thus our concern here relates to serious truth-claims, with respect to which acceptance is accompanied by the claim to adequate warrant. Admittedly "acceptance" can be even avowedly frivolous. ("I accept that that is so, though I have no real grounds for doing so" or "To be sure, I accept that contention, but since I haven't looked into the matter deeply, my view need not really count for much.") But *this* sort of acceptance is not at issue here, our concern being effectively with what John Dewey was wont to characterize as *warranted* assertion. To be sure, "acceptance-as-true" is not the only mode of *acceptance* there is: it is certainly possible to accept contentions provisionally, *pro tem*, as working hypotheses, or the like. But *this* sort of "acceptance" is not information-yielding. For acceptance to provide *information* about the world it must be a committal and earnest acceptance-as-true.

being true—we must simply abandon an information-oriented cognitive stance towards the world.[2]

Not only is this matter of acceptance central to this information-providing view of inquiry, but such acceptance must be understood in a categorical and not a hypothetical sense. Thus the pivotal idea of logic, that of conditional truth—that IF we accept some thesis P, THEN we must (in all due consistency) accept another thesis Q as well—is not presently at issue. Rather, our concern is with *categorical* theses asserting that such and such *is* (or "is sometimes" or "is always") the case about the world— that it really and actually is so.

The view of our cognitive efforts in information-acquisitive terms thus points towards the idea of an *inquiry procedure:* a systematic *modus operandi* for validating the acceptance (as true or presumptively true) of such strictly *factual* theses. Such an idea of an inquiry procedure implements the more or less orthodox conception of the goals of inquiry in information-acquisition terms.

It might perhaps be taken to go without saying that the only inquiry procedures of interest for our purposes are those which satisfy certain minimal conditions of rationality. For one thing, they must be *consistent* in that such a procedure must not enjoin us to accept both some thesis P and its contradictory denial $\neg P$. Moreover, they must encompass certain minimal principles of

---

[2] Note that this approach proceeds in the presuppositional manner introduced by Kant in his discussion of experience. That is, it does not say *categorically* that one must adopt the informational stance, but only *conditionally* what one must adopt *if* one adopts the informational stance. Now in the case of scientific inquiry, in particular, R. Carnap has opposed the idea that there should be any rules of acceptance. (See his "The Aim of Inductive Logic" in *Logic, Methodology, and Philosophy of Science*, ed. by E. Nagel, P. Suppes, and A. Tarski [Stanford, 1962], pp. 303–18. Cf. also R. C. Jeffrey, "Valuation and the Acceptance of Scientific Hypotheses," *Philosophy of Science*, vol. 23 [1956], pp. 237–46.) But apart from Carnap and his adherents, the massive majority of scientific methodologists adopt an acceptance-oriented approach. And they do so for the excellent reason—among others—that once one abandons the conception that science provides, or endeavors to provide, descriptive information as to how things work in the world, one thereby ceases to conceive of the scientific enterprise in those terms which have, from the very first, provided the core constituent of its very reason for being.

logic—especially in enjoining acceptance of anything that follows *logically* from theses whose acceptance it has already authorized. They may well, however, be *incomplete* in being prepared to suspend judgment between a pair of contradictories P *and* $\neg P$, so that nonacceptance of P does not entail acceptance of not-P. Only inquiry procedures that satisfy such minimal rationality-conditions—meeting certain basic logical requirements—will be at issue in the ensuing discussion.

The functioning of an inquiry procedure in the provision of putative factual knowledge can thus be viewed in essentially systems-theoretic terms, on the model of a production process with the applications of the inquiry procedure as the *input* and items of (putative) knowledge as the *output*, as shown in Figure 1.

Figure 1

THE PRODUCTION-PROCESS VIEW OF KNOWLEDGE

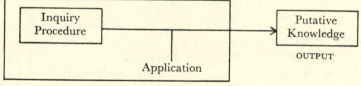

In this manner, the conception of an inquiry procedure implements the idea of *cognitive methodology* with reference to the method employed in the "production" of factual knowledge about the world. This methodological perspective brings to the fore the question of *quality control*, that is, the problem of assessing how well a cognitive method is able to accomplish its intended task. This is the central issue of the present book.

Most epistemological discussions begin, as it were, in the middle of things, by scrutinizing the sorts of evidential considerations in terms of which the acceptance of theses is to be validated. Their concern is with the probative credentials of our information. Accordingly, they begin at the *specific* level of a certain *particular* methodology of evidential argumentation rather than at the *generic* level of a consideration of probative methodology in general. The appositeness of a specific methodology is simply *assumed*, and this is then used in justifying substantive claims without itself having first received a regulative legitimation. The pivotal feature of the present approach is its insistence on the centrality of the higher-level, *activistic* question of *methodology*— of how one goes about the substantiation of theses.[3]

To be sure, the domain of cognitive methodology is much-inclusive. It encompasses various alternative issues, depending on one's focus on the methods for the *acquisition*, or the *validation*, or for the *processing*, or the *utilization* of information. Among these alternatives it is specifically the methodology of the *validation* or *substantiation* of factual claims that is to be central here. This places the *problem of the legitimation of our thesis-validating methods* at the very top of the agenda.

2. THE PROBLEM OF LEGITIMATION FOR COGNITIVE METHODS: THE DIALLELUS

How is one to determine that a fact-oriented inquiry procedure is adequate? What sort of check can be put on whether the procedure is indeed "doing its job"?

On first thought, it might perhaps seem that one can simply employ here the standard quality-control procedure of assessing the adequacy of a process in terms of the merits of its product. Unfortunately this will not do. For we immediately run up against one of the key issues of the problem disputed in antiquity between the Stoics and the Academic Sceptics under the rubric of *the criterion*—the problem, that is, of the test-process that is to represent our standard of truth.

Let C represent the criterion we actually propose to use in practice for the determination of factual or empirical truth— whatever this criterion may be, that is, whatever sort of process or procedure governs our determination of such truths. Accordingly, one will be committed to classing a fact-purporting propo-

---

[3] This approach is reminiscent of that of those cognitive psychologists (such as Jean Piaget) who insist on the primacy of *activity*—of performative knowledge of the knowing-how type—with respect to propositional knowledge of the *knowing-that* type. For a philosophically oriented introduction to his ideas see Wayne Mays, "The Epistemology of Professor Piaget," *Proceedings of the Aristotelian Society*, vol. 54 (1953–1954), pp. 49–76.

sition P as a truth if and only if $C(P)$, that is, if and only if P meets the conditions specified in C.

It will make little difference to our argument what the nature of C is. Whether it is first-hand observation, the standard processes of scientific methodology, the deliverances of immediate intuition, the indications of tea leaves, or the declarations of sacred sages—all this is totally indifferent for all immediate purposes. The discussion will for the time being proceed at a level of generality where no *particular* C is in view.[4]

Nor need C be uniform and homogeneous: it can be as complex and composite as you please. If you choose to divide the realm of potential fact up into a variety of themes or topics or subject matters, and apply an altogether different standard in each region—say a discursive process at some places and a direct one at others—then so be it. The standard C then simply becomes a complex composite of multiple subcriteria. Well and good.

All that is asked is that we be serious about C; that C really and truly be the criterion we are actually committed to using in practice for determination of factual truth.

How are we to validate our employment of C? Can it be shown that we are rationally justified in using C at all? This had better be so, considering our very libertarian approach in allowing C to range over all sorts of imaginable alternatives.

Now to all appearances the question of the appropriateness of C is simply this: Does C yield truths?

But how could one meaningfully implement the justificatory program inherent in this question? Seemingly in only one way: by looking on the one hand at C-validated propositions and checking on the other hand if they are in fact truths. But if C really and truly is our working criterion for the determination of factual truth, then this exercise becomes wholly pointless. We cannot judge C by the seemingly natural standard of the question whether what it yields as true is indeed *actually* true, because we *ex hypothesi* use C itself as the determinant of just this.

At this point it becomes altogether crucial that C really and

---

[4] One would, of course, have to impose certain *structural* requirements upon C, since what is at issue are *claims to truth*. Thus we could not possibly have that both $C(P)$ and $C(\neg P)$, where "$\neg P$" represents the contradictory denial of "P." Or again if both $C(P)$ and $C(Q)$ then we must also have $C(P \& Q)$.

truly is the criterion we actually use for truth determinations. Clearly, if the issue were that of justifying a proposed alternative procedure C', the preceding methodology would work splendidly well. For we would then simply check whether the C'-validated propositions are indeed truths—that is, whether they are also validated by C. But with respect to C itself this exercise is patently useless.

This line of reasoning has been known from the days of the sceptics of antiquity under the title of the "*diallelus*," a particular sort of *circulus in probandi*. Montaigne presented this Wheel Argument (as we may term it) as follows:

> To adjudicate [between the true and the false] among the appearances of things we need to have a distinguishing method (*un instrument judicatoire*); to validate this method we need to have a justifying argument; but to validate this justifying argument we need the very method at issue. And there we are, going round on the wheel.[5]

It is difficult to exaggerate the significance of this extremely simple line of reasoning. It proves, in as decisive a manner as philosophical argumentation admits of, that our operative standard of factual truth cannot be validated by somehow exhibiting directly that it does indeed accomplish properly its intended work of truth-determination.[6] The routine tactic of assessing pro-

---

[5] "Pour juger des apparances que nous recevons des subjects, il nous faudroit un instrument judicatoire; pour vérifier cet instrument, il nous fault de la démonstration; pour vérifier la démonstration, un instrument: nous voilà au rouet." *Essaies*, Bk II, ch. 12 ("An Apologie of Raymond Sebond"); p. 544 of the Modern Library edition of *The Essays of Montaigne* (New York, 1933). Francis Bacon, with the characteristic shrewdness of a lawyer, even managed to turn the *diallelus* into a dialectical weapon against his methodological opponents: "no judgement can be rightly formed either of my method, or of the discoveries to which it leads, by means of . . . the reasoning which is now in use, since one cannot postulate due jurisdiction for a tribunal which is itself on trial." (*Novum Organon*, Bk I, sect. 33).

[6] Notwithstanding its intrinsic significance, this line of reasoning has lain dormant in modern philosophy until D. J. Mercier's monumental *Critériologie générale ou theorie générale de la certitude* (Louvain, 1884; 8th ed. 1924). This book gave the argument a currency in Catholic circles—see, for example, P. Coffey, *Epistemology or the Theory of*

cess in terms of product is thus seemingly not practicable in the case of an inquiry procedure of the sort at issue: it is in principle impossible to make a direct check of this sort on the functioning of our truth-determining methods.

3. COGNITIVE TELEOLOGY: THE DUAL ASPECT OF THEORY AND PRACTICE

The lesson of the Wheel Argument (*diallelus*) is that there simply is no *direct* way of checking the adequacy of an inquiry procedure —at any rate with that inquiry procedure to which we are seriously committed. It is therefore necessary to explore the prospects of a different strategy of validation. It becomes a matter of urgency and interest to explore in a deeper and more sophisticated way the prospect of applying in the special case of *cognitive* methodology the sort of instrumental validation whose general structure was considered in the first chapter.

Obviously, before one can proceed along the lines of such an instrumental evaluation, the question of cognitive teleology must be dealt with. What function is actually at issue with the truths or putative truths validated by an inquiry procedure? What teleological objectives are apposite with respect to cognition? Just what are the purposes germane to a truth-determination method; what is it we propose to do with the propositions that it validates to us as truths? We must consider and resolve this question of the sorts of aims at issue with respect to our knowledge, or purported knowledge, of matters of fact.

This deceptively simple-seeming question poses profound and far-reaching issues. In particular, it forces us to give prominence to a recognition of the tritely familiar but still fundamental fact of the amphibious nature of man as a creature of mind and body, intellect and will, reason and action, theory and practice.

In keeping with this duality, our knowledge answers to two distinct categories of purpose, the theoretical and the practical. The theoretical sector of purpose is *pure* and the practical sector

Knowledge (2 vols, London, 1917). It figures centrally in two recent coincident publications, my own book, *The Primacy of Practice* (Oxford, 1973), and Roderick Chisholm's interesting lecture on *The Problem of the Criterion* (Milwaukee, 1973).

is *applied* in orientation. The theoretical relates to the strictly intellectual interests of man—the acquisition of descriptive information and explanatory understanding (to *what* and *why*)—whereas the practical relates to the material interests of man that underlie the guidance of human action: avoidance of pain, suffering, frustration, etc. The functional role of our knowledge encompasses both the intellectual/theoretical aspect of the purists' knowledge for knowledge's sake and the activist/practical aspect of knowledge as a counsel in the conduct of affairs and a guide to life. Our acceptance or nonacceptance of factual truths, of course, has profound involvements on both sides of the theoretical/practical divide, since such acceptance furnishes a guide both to intellectual belief and to overt action in the pursuit of our practical goals.[7]

In criticizing William James' theory of truth, Arthur O. Lovejoy noted that a factual belief may "work" or "succeed" in two quite different senses: it may work *cognitively*, by having its implicit predictions fulfilled, or it may work *affectively* by contributing to the welfare or well-being of those who hold it.[8] This fundamental duality points to a correspondingly dual aspect in our acceptance of truths:

(1) On the one hand there is the *cognitive or theoretical* dimension of our concern for the intellectual aspect of information or knowledge. From the purely intellectual perspective of man as knower, success is represented by the accession of correct information about things and failure entails the natural sanction of error.

---

[7] This is not the place to enlarge on the problem of *how* knowledge and belief serve in guiding rational action. The large (and rapidly growing) literature on "practical reasoning" throws much light on the relevant issues. The crucial point is the naively elemental fact that we cannot move from the objective to quench our thirst to drinking a certain liquid save by the mediation of a belief that drinking it will (or may) conduce to this goal (without offsetting side-effects).

[8] A. O. Lovejoy, *The Thirteen Pragmatisms and Other Essays* (Baltimore, 1963). Lovejoy gave the example that belief in the coming of the Messiah "worked" for the ancient Jews in the sense of contributing to the viability and attainments of their community, but it failed to "work" in the sense that the specific expectations correlated with this belief did not come to realization in the manner they envisaged.

(2) On the other hand, there are the *practical and affective* aspects of man as an *agent*—as an actor emplaced *in medias res* upon the stage of the blooming, buzzing confusion comprising the goings-on of this world. The critical element here is our welfare not as abstract intellects concerned solely to acquire information and avoid error, but as embodied agents concerned for their welfare in a context where failure entails frustration, pain, or even catastrophe.

It is sometimes said that the central, definitive function of factual knowledge is the specific prediction of the future states of natural systems, so the *prediction* represents the ultimate aim of inquiry, or else *explanation* or *control over nature* are cast in this role. But this whole quest for the uniquely definitive function of knowledge is surely misguided. It is simply wrong-headed to claim some one single factor of this sort to represent *the aim* of our endeavors to obtain factual knowledge. The fact is that *our inquiry into matters of fact has a plurality of coordinated and essentially co-equal objectives.* It seeks to facilitate retrodictive reconstruction of the past, to explain what has happened and what presently goes on, to predict what will or may probably go on, and, far from least, to afford us the instrumentalities of control (or at least partial control) over the course of events. All these objectives enter in. It thus is, or should be, quite clear that the cognitive enterprise does not have a single, monolithic aim, but a multiplicity of coordinated purposes, some largely theoretical (explanation, prediction, and retrodiction), and others primarily practical (control) in their orientation.

The crucial lesson of such considerations is that the teleology of inquiry is internally diversified and complex, and spreads across both the cognitive/theoretical and active/practical sectors. Accordingly, a truth-criterion comes to be endowed with a duality of objectives, and the relevant teleology of inquiry is both cognitive and practical.[9] Truth-acceptance is on the one hand a determining factor for belief in purely intellectual and theoretical regards, and on the other a guiding standard for the practical conduct of life. The two are inseparably interrelated. And this

---

[9] A fuller development of these considerations regarding the teleology of inquiry is given in the author's *Scientific Explanation* (New York, 1970).

second cluster of the goals pertinent to inquiry is by no means of a stature inferior to the first or subordinate to it. If anything, the reverse is the case: stress upon explanation and prediction can be viewed as derivatively subsidiary to practice. For on the one hand, explanatory adequacy is a crucial factor in guiding the practice of specifically rational beings. And on the other hand, prediction is an inevitable aspect of adequate control—even of that merely negative control of "letting nature take its course." The "correct" canalizing of expectations in predictive contexts is a crucial aspect of the "control over nature" essential to the successful guidance of practical affairs.[10]

Success in the domain of praxis is something very different from "success" in the sphere of theory (viz., "being right" about something). The success of the pragmatic context is of the *affective* order, ranging over the spectrum from physical survival and avoidance of pain and injury on the negative side to positive satisfactions such as those attending the satiation of physical needs on the other. Merely intellectual accomplishment like "predictive success" (which, to be sure, can be attended by affectively positive satisfaction) is but a small part of the picture. After all, a world-external, disembodied spectator can make predictions about the world and utter a pleased "aha—there it is" to himself when his predictions work out. But the core factor is that of the "success" of a being emplaced in this world *in medias res* who must inter-

---

[10] Though many philosophers of science maintain the primacy of prediction over retrodictive explanation in assessing the adequacy of scientific theories, others have found this puzzling. They view it as implausible that future-oriented applications should receive more weight than past-oriented ones. Thus J. M. Keynes wrote: "The peculiar virtue of prediction or predesignation is altogether imaginary. The number of instances examined and the analogy between them are the essential points, and the question as to whether a particular hypothesis happens to be propounded before or after their examination is quite irrelevant" (*A Treatise on Probability* [London, 1921], p. 305). A pragmatic point of view that stresses the centrality of control immediately rationalizes the difference between past and future in this regard: the two cases may be *logically* symmetric but there is a decisive *pragmatic* asymmetry—the past lies beyond the prospect of intervention whereas we can often still do something about the future. For an interesting treatment of some relevant issues see Alan Musgrave, "Logical versus Historical Theories of Confirmation," *British Journal for the Philosophy of Science*, vol. 25 (1974), pp. 1–23 (see especially pp. 1–3).

vene in the course of events to make matters eventuate so as to conduce to his survival and well-being. The issue here is thus not to be construed as one of cognitive success—nor even of predictive success alone (though this is bound to enter in)—but in terms of the affectively satisfying and purposively adequate guidance of action, i.e., *intervention* in the course of events so as to make things work out "satisfactorily."

Consider an example so schematic as to be almost a caricature, that of a comparison between modern and Galenic medicine—between the adequacy of the modern chemico-biologico-physiological account of morbidity and Galen's humor-imbalance account. Greater success at prediction of "the natural course of development" is only a small part of the story here. The superior claims of the modern account inhere in the fact that it provides a basis for overwhelmingly more effective manipulation of the actual course of events—an intervention that is vastly more successful to the purposive/affective mode.

This example highlights what is at issue with successful praxis as understood here. Success in the pragmatic sphere is a matter of the avoidance of affective mishaps and the attainment of affective satisfaction through the effective guidance of the actions of a being emplaced within a difficult and generally uncooperative world. The adequacy of our cognitive instruments is, on this pragmatic approach, to be assessed in terms of their effectiveness in helping us to navigate with affective success amidst the shoals and narrows of a hostile (or, at best, indifferent) environment.

To be sure, affective and cognitive success draw very close to one another in the special area of man-made predictions. For here there are significant affective implications even where our *welfare* is not engaged directly and immediately. We have on the one hand the chagrin of having been wrong and the disappointment of unrealized expectations, and on the other hand the Eureka-like satisfaction that attends the correct anticipation of events. In this area, the "purely intellectual" issue of being right or wrong thus has repercussions in the affective area of satisfaction and dissatisfaction. But, of course, the purely cognitive aspect of predictive success is in a way secondary, for we must *be there* (i.e., survive) in order to celebrate our predictive triumphs. In a ranking of operative sanctions, the simple disappointment of unfulfilled expectations is fundamentally weaker than actual harm. No doubt, the cognitive/theoretical and the noncognitive/affective aspects of success are closely interrelated (this idea is, after all, crucial to a pragmatism of any sort). But the Wheel Argument (*diallelus*) indicates that the element of practical/affective success does enjoy primacy and predominance in the order of justification. From this perspective, all rationality—cognitive as well as behavioral—is ultimately pragmatically purpose-oriented and practice-related.

4. THE PRAGMATIC TURN

In the light of these considerations regarding the teleology of cognition, it emerges that the clear moral of the seemingly devastating *diallelus* argument is not the establishment of scepticism, but merely the less drastic conclusion that one should interpret the quality-control factor of the "success" of a cognitive method or criterion in the *practical* rather than the theoretical mode. Practical or pragmatic efficacy thus comes to be seen as the appropriate standard of instrumental justification for our criterion of factual truth. Since truths serve us amphibiously on both the theoretico-cognitive and the practico-active sectors, and since considerations on the strictly theoretical side are revealed as inadequate to the needs of the justificatory situation, we are thrown back upon the latter, practical domain. One is, accordingly, led to surmise that the natural and appropriate step is to use success in the *practical* mode as the justificatory standard proper to a criterion of factual truth.[11] The practically *purposive* aspect of cognition thus comes to the fore, an aspect to which philosophical pragmatists have always accorded a central role on the epistemological stage. We are brought back through our methodological detour to their doctrine that *praxis* is the ultimate arbiter of *theoria*.

To be sure, the hard core of the *praxis* at issue relates to man's

---

[11] We are not, of course, saying that *practical* controls are wholly self-sufficient to the exclusion of any *rational* controls. Indeed we granted at the outset that any truth-criterion must be subjected to certain minimal (logical) requirements of rationality. The crucial point is, rather, that these rational controls are so minimalistic as to require pragmatic supplementation.

survival, welfare, and affective well-being—it has to do with making life possible, easier, and pleasanter. But this, of course, is only the hard core. In the more advanced stages of the development of human societies, practice ramifies far beyond this restricted region to embrace a much enhanced sphere of "practical" activities whose relationship to the issue of welfare is rather remote. Think here especially of that sector of *praxis* which might be characterized as *cognitive practice* related to the technology of inquiry. Much of the practice of sophisticated societies is itself cognitively oriented and relates to the acquisition and processing of information, involving the use of such sophisticated cognitive tools as: computers, radio-telescopes, electron microscopes, atom-smashers, space rocketry, etc. The point is that the "practice" of a scientifically sophisticated and technologically advanced civilization is itself largely geared not towards the conduct of everyday life but towards the enlargement of knowledge. The factor of successful practice ("control over nature") envisaged as arbiter over the concerns of theory and cognition must thus be construed in a relatively wide way to include also the sector of cognition-oriented practice related to the technology of inquiry. This crucial consideration brings to the fore the range of practical/affective purposes in fact complexly interwined with those of the "purely cognitive" sector, with the result that our insistence upon the *legitimative* primacy of practice is not somehow insulting or derogatory to the more lofty claims of the intellectual sector.

All the same, the *pragmatic* aspect of this approach deserves emphasis. The central concern of pragmatism has always been oriented to the teleology of human thought. Its fundamental theses are (1) that human cognition has a *telos*, (2) that this *telos* is complex and embraces not only the furtherance of knowledge *per se* but also practice in the successful conduct of the affairs of life, and (3) that the rational legitimation of cognition can properly be accomplished only by reference to the full range of man's purposive concerns, specifically and preeminently including those of the practical sector. All of these points will play a prominent role in the position to be developed here.

Chapter III

THE PRAGMATIC APPROACH TO COGNITIVE JUSTIFICATION

1. THE PRAGMATIC JUSTIFICATION OF COGNITIVE METHODOLOGY

The teleology relevant for the evaluation of cognitive methods must—so we have argued—be located ultimately in applicative "success" in the practical area. But how is such an approach to be implemented? Let us now try to exploit in the special case of an inquiry procedure the generic process of instrumental justification as previously outlined, recognizing the specifically *pragmatic* aspect of the relevant teleology. Approached from this angle, the justificatory process will have the systematic structure exhibited in Figure 1.

Figure 1

THE INSTRUMENTAL JUSTIFICATION OF AN INQUIRY METHOD

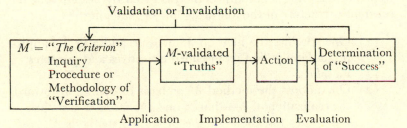

This schema presents—at least in barebones outlines—the process of the "pragmatic justification" of an inquiry procedure or truth-criterion. Its workings are virtually self-explanatory. The pragmatic factor of the practical success realized in *applying* the findings of the procedure comes to represent the governing consideration for the evaluative issue of its legitimacy.

This pragmatic approach to cognitive legitimation raises a

deep question: Do the results justify the method or does the method justify the results? Ordinarily and in general, instrumental justification moves along a one-way street: a method is justified by its results—and this was exactly the general circumstance we envisaged in Chapter I. But in the special circumstances of *cognitive* methodology the case is altered, because a situation of *reciprocity* can and must prevail: justification is here an essentially two-way process—its results legitimate the method as proper and appropriate, and the method justifies its results as "correct". This raises immediate problems, for is not the circularity involved vitiatingly vicious?

2. THE PROBLEM OF CIRCULARITY: PLAUSIBLE PRESUMPTIONS AS A WAY OUT

There is no denying that a pragmatic approach to cognitive legitimation has its difficulties. To begin with, one must face up to the critical point that any use of the instrumental approach to methodological justification which invokes the record of actual experience will require some empirically factual inputs. To establish the record inevitably requires one to talk about such plainly factual matters as past actions and their subsequent developments. For an instrumental defense in terms of the actually experienced results of adopting a certain method is given by fleshing out the schematic structure of the following line of reasoning:

(1) One specifies the method M at issue and also the appropriate family T of its intended objectives and purposes (T for *telos*).

(2) One adopts the method M as basis of operation towards the realization of T—that is, one *applies* M in practice.

(3) One notes that none of the promising methods M', M'', etc. alternative to M prove on balance as effective as M in leading to the realization of T.

Accordingly, the conclusion is drawn that one is relatively justified in adopting M for the realization of T. Now it is clear that this line of argument is heavily laden with factual commitments, since the premises at issue in both items (2) and (3) represent a significant incursion into the realm of empirical fact.

It is in principle impossible to attempt "the appeal to experience" regarding the effectiveness *in practice* or the success *in actual employment* of a method in the absence of any and all factual data regarding the actual occasions of use of this or alternative methods and the subsequent occurences. The generic structure of an *experientially* instrumental justification requires us to recognize that we have adopted and implemented certain courses of action; to note that certain occurrences supervened upon these steps; and finally to assess these occurrences in point of their conduciveness to our objective T. Putting the evaluative issues of this final item aside, we remark that the remaining points are entirely matters of record relating to past activities and observations. To implement the pragmatic program of determining whether a certain procedural method works out, we must inevitably have some informative *data regarding what was done and what happened*. It is self-evident that to apply any argument from experience we need factual records to tell us what experience has been.

If we were to hold (say) that medical practice has improved over the years, then we would require (*inter alia*) the patently factual data needed to establish that there are diseases and disabilities that used to be incurable but can now be cured. And it would seem that this will constitute a knowledge-claim which our inquiry procedure must endorse before we are entitled to accept it. And so we must—seemingly—appeal to the procedure itself to sustain the claim that is to be its "external" support. Does this sort of circularity not block any sort of instrumental justification of our cognitive methods at the very outset?

This leads to the crucial question: Given that factually informative data are needed for any application of the instrumental line of justification, just whence is one to obtain these factually informative historical inputs when this justification concerns one's very criterion of factual truth itself? Clearly, if the factual premises are to come from the methodological criterion M itself, then one moves in the unhappy circle of invoking M to validate certain claims, claims are then in turn used themselves for the validation of M.

If the experientially pragmatic justification of a criterion M of factual truth is to succeed, this circle must be broken. But how can this be done?

Only one way seems to be open. Insofar as they function as premiss-inputs into the justificatory argument for M, the experiential data must be seen *not as validated truths but merely as plausible presumptions.* One must carefully distinguish the claim of *certainty* (a truth is, after all, in principle not defeasible—otherwise it would not be a truth) from the claim of *plausibility.* To class a proposition as a certified *truth* is (as John Dewey was wont to insist) very different from characterizing it as having some suitable degree of *warranted assertability.* From an epistemic standpoint there is a vast gulf between an established truth and a provisionally accepted supposition—between characterizing a thesis as *prima facie* correct and acceptable in the first analysis (plausible or credible), and claiming it as ultimately correct and acceptable in the final analysis (actually true). To limit our epistomological purview to *certified truths* alone is to ignore that vast and important class of theses which are *tentatively* acceptable, but subject to abandonment in the light of systematic considerations, and so ultimately defeasible.[1]

This distinction between genuine truths and merely presumptive truth-candidates demands emphasis because it is crucially central to present purposes. Any *experiential* justification of a truth-criterion must pull itself up by its own bootstraps—it needs factual inputs, but yet these factual inputs cannot at this stage already qualify as truths. To meet this need it is natural to appeal to truth-candidates, data which are no more *truths* than candidate-presidents are presidents—though some of them are ultimately bound to win out.

Accordingly, it is quite sufficient for present purposes to have it that the retrospective record and memory yields informative yet infirm data: data of merely *prima facie* correctness that need not be ultimately true but merely plausible truth-candidates. Not the outright *truth* but the mere *plausibility* of retrospective records can provide the information-base needed for the pragmatic argument from experience. To be sure, it must be granted that only an argument from true premisses can possibly *demonstrate* its conclusion. But this undoubted fact does not entail the (surely

---

[1] This conception of *data* not as truths as such, but as promising truth-candidates, is elaborated in greater detail in the author's *The Coherence Theory of Truth* (Oxford, 1973).

incorrect) consequence that arguments from merely plausible premisses cannot carry substantial probative weight. Nothing untoward ensues from a recognition that the present line of justificatory argumentation is presumptive rather than demonstrative, in that some of its premisses figure in the role of plausible data rather than certified truths.

3. THE PROBLEM OF ATTRIBUTABILITY: POST HOC AND PROPTER HOC

Another fundamental difficulty resides in the very nature of the premiss pivotal to *any* instrumentally teleological validation of a method, namely the premiss to the effect

> M works; that is, employment of M is appropriately conducive to realization of the objective T.

For when we take the experiential route to the establishment of this decidedly factual premiss, the only information we can obtain on the basis of the matters-of-historical-record takes the following form:

(1) The method M has been tried (as have its alternatives M', M'', etc.).

(2) The objectives T were realized sooner or more fully (more efficiently, more effectively) by M than by employing its competitors (M', M'', etc.).

So much can be available as a matter of historical record. But this will not suffice to establish the requisite degree of intimacy between the method M and the correlative desideratum T. What is clearly needed to warrant the "is conducive" claim of the premiss is not just the *post hoc* information that M was adopted and the sought result T achieved, but the *propter hoc* information that T was attained because of the adoption of M. If the realization of T is to validate M, then its *attributability to the use of M* must be established. To (1) and (2) above we must add yet another premiss:

(3) In all (most) particular instances i: attainment of T in instance i is attributable—or at least presumptively attributable—to the use of M.

Accordingly, the thesis that "M works" appears in the light of a generalization from a host of specific cases attributing successful realization of T to the use of M.

Now in general there is nothing in this state of affairs to create problems for a pragmatic validation. But in the specific cases of a *cognitive* method for the validation of factual truth-claims a serious difficulty crops up with respect to (3). For if the argument is to have proper probative weight, then all its premises must be established, and while the matters of record at issue in (1)–(2) can be handled by the approach of the preceding section, the patently fact-claiming premiss (3), which is clearly *not* just a matter of historical record, poses altogether new difficulties. For any attempt to show that this attributability thesis (3) is *true* once again activates the specter of circularity: its truth will obviously be a matter of fact, while it is a criterion of factual truth we are endeavoring to validate. We seem once more to be plunged into the patently circular position that our validation of a criterion of factual truth calls for our *already* being in the possession of a validated factual truth.

The resolution to this problem of validating a *propter hoc* attributability-claim is to see its appearance in the over-all justificatory argument in the status of a *warranted postulate* rather than in the status of a *validated truth* (since this would indeed be circular). Not that it does not even make sense to ask with respect to postulates (unlike theses, conjectures, assumptions, or hypotheses) whether they are true (*qua* postulates). This approach maintains that when the *post hoc* facts are suitably adjusted—*subject to all of the appropriate controls and cautions of the theory of the design of experiments*—than a certain postulation is warranted or justified.

Accordingly, we would adopt at the *regulative* level (rather than the factual or constitutive level) an operative precept of the type:

(P) To treat a certain *postulation* of propter-hocness as warranted under suitable circumstances regarding post-hocness.

This is itself a practical/procedural principle rather than a cognitive/factual thesis. It indicates a mode of action rather than a claim to truth. Its status is methodological, and its validation is part and parcel of the over-all program of instrumental validation of our cognitive methods.[2] (It deserves note, incidentally, that treating such a thesis of attribution as a justified postulate within the framework of the pragmatic justification of a method does *not* preclude the prospect of *eventually* reclassifying it as a truth *ex post facto*, once this—duly justified—method is itself *applied*.)[3]

On this line of approach, then, we start with the validating force of an operative precept of regulative status, affording us with a requisite factual input whose standing is initially that of a warranted postulate rather than an established truth. Some such prejustification-as-truth warrant is clearly needed to avoid circularity in the justificatory argument. But nothing vicious ensues if it turns out from the *post-justificatory* standpoint—as indeed if all goes well it must, at least by-and-large—that the thesis whose *antecedent* epistemic status is merely that of a postulate should ultimately acquire the *consequent* status of a truth. Such cognitive upgrading of theses whose *content*, of course, remains uniform throughout is, after all, at the very core of the cyclic feed-back process envisaged in the present analysis. Moreover, there is nothing fatal if in some instances the results of postulation turn out to be such that their consequent status is that of falsehood. A warranted postulate—unlike an established truth—is defeasible and can in the final analysis turn out to be untrue without thereby

---

[2] However, the fact that in a case of this sort a *plurality* of principles comes into play concurrently gives to the over-all analysis a holistic character whose implications are far-reaching. On the one hand, it means that when the justificatory principles P_1, P_2, . . ., P_n jointly lead to the correctness of the appropriate conclusion C, then the entire collection of principles P_1–P_n is supported at one stroke. But on the other hand if P_1, P_2, . . ., P_n fail to yield the appropriateness of C, then it becomes in principle impossible to pinpoint the specific sources of the difficulty in one of the P_i. Negative results are accordingly not very useful. The reader familiar with the discussion of Duhem's thesis in the recent literature of the philosophy of science will be able, *mutatis mutandis*, to apply the lessons of that problem to the present case.

[3] Regarding the process of imputation that underlies such postulational attributions of *propter-hoc* status (on the basis of evidence relating to *post-hoc* relationships) see Chapter IV below, and also the author's *Conceptual Idealism* (Oxford, 1973).

undoing its initial status as warranted. Its acceptance in a regulative and facilitating role in the framework of inquiry does not render it incorrigible at the constitutive level.[4]

4. HUME'S PROBLEM

We come, finally, to yet another serious—and seemingly decisive —obstacle in the way of an experientially pragmatic justification of a methodology of inquiry or thesis-substantiation, namely Hume's problem of the validation of reasoning from past to future.

To begin with, it would seem that any *experiential* justification of a methodology *M of* substantiation in the factual domain envisages a line of argument whose direction of motion is as follows:

M has provided truths → *M* provides truths in general

This form of argument patently comprises *a fortiori* a sub-argument of the form:

M has provided truths → *M* will provide truths[5]

---

[4] This conception of a pragmatically warranted postulate of essentially regulative import bears some points of resemblance to the theory of "fictions" developed in Hans Vaihinger's *Philosophy of "As If"* (tr. C. K. Ogden, London, 1924)—the key point of difference being that Vaihinger's fictions have to be *express falsehoods*. It would be unjust, however, to fail to acknowledge the kinship of ideas, whose actual source is, simply enough, the common influence of Kant.

[5] The "problem of induction" is often formulated specifically in the context of this second thesis, but it is clearly the first that is fundamental, as logicians have stressed since J. S. Mill's day:

> Now it has been well pointed out, that . . . [with inductive generalization] Time, in its modifications of past, present, and future, has no concern either with the belief itself, or with the grounds of it. We believe that fire will burn to-morrow, because it burned to-day and yesterday; but we believe, on precisely the same grounds, that it burned before we were born, and that it burns this very day in Cochin-China. It is not from the past to the future, *as* past and future, that we infer, but from the known to the unknown; from facts observed to facts unobserved; from what we have perceived, or been directly conscious of, to what has not come within our experience. (*A System of Logic*, Bk III, ch. III, sect. 1.)

Now it is clear by parity with our earlier arguments that—quite apart from any special difficulties posed by Hume's problem—no justificatory reasoning of such a form can succeed with respect to that methodology of substantiation which really and truly is in the final analysis to provide our truth-criteria, because the essential premiss that M has provided truths is vacuous in having us judge the products of M by the circulatory trivializing standard of M itself.

But we shall endeavor to show that no comparable difficulty will affect the cognate reasoning that proceeds on the practical (rather than theoretical) side, and has the surface aspect of the following line of reasoning:

M has provided satisfactory results $\rightarrow$ M provides satisfactory results in general

To be sure, this reasoning would comprise *a fortiori* the sub-argument whose principal direction of motion is as follows:

M has provided satisfactory results $\rightarrow$ M will provide satisfactory results

And such an argument, while evading the previous obstacle of circularity, at once encounters Humean difficulties. For it seems that what is at issue here is still an *argument*, though now one of the *practical* form:

works in the past $\rightarrow$ works in the future

rather than the theoretical/cognitive form:

true in the past $\rightarrow$ true in the future

And it would seem that such a line of trans-temporal argument will at once run into the roadblock erected by Hume to preclude inferences regarding the future from premisses relating to the past.

But any such *discursive* appearance is in reality misleading. For our actual concern here is not really at all with an *argument to establish a factual thesis* regarding the relationship of past and future occurrences—such as the regularity of nature—but with *the validation of a practice*: namely the implementation of the precept inherent in the following *practical* policy:

To continue to use a method that has proven to be successful (i.e., more effective than alternatives) in those cases (of suitable numerousness and variety, etc.) where it has been tried.

The validation of this methodological precept lies deep in the nature of practical rationality itself, since it is quintessentially rational to continue to use for the attainment of specified objectives methods and procedures that have proven themselves effective in their realization. And the grounds of this rationality are simple—they are provided by the *faute-de-mieux* consideration that *this is the best one can do.*[6]

There is no need here to deny the sound Humean point that the fact that a certain method has proven successful up to time *t* does not *guarantee* that it will succeed after time *t*. But the thesis that past-success is future-indicative is not and need not be at issue. The critical point is that in the context of our justificatory reasoning we are not dealing with the establishment of a factual thesis at all—be it demonstrative or presumptive—but merely with the rational validation of a practical course of action. And the practical warrant that rationalizes the use of a method need not call for any assurance of success of a type which it is, in the circumstances of the situation in view, altogether impossible to give. Such guarantees being impossible in the very nature of the case, all that need be done in the context of practice-justification is to provide as good reasons as, under the circumstances, one can reasonably hope to have.[7] Accordingly, the pragmatic legitimation of induction does not claim to demonstrate that this method is "correct" but that it is a rational practice to adopt on the ground that if *anything* can count as a sound reason for adopting a practice of inquiry, then the pragmatic success of its past applications must do so.

Of course, the issues that arise here are so complex that these brief indications can do no more than show the general direction

---

[6] The man lost in the woods may well pick a random direction and keep to it. He has no guarantee that it will lead him to a desired destination. But he has the assurance of realizing that under the circumstances no superior avenue of action is open to him.

[7] We shall have occasion to return to this issue of the differences in the ground-rules of rationality as between practical and theoretical contexts in Chapter XII below.

of the proposed resolution. But for present purposes, the important fact is that the rational warranting of action-performance and thesis-acceptance are so different that a promising avenue is open for resolving the Humean difficulty by an experientially pragmatic approach to the justification of a method of inquiry.[8]

5. THE STRUCTURE OF THE PRAGMATIC JUSTIFICATION OF A COGNITIVE METHOD

The resources of presumption and plausibility introduced in the preceding discussion enable us to give a more detailed analysis of the proposed pragmatic legitimation of cognitive methodology. In its fuller perspective, the logical structure of the justificatory process appears as is set out in Figure 2.

Figure 2

THE PRAGMATIC JUSTIFICATION OF A METHODOLOGY OF INQUIRY

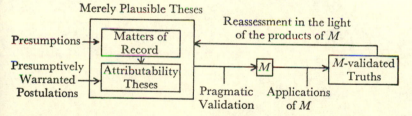

The over-all process envisages a feed-back loop leading from the M-validated truths back to the initial "merely presumptive" truths.

The closure of this cycle affords a test of the adequacy of the presumptions and postulations at issue. Their own appropriateness —and thus that of our means of obtaining such initial, tentative, merely plausible truths—can be reassessed *ex post facto* by deploying the testing capabilities of M against them. To be sure, it

[8] The line of reasoning sketched in this section is worked out in somewhat greater detail in Chapter II, "A Pragmatic Justification of Induction" of the author's *The Primacy of Practice* (Oxford, 1973). Parts of the present discussion have been drawn from this book.

would not count as seriously invalidating if *in occasional particular instances, propter hoc* attributability-contentions should be ultimately classed as false by the method of substantiation (that the method should, so to speak, *on occasion* bite the hand that feeds it with substantiating materials). But clearly if *most* of these were to turn out false in the light of M, something would have gone seriously amiss. The *reasonableness* of the over-all process thus rests not only on the (external) element of success inherent in the factor of pragmatic efficacy, but also on the (internal) factor of intrinsic coherence and the mutual support of self-substantiation that the various stages of the whole are able to lend to one another. The justificatory rationale must as a whole be coherent and self-sustaining—a theme to which we shall later have occasion to return from various directions of approach (especially in Chapters VII and X).

Chapter IV

DEFICIENCIES OF THESIS PRAGMATISM

I. THE NATURE OF THESIS PRAGMATISM

This chapter will deal specifically with those epistemological theories that attempt to employ pragmatic tests directly as a criterion or standard of warranted-acceptability-as-true at the level of individual claims or beliefs—theories that envisage a direct relationship between the utility of accepting theses and their (presumptive) truth.[1] According to the traditional pragmatic theory of truth, what determines the truth-acceptability of propositions is the factor of their *utility:* a proposition is to count as true if the practical consequences of its acceptance outweigh those of its non-acceptance or perhaps rather—and better—those of its rejection (i.e., the acceptance of its contradictory denial). The rationale of this pragmatic theory seems to reside in the (surely ill-advised) view that one cannot profit by error, and fare better by rejecting a true proposition than by accepting it (or by accepting a false proposition than by rejecting it.) Perhaps by contraposing the plausible thesis that being right is the most advantageous circumstance, such an approach construes maximal utility as a safe indicator of truth. Accordingly, we are to determine whether or not a proposition qualifies as true by assessing the *utility* of endorsing this thesis as compared with its possible alternatives. The truth, to put it crudely, is that whose acceptance is maximally utile and "works out for the best." As William James puts it, "ideas become true in so far as they help us to get into satisfactory relation with other parts of our experience."

Let us consider more clearly this sort of relationship claimed to obtain by philosophers of the Pragmatist school between the

[1] The force of the words "direct" and "immediate" here is to rule out of consideration our own present theory which sees an *indirect* relationship between utility and truth through the mediation of methods, with methods of inquiry validated through their practical success and theses then in their turn verified by the use of such duly validated methods.

truth of our beliefs and their practical utility. William James, the classic exponent of this doctrine, put the matter as follows:

> The possession of truth, so far from being here an end in itself, is only a preliminary means towards other vital satisfactions. . . . True ideas would never have been singled out as such, would never have acquired a class-name, least of all a name suggesting [positive] value, unless they had been useful from the outset in this way. . . . Primarily, and on the common-sense level, the truth of a state of mind means this function of *a leading that is worth while*. . . . Our account of truth is an account of truths in the plural, of processes of leading; realized *in rebus*, and having only this quality in common, that they *pay*.[2]

James and his followers in what might be called the mainstream of pragmatic tradition saw a straightforward relationship between truth and the success of implementing accepted propositions in action. The rationale of their thinking seems to have been that acting on false suppositions is ultimately bound to produce failure in realizing one's objectives, so that, conversely, the success of belief-implementing actions can serve as an indicator of truth for the guiding beliefs.

This position is not confined to the traditional philosophical pragmatists. For example, various recent methodologists of science have reacted against Rudolf Carnap's thesis that science can dispense with accepting hypotheses as true by holding that scientists *do* accept hypotheses, albeit on purpose-oriented rather than strictly cognitive grounds. On the view of this school of thought, "accepting a hypothesis as true" is to be reinterpreted to amount to "acting or being disposed to act in the manner which would be best (relative to the objectives in view) if the hypothesis

---

[2] *Pragmatism* (New York, 1907), pp. 203–5 and 218. Compare a similar passage in another place:

> First, ideas *are* practically useful in the narrow sense . . . most often ideas which we can verify by the sum total of all their leadings, and the reality of whose objects may thus be considered established beyond doubt. . . .This manner of their practical working was the first thing that made truths good in the eyes of primitive men; and buried among all the other good workings by which true beliefs are characterized, this kind of subsequential utility remains. (*The Meaning of Truth* [New York, 1912], pp. 207–8.)

were true."[3] Accordingly, such a view of scientific cognition also proposes to determine acceptability-as-true with reference to successful action.[4] The position at issue here is in line with that of Richard Rudner's much-discussed 1956 paper, "The Scientist *Qua* Scientist Makes Value Judgments,"[5] where it is maintained that:

> For, since no scientific hypothesis is ever completely verified, in accepting a hypothesis the scientist must make the decision that the evidence is *sufficiently* strong or that the probability is *sufficiently* high to warrant the acceptance of the hypothesis. Obviously our decision regarding the evidence, and respecting how strong is "strong enough," is going to be a function of the *importance*, in the typically ethical sense, of making a mistake in accepting or rejecting the hypothesis. . . . *How sure we need to be before we accept a hypothesis will depend on how serious a mistake would be.*[6]

Clearly, this idea of the seriousness of mistakes ensuing upon acceptance of a scientific thesis points to a rationale of propositional acceptance (within a practical context) based on the pragmatic criterion of the *practical consequences of acting in implementation of the accepted thesis.*

The "utility" of thesis-acceptance can, of course, be conceived in two ways, according to whether the issue is taken to be one of

    (i) *practical utilities* having to do with the concrete effects for the conduct of the affairs of life, be they beneficial or malign, or

---

[3] See Richard C. Jeffrey, "Valuation and Acceptance of Scientific Hypotheses," *Philosophy of Science*, vol. 23 (1956), pp. 237–46. Reprinted in B. A. Brody (ed.), *Readings in the Philosophy of Science* (Englewood Cliffs, 1970). In this article Jeffrey criticizes the invocation of this decision rule to validate propositional acceptance in the Churchman-Rudner manner, but does so for reasons only remotely related to those canvassed in this chapter.

[4] Cf., for example, C. W. Churchman, "Science and Decision Making," *Philosophy of Science*, vol. 23 (1956), pp. 247–9.

[5] *Philosophy of Science*, vol. 20 (1953), pp. 1–6. Reprinted in B. A. Brody (ed.), *Readings in the Philosophy of Science* (Englewood Cliffs, 1970).

[6] *Ibid.*, p. 2.

(ii) *cognitive utilities* that are purely theoretical and have to do not with success in practical matters, but only with cognitive success in "being right" in one's judgments and in being effective in the construction of explanatory mechanisms and in yielding verifiable (i.e., correct) predictions.

Now the second category of *cognitive* or *epistemic* utilities shall not concern us here, any more than they concerned the classical pragmatists (putting aside a bit of wavering on the part of the later William James). Our present interest is wholly in the *practical* or *pragmatic* aspect of the utility of beliefs that relates to their role in the guidance of human action.

We shall endeavor to exhibit the serious difficulties in the way of maintaining this pragmatist doctrine of a direct relationship between the pragmatic utility of beliefs on the one hand and their truth on the other. It will be argued that genuinely pragmatic utility is simply not capable of bearing the weight imposed on it when it is used in the role of a decision-criterion for the determination of truth or acceptability.

2. PRAGMATIC UTILITY AS A TEST OF ACCEPTABILITY

What might be called the *standard approach* to the issue of pragmatic utility proceeds on the following basis:

The pragmatic utility of *theses* is derivative in nature, and is determinable in terms of the ground-floor utility of *states of affairs*. For the pragmatic utility of a belief is to be determined in terms of the utility of the states of affairs whose actual or probable realization is attributable to acceptance of the thesis.

Accordingly, three key steps comprise the over-all process of utility-of-belief determination

(1) The acceptance of a thesis (or holding of a belief) is seen as issuing in a duly accordant *course of action*.

(2) A course of action is seen as issuing—in fact or probabi-

listically—in a resulting *state of affairs:* an "outcome" which is an objective "condition of things" obtaining in the world.

(3) A utility-calculus at the level of world-states is applied at *this* point, and its result projected back unto the result-initiating beliefs.

On this account, the pragmatic utility of a thesis becomes, in effect, that of the state of affairs that would result as outcome from its acceptance (be it *determinate* or probabilistic, i.e., *expected*, values that are at issue). The basic model operative here is that the holding of a belief P induces a series of actions a_i that produce a state of affairs S. On this approach, the *pragmatic* utility of accepting P is to be identified with (or otherwise calculated in terms of) the *situational* utility of S, and the acceptance of P is to revolve about this consideration. It is this approach that we are now concerned to examine critically.

In somewhat more formal terms, a pragmatic criterion of thesis-acceptability takes on a shape that can best be apprehended by introducing a bit of symbolic machinery. Let P, Q, R, etc., represent theses. There will now be two correlative modes of "cognitive action" in terms of an acceptance-operator α.

$\alpha(P)$ = accepting the thesis P
$\tilde{\alpha}(P)$ = not accepting the thesis P

(Note that not accepting P, i.e., $\tilde{\alpha}(P)$, is very different from accepting not-P, i.e., $\alpha(\neg P)$.) Let us begin on this basis by contemplating the four theoretically available alternatives. (1) $\alpha(P)$ & $\tilde{\alpha}(\neg P)$, (2) $\alpha(\neg P)$ & $\tilde{\alpha}(P)$, (3) $\alpha(P)$ & $\alpha(\neg P)$, and (4) $\tilde{\alpha}(P)$ & $\tilde{\alpha}(\neg P)$. Since *rational* acceptance is to be at issue, the principle of operation for the acceptance-operator α must clearly embody the rule: If $\alpha(P)$, then $\tilde{\alpha}(\bar{P})$. (Note: We shall henceforth abbreviate $\neg P$ as $\bar{P}$.) We thus arrive at the following upshot: Case (1) is tantamount simply to $\alpha(P)$ itself, case (2) simply to $\alpha(\bar{P})$ itself, and case (3) is inherently impossible. The alternatives regarding the acceptability of P are thus reduced to three mutually exclusive and exhaustive cases:

αP, $\alpha\bar{P}$, $\tilde{\alpha}P$ and $\tilde{\alpha}\bar{P}$ [We now drop unneeded parentheses.]

Only three possibilities exist: acceptance, rejection, and agnosticism. (We shall henceforth abbreviate the third as $\alpha^*(P)$.)

At this stage, we can return to the idea of a utility-measure for actions along the lines envisaged above:

> *Util* [an action] = the utility of the state of affairs resulting from its execution

Given any utility measure, one can implement a *Bayesian* decision program by guiding action in terms of a program of maximizing the expected utility of its outcome. On this approach, one applies the general decision-rule:

> Within the range of available action-alternatives adopt that for which the estimate of the resulting utility (or the expected value thereof) is a maximum.

This decision-rule is sometimes called the "Bayesian criterion" for rational choice among action-alternatives.[7] Applying this rule to our special case of propositional acceptance, we must examine in its light the three exclusive and exhaustive alternatives of acceptance, rejection, and suspension of judgment.

How serious a matter is error? Some regard it as akin to a heinous crime. W. K. Clifford certainly thought so. In his classic 1877 essay on "The Ethics of Belief" (to which William James's even more famous essay of 1895 on "The Will to Believe" offered a reply) Clifford maintained that:

> It is wrong, always, everywhere, and for everyone to believe anything upon insufficient evidence.[8]

Some writers have even gone so far as to push this sort of judg-

---

[7] See R. Duncan Luce and Howard Raiffa, *Games and Decisions* (New York, 1957), pp. 312–13.

[8] *Lectures and Essays*, Vol. II (London, 1879); originally published in the *Contemporary Review*, vol. 30 (1887), pp. 42–54. For a useful outline of the James-Clifford controversy and its background see Peter Kauber, "The Foundations of James' Ethics of Belief," *Ethics*, vol. 84 (1974), pp. 151–66, where the relevant issues are set out and further references to the literature are given. For a particularly interesting recent treatment see Roderick Chisholm, "Lewis' Ethics of Belief" in *The Philosophy of C. I. Lewis*, ed. by P. A. Schilpp (La Salle, 1968), pp. 223–42.

ment to its logical conclusion by pressing it towards the boundaries that separate the morally reprehensible from the legally criminal. For example, in Janet Chance's ardent little book on *Intellectual Crime*, one finds "the making of statements that outstrip the evidence" prominently enrolled on the register of this category of "crimes."[9]

William James quite properly argued against W. K. Clifford that the enterprise of inquiry is governed not only by the negative injunction "Avoid error!" but no less importantly by the positive injunction "Achieve truth!" And, in the factual area—where the *content* of our claims outstrips the evidence we can ever gather from them—this (so he insists) demands the risk of error. There is nothing irrational about this risk, quite to the contrary: "a rule of thinking which would absolutely prevent one from acknowledging certain kinds of truth, if those kinds of truth were really there, would be an irrational rule."[10] There are in fact very different sorts of "errors." There are errors of the first kind, errors of omission arising when we do not accept P when P is in fact the case. These involve the penalty (disvalue) of *ignorance*. And there are also errors of the second kind—errors of commission —arising when we accept P when in fact $\bar{P}$. These involve the penalty of cognitive dissonance and outright *mistake*.

Let us look at the matter in a Jamesian perspective as one of combining balancing the desideratum of error-avoidance off against that of information-loss. We then arrive at a situation

---

[9] Janet Chance, *Intellectual Crime* (London, 1933), pp. 33–4.

[10] *The Will to Believe and Other Essays in Popular Philosophy* (New York, 1956), pp. 27–8. Clifford's tough line on belief in the religious sphere is not matched by a corresponding toughness in the sphere of scientific knowledge, where he took a confidently realistic position. Rejecting the possibility of certainty here, he stressed that what we accept as our "knowledge" of nature rests on various interpretative principles, which, though indemonstrable, are nevertheless necessary for man's survival, and whose acceptance is thus to be accounted for (though not *established*) in evolutionary terms. He held the uniformity of nature to be such a principle, maintaining that "Nature is selecting for survival those individuals and races who act as if it were uniform; and hence the gradual spread of this belief over the civilized world" (*op. cit.*, p. 209). James' own position against Clifford comes down to saying that what's sauce for the scientific goose is sauce for the religious gander as well.

somewhat as follows (where $v(P)$ is to be a measure of the "value" or raw utility of the thesis P):

Payoff Matrix

Actual Situation	Course 1 Accept P (αP)	Course 2 Accept $\bar{P}$ ($\alpha\bar{P}$)	Course 3 Suspend Judgment re. P ($\alpha*P$, i.e., $\tilde{\alpha}P$ and $\tilde{\alpha}\bar{P}$)
P obtains	$+ v(P)$	$K \times - v(P)$	$- v(P)$
$\bar{P}$ obtains	$K \times - v(\bar{P})$	$+ v(\bar{P})$	$- v(\bar{P})$

Here K is a constant that fixes the seriousness of the penalty of "falling into error"—the larger the value we assign to K, the more cautious we will be in running the risk of error, and the more weight we give to errors of the second kind *vis-à-vis* those of the first. (A Cliffordian will make K relatively large, a Jamesian relatively small.[11])

We can now do some expected-value calculations regarding the utilities of various acceptance-postures towards P:

Expectations (with x as the probability of P):

$$E(\alpha P) = x \cdot v(P) + (1 - x) \cdot K \cdot -v(\bar{P})$$
$$E(\alpha\bar{P}) = x \cdot K \cdot -v(P) + (1 - x) \cdot v(\bar{P})$$
$$E(\alpha*P) = x \cdot -v(P) + (1 - x) \cdot -v(P)$$

Let us adopt the abbreviation U for the value of a thesis as weighted by its probability:

$$U(P) = \text{pr}(P) \cdot v(P)$$

Then we have

---

[11] But K would never be very small (very close to 1). As long as we keep our acceptance-set consistent, the inclusion of error *blocks* accepting further truths, while non-acceptance never blocks anything. Errors of the first kind are thus substantially more serious than those of the second (for which $K = 1$, in effect).

$$E(\alpha P) = U(P) - K \cdot U(\bar{P})$$
$$E(\alpha \bar{P}) = -K \cdot U(P) + U(\bar{P})$$
$$E(\alpha^* P) = -U(P) - U(\bar{P})$$

Thus we are to accept P in the following circumstance:

$E(\alpha P) > E(\alpha \bar{P})$ iff
$$U(P) - K \cdot U(\bar{P}) > -K \cdot U(P) + U(\bar{P}), \text{ and so}$$
$$U(P) \cdot (1 + K) > U(\bar{P}) \cdot (1 + K), \text{ or equivalently}$$
$$U(\bar{P}) < U(P)$$

And, of course, by symmetry

$$E(\alpha \bar{P}) > E(\alpha P) \text{ iff } U(P) < U(\bar{P})$$

Note that when it comes to the choice of P *vs* $\bar{P}$, the value of the penalty-constant K does not matter.

Let us next take up the case of a suspension of judgment

$E(\alpha^* P) > E(\alpha P)$ iff
$$-U(P) - U(\bar{P}) > U(P) - K \cdot U(\bar{P}), \text{ or}$$
$$U(\bar{P}) \cdot K - 1 > 2U(P), \text{ or equivalently}$$
$$U(\bar{P}) > \frac{2}{K-1} U(P)$$

$E(\alpha^* P) > E(\alpha \bar{P})$ iff
$$-U(P) - U(\bar{P}) > -K \cdot U(P) + U(\bar{P}), \text{ or}$$
$$U(P)(K-1) > 2U(\bar{P}), \text{ or equivalently}$$
$$U(P) > \frac{2}{K-1} U(\bar{P})$$

Suspension of judgment is indicated just when both of these conditions are satisfied.

The general position of affairs is depicted in Figure 1.

In the region below Line I, accepting P is preferable to a suspension of judgment. In the region above Line II, rejecting P (accepting $\bar{P}$) is preferable to a suspension of judgment. In the region between the lines a suspension of judgment is preferable to either alternative. The angle between Lines I and II depends on the size of the number K which determines how serious a sanction "falling into error" actually is. When $K = 3$ we're in the straight comparison case. When $K > 3$, then, as K gets bigger, the region of uncertainty grows, until it becomes all-pervasive as $K \to \infty$. The broken central line indicates the boundary above which we are

Figure 1

ACCEPTABILITY RELATIONSHIPS

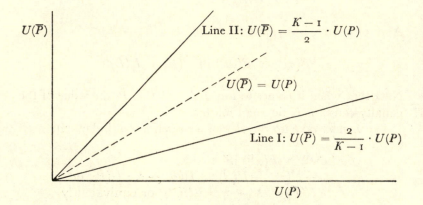

better off accepting $\bar{P}$ and below which $\bar{P}$ is preferable in a forced choice between P and $\bar{P}$. (This is, of course, independent of K.)

The picture of Figure 1 makes it graphically clear how telling James' argument against Clifford in fact is. In viewing "falling into error" as virtually a fate worse than death—taking K to be very large indeed—Clifford cuts himself off from Butler's view of probability as a guide to life. Any sort of calculated risk in the whole empirical sphere of the inherently less-than-certain is now precluded. As James saw, Clifford failed to sail between Scylla and Charybdis—he avoids error of the second kind (errors of commission) only at the price of massive errors of the first kind (errors of omission).

All the utility-models of propositional acceptance lead to an upshot of the same general structure: A thesis P is to be accepted iff the expected utility of its acceptance exceeds some specified quantity which may or may not be allowed to vary with P itself.

The pragmatic approaches in view all adopt the same general idea: acceptance is to be correlative with possession of a "sufficiently large" utility.

Having considered how a pragmatist theory of thesis-acceptability proposes to proceed, we shall now see the substantial obstacles which such a program is bound to encounter.

3. THE MACHINERY OF UTILITY ASSESSMENT

To begin with, it is necessary to introduce a bit more machinery to facilitate the handling of utility-considerations. Let us examine the workings of a utility-of-acceptance model a little more closely by way of a specific illustration. The sorts of examples we shall be dealing with throughout envisage a person who is asked to select (on the basis of otherwise unspecified cues and clues) a position at which an object is to be found within a (nonpresented) tic-tac-toe configuration—subject to some reward for getting the matter right or some penalty for getting it wrong. Specifically, suppose a person hunts for the object—valued at 12 utiles— placed at a position (unknown to him) in a 9-place network. Suppose that in actual fact such an object is placed in the following x-indicated compartment:

If the searcher believes the sought object to be placed at the row/column position 1/2, the pragmatic utility value of this belief—producing, as it does, the *situational* result of "finding the object", a result whose value is (*ex hypothesi*) 12 utiles— will itself be 12u. On the other hand, if the person believes that the object is at the central row/column position 2/2, the pragmatic utility of this belief will be 0.

Of course beliefs—unlike concrete situations outside the quantum-mechanical realm—can be *indefinite* or fundamentally *disjunctive* in nature. That is, our searcher might well believe simply that the sought object is placed in the first row (i.e., *some-place* in the first row—without any more definite idea). Since the searcher is (*ex hypothesi*) indifferent as between the three situations 1/1, 1/2, and 1/3, whose situation-utility value is 0, 12, and 0 units, respectively, we may in this case suppose an effectively random resolution to be made, and so assign *the expected value* as the resultant pragmatic utility, thus arriving at a result of 4*u*.

These considerations provide the machinery for dealing with the utility of theses by means of which the ensuing critique of thesis pragmatism can be developed efficiently and economically.

4. THE CLAIMS OF PRAGMATISM AND THE LINK BETWEEN UTILITY AND TRUTH

Given the machinery of the preceding section we can analyze with precision a pragmatist rule for the acceptance-as-true of beliefs regarding the make-up of our tic-tac-toe configurations. The analysis proceeds on the basis that such a claim is to count as true if *both* of two conditions obtain:

(1) *its acceptance is itself of a relatively high utility* (say two-thirds of the maximum of 12 units, that is, 8 units or greater), and

(2) *its acceptance is of greater utility than acceptance of its contradictory denial.* (These two conditions accord with the general principles laid down in section 2 above.)

Let us consider how such a pragmatist standard of truth fares. The queries we shall now raise are intended to throw doubt on this part of the pragmatic program by showing just how great the gap between truth and utility in fact is.

Query 1: Need an actually true belief be more utile than a false one?

Consider *A*'s mistaken belief that there are no *x*'s on the principal diagonal of the following set-up:

So long as *A* holds this belief (in a context of agnosticism at other points, apart from the conviction that there are some *x*'s within the configuration), he is *bound* to succeed in selecting an *x*'d position. The mistaken belief at issue is thus worth $12u$. On the other hand, suppose that *A* believes (again more or less *in vacuo*) that there are two *x*'s in the first row. The expected value of this true belief will merely be $8u$. Clearly, a true belief need not prove more utile than a false one (in the present sense of "utility" in terms of the pay-off resulting from implementation in action).[12]

Query 2: Need a more utile belief prove a better-qualified candidate for truth than a less utile one?

An example will serve to show that the query in view must once again be answered in the negative. In fact, it is simple to see that even a *maximally* utile belief need not be true. Assume the following set-up:

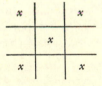

Consider now *A*'s belief: "*x*'s occur *just* (i.e., *only*) at the four extreme positions." Clearly this belief, albeit false, will unfailingly

---

[12] Bertrand Russell repeatedly argued just this point against William James and F. S. C. Schiller:

> [On a pragmatic theory of truth] persecution can actually make a doctrine true which would otherwise be false, since it can make a doctrine "useful to our lives." In the absence of any standard of truth other than success, it seems evident that the familiar methods of the struggle for existence must be applied to the elucidation of difficult questions, and that ironclads and Maxim guns must be the ultimate arbiters of metaphysical truth. (*Philosophical Essays* [London, 1910], pp. 123–4.)

C

lead *A* to *act* (i.e., make his one-shot selection) in a way that is as utile as any belief can be. In particular, the true belief that there is an *x* in the second row is clearly less utile than the false belief at issue.

Thus the linkage of the utility of beliefs to their truth is more problematic than might appear on first thought to be the case.

The attacks launched in this section against the claim of a direct linkage between utility and truth are variations on an old theme. Examples of the sort envisaged here have been the stock in trade of critics of pragmatism since the early days of B. Russell and G. E. Moore in the first decade of this century.[13] The linkage between truth and utility, they insisted, is just too loose: a false thesis may be useful (we can do very effective astronomy on a Ptolemaic basis!) and a true thesis may not be useful (as the fearful man who rightly believes his own life in danger may panic and further endanger himself and others). But behind these *substantive* objections there lurks yet another that is more discomfiting and more far-reaching.

5. THE "ILLOGICAL" NATURE OF UTILITY

The discrepancies between truth and utility brought out in the preceding examples are symptomatic of the decisively damaging fact that utility simply fails to comport itself in accordance with logical principles that do and must govern the behavior of truth.

---

[13] Already in 1891 C. S. Peirce had suggested that while the axioms of Euclidean geometry had served man so well that evolution had rendered them "expressions of our inborn conception of space" still "that affords not the slightest reason for supposing them exact," and and indeed the universe may well be non-Euclidean. (*Collected Papers*, VI: 6.29) Russell, for example, argued that, since the contrary of what is utile for one person might be utile for another, James is caught in the trap that "his doctrines lead to the conclusion that different people ought to have incompatible beliefs" (*op. cit.*, p. 308). (A convenient avenue of access to the relevant discussions is A. Rorty [ed.], *Pragmatic Philosophy: An Anthology* [New York, 1966].) An interesting modern perspective on the issues is given in the section "Does Practice Validate Theory?" of Mario Bunge, "Technology as Applied Science" in F. Rapp (ed.), *Contributions to a Philosophy of Technology* (Dordrecht, 1974), pp.19–39, where it is forcibly argued that "the practical success or failure of a scientific theory is no objective index of its truth-value" (p. 24).

This can be brought out by the consideration that a utile belief can be undone as such by others copresent in its context. For this means that utility must behave in a manner altogether at odds with truth.

Thesis 1: The utility of beliefs (unlike their truth) cannot be appraised independently but must be judged *en bloc* in the setting of an entire belief-system.

For consider a person A operating in the context of a selection-configuration set-up of the by-now familiar sort:

Let it be supposed that A believes (otherwise *in vacuo*) that an x is located in the second row. This yields an expected value of success of $8u$, and so seems far more utile than, *inter alia*, its contradictory, the belief that no x is located in the second row. But note that if A *already believes* the (also relatively utile) thesis that all the x's there are are located along the principal diagonal, then the belief initially at issue is a decisively unfortunate one because it ensures utter failure (whereas its contradictory would produce certain success in the context of the "background" belief).

The *truthfulness* of a proposition can never become unstuck in this manner: the truth of a complex entails the truth of its parts. But the issue of utility leads us into a connected-nexus situation that must be approached holistically. For utile beliefs present a composite ensemble from which no separations are possible in such a way that "all else remains intact."

Let us pause for a moment to consider the posture of the utilitarian who, conceding this line of argument, takes the following position:

In the face of such considerations (so says our utilitarian) we must clearly take a holistic stance as to the relationship of truth to utility. One must accordingly refrain from imputing truth to *individual* theses on the basis of their isolated utility, but must proceed with a view to the utility of entire *belief systems*. Only when a thesis is a member of a belief system that is utile over-all should one claim truth for it.

This holistic position still has its difficulties. For what is "whole and complete" to mean here? Is such completeness to be *internal* to the belief-system, or is it a matter of the *external* relationship of the system to "the real world" (and *ergo* something which renders the idea at issue effectively inoperable)? Thus, consider the man *A* whose belief-internal picture of some sector of reality looks thus:

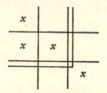

Now while this is to be the sum and substance of *A*'s belief-world, as pictured within the horizons of his own knowledge, the "real"-world actually looks thus:

Note that *A*'s (incorrect) belief-picture is such that he will never make an improper choice in practical action. Thus *A*'s incorrect picture cannot be faulted on practical grounds. But on the one hand, he will *undeservedly* possess certain truths (e.g., "There are *x*'s all along the main diagonal"). And on the other hand, *A* will be also committed to certain outright falsehoods (e.g., "Only the position 1/2 lacks an *x*").

So much, then, for the idea that the utilitarian can extricate himself from the difficulties generated through Thesis 1 by adopting a holistic line of approach.

Resuming the principal line of thought, let us now consider a fact closely related to the preceding thesis, viz.:

Thesis 2: A conjunction of separately utile beliefs need not be conjunctively utile.

This thesis may be established by means of the same example:

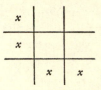

Note that "There are no x's in the first two rows" and "There are no x's in the last two columns" are both relatively utile beliefs. But their *conjunction*—which is equivalent with "All the x's there are, are in the lower left-hand corner"—is emphatically disutile, indeed of zero utility. This clearly illustrates the fact that the pragmatic utility of beliefs will behave in a way radically at variance with the behavior of truthfulness. (Clearly, beliefs that are severally true cannot but prove true in conjunction.)

But even worse is yet to come concerning the "logical" aspects of the matter:

Thesis 3: The logical consequences of utile beliefs need not themselves be utile.

Consider the situation:

Now the belief "There is an x in the upper left-hand position" is definitely utile, but its *disjunction* with "There is an x in one of the two rightmost positions of the first row" yields a result tantamount to "There is an x someplace in the first row." And *this* thesis, itself clearly a logical consequence of the initial one, is emphatically disutile (having a utility of 4, while that of its negation is 12). Since the logical consequences of truths must inevitably be true themselves, this thesis again brings out the drastic disparity between the comportment of utility and that of truth.

The upshot of these considerations is that while truth must

behave in a manner conformable to the inferential principles of logic, pragmatic utility emphatically does not. The cold—and, from the standpoint of a pragmatic theory of verification, cruel—fact is that pragmatically utile theses do not in general behave like truths. This at bottom is the reason why the pragmatic doctrine that the truthfulness of beliefs hinges upon the extent of their utility must come to grief as long as the utility-appraisal is made in the manner standardly envisaged, viz., as a utility-assessment of the states of affairs produced by actions that implement an acceptance of the theses at issue. Utility is ill-fitted to serve as straightforward arbiter of truth. The discrepancy in behavior between the truth-status of theses and their utility-ramifications darkens the prospects of a pragmatic standard of acceptability in anything like its classic Jamesian form.[14]

6. THE ROOTS OF THE DIFFICULTY

It is illuminating to probe more deeply into the bases of our argument and so set out its structure with somewhat greater precision and detail.

The starting point is the idea of a pragmatic criterion of thesis-acceptability as per the following fundamental equivalence: P is to be classed as acceptable—let us abbreviate this as $!P$ by pressing an acceptance-imperator ($!$) into service—provided that the utility of its acceptance exceeds some suitable function of the utilities of the available alternatives, viz., the nonacceptance of P or the acceptance of $\neg P$:

(I) $!P$ iff $u[\alpha(P)] > \Phi[u[\alpha \neg P], u[\tilde{\alpha}(P)]]$, for some suitable combination function Φ

Now clearly the acceptance-imperator $!$ must in any event function in such a way at least that the principles of logic are satisfied, principles such as:

(1) $!P$ entails that not $!(\neg P)$
(2) $!(P \& Q)$ iff both $!P$ and $!Q$

14 Sections 3–5 draw on a paper "On the Truth-Relevancy of the Pragmatic Utility of Beliefs" written in collaboration with Thomas C. Vinci and published in *The Review of Metaphysics*, vol. 28 (1975), pp. 443–452.

(3) $\vdash P$ entails $!P$ (here $\vdash$ represents truth on logical grounds)
(4) $!P$ and $P \vdash Q$ together entail $!Q$ (here $\vdash$ represents logical consequence)

Now given the fundamental equivalence (I), these principles become tantamount to conditions upon the utility-measure u. In setting this out it is handy to abbreviate $\Phi[u[\alpha(\neg P)], u[\tilde{\alpha}(P)]]$ as simply $\Gamma(P)$. On this basis the principles (1)–(4) can be transposed into:

(1′) $u[\alpha(P)] > \Gamma(P)$ entails $u[\alpha(\neg P)] \leqslant \Gamma(\neg P)$
(2′) $u[\alpha(P \& Q)] > \Gamma(P \& Q)$ iff both $u[\alpha(P)] > \Gamma(P)$
and $u[\alpha(Q)] > \Gamma(Q)$
(3′) $\vdash P$ entails $u[\alpha(P)] > \Gamma(P)$
(4′) $u[\alpha(P)] > \Gamma(P)$ and $P \vdash Q$ together entail $u[\alpha(Q)] > \Gamma(Q)$

Let us characterize as X-utility a construction of an acceptance-utility measure u that conforms to these various abstract conditions needed to underwrite the operation of the usual principles of logic. Only such an X-utility can serve to make a pragmatic criterion of thesis-acceptability satisfy the at least minimally necessary condition of accommodating basic logical principles.

Now the entire point and purport of the preceding argument is simply this, that there is a decisive gap between this artificial X-utility of the theoreticians and the sort of genuine, real-life utility which alone can serve the traditional pragmatists' program of determining thesis-acceptability. A fundamental dilemma arises: the *sort* of "utility" (viz., X-utility) needed to make the theory adequate on the logical side is not conformable to the real-life utility-considerations espoused by the pragmatists; and the realistic modes of utility which pragmatists have in fact envisaged are not capable of bearing the logical burdens which a workable criterion of propositional acceptance will have to bear.

The difficulties encountered by the pragmatic theory are now readily characterized in terms of a dilemma:

(1) If it is *practical* utilities that are at issue, then the bridge from utility to truth is broken. There is no reason of principle why acceptance of a falsehood should not be enormously benefit-conducive, or why something that is

benefit-conducive should be true.[15] There may well be *some* positive correlation between the truth of propositions and the practical utility of their espousal, but this is by no means enough to warrant taking the one as a criterion for the other.[16]

(2) If it is *cognitive* utilities that are at issue, then a link between utility and truth is indeed maintained. But now pragmatism is effectively abandoned as an ultimate standard of truth, since the conception of "working out" in the specifically cognitive sense of "being correct" can be implemented only through an *independent* criterion of truth of an essentially non-pragmatic character. In taking the view that the ideas of "having positive effects" and "working out" are to be interpreted as "being right" and "being correct," we in effect *bypass* the pragmatic formulation and go over to a different (presumably correspondentist) criterion of truth. Insofar as practical utilities are abandoned in favor of strictly cognitive ones, the characteristic genius of the pragmatic theory is simply ignored.

These considerations point to the dilemma that we either (1) maintain the link between utility and truth through the cognitive construction of utilities, but then risk abandonment of an essentially pragmatic approach; or else (2) maintain an emphatically pragmatist perspective through the genuinely practical construction of utilities, but then sacrifice the prospect of a warrant for the move from utility-maximization to truth. The critical—and

---

[15] The literature of the subject is replete with examples of the following sort: a man mistakenly believes he has a certain disease and mistakenly believes a certain medication is called for by way of treatment. Unbeknown to himself, he actually has another, more serious malady against which this medicine is highly effective. If he "knew the truth" he would suffer badly, being altogether ignorant of any remedy for his actual condition. For variations on this theme see the Appendix to this chapter.

[16] In the first decade of this century, this line of objection was heavily pressed against William James by A. O. Lovejoy in "The Thirteen Pragmatisms," *The Journal of Philosophy*, vol. 5 (1908), pp. 1–12 and 29–39, and by Bertrand Russell in *Philosophical Essays* (London, 1910). Even John Dewey, his own pragmatist ally, criticized James to the effect that he had confounded the intellectual issues of what can satisfy the inquiring mind with the issue of genuinely pragmatic values.

ultimately fatal—tension between the role of purely cognitive satisfactions (utilities, etc.) and those that are strictly practical has never been fully resolved by the pragmatists.[17]

Of course nothing in our discussion precludes the inherently not implausible prospect that the pragmatic utility of theses might somehow serve as a *plausibilistic or probabilistic indicator* of their truth. However, the Jamesian version of pragmatism goes far beyond this very modest sort of relationship to establish the factor of pragmatic utility as a *criterion* of truth. But this—as our argument shows—involves pressing its claims beyond tenable limits.

7. A VARIANT FORM OF THESIS PRAGMATISM: PEIRCE'S THEORY OF TRUTH

A "pragmatic theory of truth" is generally construed with reference to a criterion which assesses the claims to truth of a thesis in terms of the *success* engendered by its acceptance (its conduciveness to the realization of some sort of "utility"). But this construction takes an overly restricted view of the matter, for it interprets the theory in its specifically Jamesian form, slighting the

[17] William James, for example, sometimes wrote as though the purely cognitive, theoretical satisfactions were the principle issue: "But particular consequences can perfectly well be of a theoretic nature. Every remote fact which we infer from an idea is a particular theoretic consequence which our mind practically works towards. The loss of every old opinion of ours which we see that we shall have to give up if a new opinion be true, is a particular theoretic as well as a particular practical consequence. After man's interest in breathing freely, the greatest of all his interests (because it never fluctuates or remits, as most of his physical interests do), is his interest in *consistency*, in feeling that what he now thinks goes with what he thinks on other occasions. We tirelessly compare truth with truth for this sole purpose. Is the present candidate for belief perhaps contradicted by principle number one? Is it compatible with fact number two? and so forth. The particular operations here are the purely logical ones of analysis, deduction, comparison, etc.; and although general terms may be used *ad libitum*, the satisfactory *practical working* of the candidate-idea consists in the consciousness yielded by each successive theoretic consequence in particular. It is therefore simply idiotic to repeat that pragmatism takes no account of purely theoretic interests" (*The Meaning of Truth: A Sequel to Pragmatism* [New York, 1909]; quoted from A. Rorty [ed.], *Pragmatic Philosophy* [New York, 1966], p. 188).

fact that other pragmatists approached the matter quite differently. Peirce is a prime example. His criterion for assessing the truth of a factual thesis was not at all the factor of its applicative *success*, but its stability or staying-power: the simple temporal constancy of its long-run espousal within the scientific community.

The structure of Peirce's approach is roughly as follows: There is an established methodology of investigation—the scientific method—which is used in an ongoing way within the community of rational inquirers. The key determinant of the correctness of a thesis appears from the historical record of the rulings regarding it through continued reassessments by means of this methodology. (Note that the issue of the continuity of the scientific method as one historically uniform methodology is crucial here. If the methods at issue here differed over time, then the fact that some rule for and others against a thesis is probatively useless, and the significance of the time-series aspect of how the theses fare on different occasions would be undone.) But if we suppose that a *uniform* methodology is applied over time in a way that is successively more refined and sophisticated (for example, with a constantly improved data-base), then it is certainly reasonable to suppose that a scientific thesis deserves recognition as true if it manages to secure ongoing acceptance by the community of inquirers.

In somewhat more formalistic terms, the issue may be viewed as follows: On any given scientific question Q various responses will be forthcoming as the history of inquiry proceeds. We thus obtain a temporally indexed series A_t presenting the response to Q afforded by "the science of the day" at time t. The real or true answer to Q will be that which is ultimately stable and unchanging, that which is attained once a temporal juncture t^* is reached after which the answer remains constant:

$$(\forall t)(\forall t')[(t \geqslant t^* \ \& \ t' \geqslant t^*) \supset A_t = A_{t'}]$$

If and when such a point is reached, then A_{t^*} is the *real* answer to Q and presents the truth on this particular issue.

Several aspects of Peirce's approach deserve remark:

(1) The Peircean doctrine that what ultimately prevails must be recognized as the truth is the converse counterpart of J. S. Mill's doctrine (in the essay *On Liberty*) that the

truth is bound to prevail over the long run in open competition within a community of unfettered (free and open-minded) inquirers. (Peirce's position is an inverted version of Mill's: Mill says that if a maintained thesis is true, then it must ultimately prevail; Peirce says that if a thesis ultimately prevails, then it must be true.)

(2) Peirce's survivalistic truth-criterion approximates rather closely to James' success-oriented standard, provided one is prepared to reconstrue Jamesian success not (as with earlier James) in pragmatic/affective terms, but rather (as with the later James) in an intellectualized manner, in the essentially cognitive/epistemic terms of "satisfying" inquirers with regard to their specifically theoretical demands. For *this* sort of success comes to be tantamount to continued acceptance, i.e., "survival."

(3) Or, alternatively, suppose one took the—not altogether far-fetched—position that the pragmatic success of the implementation of a factual belief was a necessary condition of its continued acceptance in the scientific community. Then Peircean staying-power would, in effect, be carried back to the Jamesian condition of pragmatic success.

(4) A striking facet of the Peircean theory is its altogether Darwinian aspect, through the equation:

$$\text{retention-stability} = \text{survival in point of acceptance}$$

Peirce's approach invites a Darwinian picture of scientific progress, with scientific innovation (= the springing up of new "varieties"), leading to eliminations in the "struggle for existence," represented by the contest for acceptance in the scientific community. Only the "fittest" varieties (hypotheses) settle into stable species (theories) that can attain adaptive stability needed for survival over time. And so the very fact of survival manifests the appropriateness of scientific beliefs, with "truth" tantamount to "fitness in the final analysis" as manifested by *ultimate* survival.

One issue must be confronted face to face in regard to the legitimation of Peirce's view. For a sceptic can readily press the question: "Why, in heaven's name, should the stability of its espousal over time—mere temporal endurance and survival among the community of scientific inquirers—be accepted as indicative of the *truth* of a thesis?" The only convincing line of reply open here presupposes the interpretation of "survival" as a *survival of tests*—that is, success in frustrating attempts at experimental or observational falsification. Peirce's view of survival as probatively truth-indicative is wedded to a proto-Popperian conception of science as committed to efforts to falsify accepted theses, so that the survival of a factual thesis over time becomes an indicator of its acceptability. Peirce's theory is geared to a position of the Popperian type in its view of scientific inquiry as fundamentally falsificationist in orientation.[18]

[18] The following passage elegantly depicts Peirce's position:

> It is a great mistake to suppose that the mind of the active scientist is filled with propositions which, if not proved beyond all reasonable cavil, are at least extremely probable. On the contrary, he entertains hypotheses which are almost wildly incredible, and treats them with respect for the time being. Why does he do this? Simply because any scientific proposition whatever is always liable to be refuted and dropped at short notice. A hypothesis is something which looks as if it might be true and were true, and which is capable of verification or refutation by comparison with facts. The best hypothesis, in the sense of the one most recommending itself to the inquirer, is the one which can be the most readily refuted if it is false. This far outweighs the trifling merit of being likely. For after all, what is a *likely* hypothesis? It is one which falls in with our preconceived ideas. But these may be wrong. Their errors are just what the scientific man is out gunning for more particularly. But if a hypothesis can quickly and easily be cleared away so as to go toward leaving the field free for the main struggle, this is an immense advantage. (*Collected Papers*, Vol. I:1.120.)

And again:

> It is a grave mistake to attach much importance to the antecedent likelihood of hypotheses, except in extreme cases; because likelihoods are mostly merely subjective, and have so little real value, that considering the remarkable opportunities which they will cause us to miss, in the long run attention to them does not pay. Every hypothesis should be put to the test by forcing it to make verifiable predictions. (*Op. cit.*, Vol. V:5.599.)

Note that these remarkable passages were written by Peirce around 1900, and not by Karl Popper a generation later.

The shortcomings of this view are encompassed in the sorts of reasons for which Popper himself is anxious to extrude truth-claims from the arena of discussion: the range of the available alternatives—mutually incompatible possibilities that remain unfalsified—is always too large for survival-to-date to be unproblematically truth-indicative. In cases when we can produce theses or theories faster than we can test and refute them, the fact that a thesis stands as so-far-unrefuted can move only a precious little way towards establishing its claims to truth.

The main defect of Peirce's position is in fact one it shares with that of James's, namely its *orientation toward theses*. The survival of a thesis as generally accepted within the scientific community may well reflect a matter of mere historical accident, a fact whose factuality is due simply to fortuitous factors. Thus, for example, a false thesis might not have been falsified—and might never be—either because (1) we imperfect intellects simply lack the ingenuity to contrive a confrontation with the falsifying circumstances, or because (2) we limited beings lack the technical means of contriving the falsifying circumstances—say because they call for lower (or higher) temperatures, greater voltages, longer distances (etc.) than we are able to have at our disposal.

Of course, this line of thought does not gainsay the *truth-presumptiveness* of thesis-survival in a community of properly competent inquirers. But it does show that the presumption at issue is very weak, too weak to underwrite any warrant for the substantial step from a probatively feeble truth-presumptiveness to a rationally warranted claim of truth as such.

The upshot of these considerations is clear. As cases of the sort considered here show, the relative success (or failure) of action need not prove reliable indicators of the truth (or falsity) of the beliefs on which the action is predicated. Because the element of success includes various pivotal factors other than correctness alone, success or failure cannot provide a controlling determinant of the truth of theses. At the level of specific *theses,* the linkage between truth and applicative success is too remote to place these factors into a correlation sufficiently tight for the purposes of criteriology.

This, to be sure, is not the end of the matter. Throughout the chapter we have been concerned to call the merits of a pragmatism oriented to the acceptance of specific *theses* (or groups thereof). It is time to return to the *methodological* theme central to our present theory.

APPENDIX: A CAUTIONARY TALE AND ITS LESSONS

1. *The Tale*

The small semitropical republic of Atopia is a happy, sunny land, populated by the Atopians, a cheerful and optimistic—if slightly unenterprising and somewhat contentious—people. Its agriculturists are unanimously agreed that the growing season extends over 364 days of the year, although there is considerable disagreement over where the off-day falls. Sunny days are the rule in Atopia; it does not rain very often, and there are never more than two rainy days in succession. Because of the peculiar soil-conditions of the land, planting can succeed only when done in the morning of a rainy day. And, on account of the regrettable but ineradicably ingrained lethargy of Atopian agriculturists, it requires a full day's preparation to get ready for planting. In consequence, weather-prediction is a matter of substantial importance.

For years now, Atopian discussions about weather-prediction have crystallized around the Great Weather Forecasting Controversy. On the one hand is the school of a most sanguine sage whose predictive rule is optimistic simplicity itself: *Always predict a sunny day.* The adherents of this school soon came to be known as the "Eternal Optimists." The opposition, known as the "Fair Weather Optimists," follow a rival sage whose predictive rule exhibited greater caution: *If the day is sunny, or is the second of two successive rainy days, predict sun; but otherwise predict rain.*

Some years ago, the National Agriculturists League commenced an agitation that brought this vexed-prediction issue to a head in Atopia's Parliamentary Congress. The matter was referred thence to Atopia's national academy of science, COW ("Council of Wisdom"). After considerable study of the problem, COW issued a report which gave unqualified support to the school of the Eternal Optimists. The key passage of this report read as follows:

While it has thus far been the case that both weather-forecasting methods have accumulated records of substantial success, the superiority of Method 1 (i.e., that of the Eternal Optimists) can be established with mathematical precision. For let it be supposed that during a given period there is a total of x rainy days, of which the subtotal y are the first of "pairs" (of rainy days). The Method 1 will, under these assumptions, result in exactly x erroneous predictions. Method 2, on the other hand, will make two erroneous predictions in the case of each "single," and one in the case of each "pair," leading to a total of

$$\text{(A)} \qquad 2(x - 2y) + y = 2x - 3y = x + (x - 3y)$$

erroneous predictions. But consider now the quantity $x - 3y$. Statistical evidence shows that the ratio of "singles" to "pairs" is around 3:1 over any substantial period, so that the ratio x:y is around 4:1. Thus the $x - 3y$ of equation (A) is a positive quantity. Therefore it is clear that the failure rate of Method 2 must exceed that of Method 1. *The Predictive superiority of Method 1 over Method 2 can thus be taken as established.*

Upon receiving COW's report, the Parliamentary Congress enacted the Meteorological Settlement Act, prescribing official adoption of the forecasting rule of the Eternal Optimists for a period of one year.

But things did not work out well. Although the Weather Department's prediction records have never been brighter, rumblings could be heard from the agricultural community. *Planting days somehow never came around.* Drastic shortages of many foodstuffs dearly beloved of all Atopians developed. (Famine was, needless to say, never a problem: happy Atopia being bountifully supplied by nature with all necessities of subsistence.) In several villages there were riots when the Annual Tomato Festival (this vegetable being a great Atopian favorite) had to be celebrated with only carved wood specimens of this delicacy on hand. There was much adverse comment in the capital on the absence in the Lord Mayor's palace of the traditional groaning board of tomato pies. (Importation was, alas, impossible, Atopia's trade being balanced at level 0, and even tourism, that domestic export, nonexistent, since the Atopians are too occupied with enjoying themselves to operate hotels and tourist facilities for others to enjoy themselves.)

In the uproar that ensued, the Parliamentary Congress shelved the Meteorological Settlement Extension Bill; public opinion shifted, and political opinion moved with it. The Fair Weather Optimists came to carry the day, if not among the learned, at any rate among the agriculturists and the common people. (The National Agriculturists League officially adopted their forecasting method.) Slowly the state of the gastronomic affairs of Atopia moved—was it merely by chance?—from worse to better.

The Eternal Optimists stood stoutly by their cause, and continued to get powerful support from adherents in the national academy, COW, and from their adherents in Atopia's miniscule literary, journalistic, and academic circles. But among the population at large, their stock stood low indeed.

The intelligentsia felt this alienation keenly. "We have on our hands a shocking decline of intellectual standards, and a most regrettable drift to anti-intellectualism," remarked one litterateur. The daily press quoted a shoemaker as saying: "I don't really know what's agitating those schoolteacher fellows so, and I know nothing of their systems or theories. What I do know is that in the time of that law they're all so eager to restore we had to do without tomatoes, and now they're plentiful again, and cheap too." "There you have it in a nutshell," an academician of COW quipped bitterly, "that's just what we've got on our hands: a beastly victory of the stomach over the head."[1]

2. *The Lessons*

The idea of the "predictive success" of a forecasting rule exhibits a now familiar duality of aspect, for the success of a thesis of generalized rule such as is at issue in the story may be either (1) purely *theoretical* success in terms of the *correctness-ratio of predictions*, or (2) *practical* success in terms of the character of the actual *concrete results* to be achieved by adopting the rule-thesis as a guide to action. Our tale shows that these two modes of success may well diverge and must thus be distinguished with care: practical/pragmatic success is not necessarily to be correlated with theoretical/cognitive success, and these two will clash

[1] This tale was originally published by the author in *Philosophy*, vol. 39 (1964), pp. 346–8.

in an operating environment in which people are unintelligent or nature is uncooperative.

And this points towards what is, from the angle of present purposes, the key lesson of the cautionary tale. Not only a successful particularized thesis but *even a thesis-cluster* whose acceptance and implementation proves pragmatically successful at a level of implementation of considerable generality need not be true. Not only does the one-shot success of a particular thesis fail to assure attainment of the truth—as we saw in the preceding discussion—but even the regularized and repeated pragmatic success of a general-rule thesis fails to do so.

Chapter V

METHODOLOGICAL PRAGMATISM

I. THE METHODOLOGICAL APPROACH TO COGNITION

The preceding chapter has maintained the unsuitability of pragmatic standards as a means for the verification of factual theses. It will be argued now that the case is dramatically altered when pragmatic considerations are brought to bear not upon *theses*, but upon the *methods* used for their substantiation or verification, implementing the approach to cognitive methodology mooted in Chapter II.[1] The rational structure of a pragmatic justification of a methodology of inquiry would thus have the (by now familiar) format outlined in Figure 1.

Figure 1

THE PRAGMATIC JUSTIFICATION OF AN
INQUIRY-METHODOLOGY

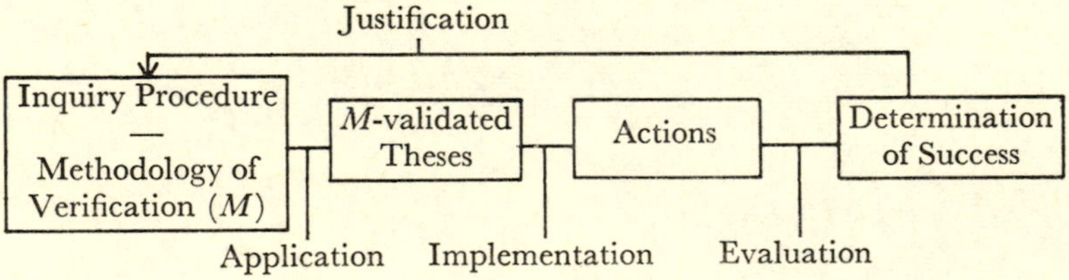

Justification

Inquiry Procedure — Methodology of Verification (M)	*M*-validated Theses	Actions	Determination of Success

Application   Implementation   Evaluation

---

[1] There is no denying that methods and theses may be connected in various ways (e.g., that methods might have "presuppositions" that can be stated as theses, or that theses might have "implications" of a methodological sort). A general thesis or theory (e.g., Galenic medicine) will usually have methodological ramifications (say for the *modus operandi* of diagnosis and therapy). The point, however, is that it is specifically the methodological aspect that is germane to our discussion. And the distinction remains important because the viability of a method (e.g., "Treat everyone as though he were a responsible and intelligent person") does not require the truth of the correlative proposition.

The motivation for this approach to cognitive justification lies in a recognition that the things one rationally accepts are not of a piece. Specifically, careful heed must be given to the distinction between *theses* on the one hand and *methods* on the other. It is indeed ultimately problematic to go about justifying theses in terms of further theses in terms of further theses, and thus onwards. But there are alternatives to such an approach to the methodology of truth-determination. For one can also justify the acceptance of specific theses on the grounds that they are validated by an appropriately warranted inquiry procedure (in effect the scientific method, on our view). Accordingly, it becomes possible to break the regress of justifying theses by theses: a thesis can be justified by application of a method, and the adoption of this method is justified by reference to certain *practical* criteria (preeminently, success in prediction and efficacy in control). This two-stage division of labor represents the characteristic idea of a specifically *methodological* pragmatism.

To be sure, most recent epistemologists prefer to focus directly on our knowledge by itself, without considering it in the light of the methodology that produces it; they tend to agree with K. R. Popper's claim that "the study of the products [of cognition, viz., theses and theories] is vastly more important than the study of the production, even for an understanding of the production and its methods."[2] The present approach departs drastically from this position. It views methodology as a factor of prime importance in the arena of validation—an importance not inferior but strictly *correlative* with that of the products (viz., substantiated theses) which are the fruit of its application.

The idea of a cognitive method is a ramified one. There are many sorts of cognitive methods: methods of investigation, methods of explanation, as well as methods for the discovery, acquisition, confirmation, processing, utilization, transmission of information. However, we shall focus here on only one group of cognitive methods—viz., those for the *validation or substantiation of thesis-acceptance*. The methods of present concern are thus specifically those by whose means factual theses are *tested*, i.e., the methods of investigation by whose means factual claims are evaluated in evidential terms with a view to their validation or

---

[2] *Objective Knowledge* (Oxford, 1972), p. 114.

invalidation. We are thus dealing with cognitive methods, and specfically with *the probative methods of factual substantiation.* (However our principal doctrine regarding these—viz., that they must in the final analysis rest upon pragmatic considerations of success or effectiveness in application with this success construed in primarily pragmatic terms—represents a contention that will obtain also throughout the remainder of this range.)

The ensuing deliberations will thus focus upon the methodology of thesis-substantiation, the canons of evidence and probative inference from factual data. (Deductive logic, the rhetorician's study of effective argumentation, the theory of statistical inference and of the design of experiments, as well as the process of inductive argumentation from factual data, all form part of the "cognitive methodology" at issue.) However, there is nothing in principle unique and inevitable about our cognitive methods. The history of human knowledge indicates a good deal of variation and experimentation of this sort: animistic, numerological, astrological and many other sorts of occult devices have been used for the evidential extraction of facts from data and the probative utilization of data. And even stranger inquiry-methods have been envisaged in speculation. Perhaps the oddest of these is *counterinductivism.*

Counterinductivism represents the following purely fictive line of policy of validation for empirical generalizations:

If a generalization has been applied *un*successfully (sic) in prior applications, you may infer its (probable) success in the application presently in hand; and if it has been applied successfully in prior applications, you may infer its (probable) failure in the case in hand.

Clearly this manner of supportive reasoning is nothing short of perverse from ordinary standpoint. Granted. But just where does it go amiss? And what sort of considerations render such an (undoubtedly queer) substantiation-process rationally unacceptable? It must be a key task of any program for the rational legitimation of knowledge to show *that* and *how* cognitive methodologies of the more bizarre variety go wrong, given that the Wheel Argument (*diallelus*) blocks the way to the easy solution of maintaining that they "produce falsehoods." It will transpire at just this point that the pragmatic aspect of our methodological approach comes crucially into play. (See also pp. 104–5 below.)

2. THE METHODOLOGICALLY PRAGMATIC VALIDATION OF KNOWLEDGE

Knowledge, so the traditional—albeit much-controverted—formula has it, is true, justified belief. A critical literature of vast scope on this subject has sprung up in recent years.[3] But whatever the strengths and weaknesses of this formula may be, it at least points out, quite appropriately, that knowledge-claims must have some sort of justification; they must be supported or supportable. A theory of knowledge must come to terms with what Dewey treated under the rubric of *warranted assertability*. It is the methodological aspect of this warrant that will concern us here.

The standard view of cognitive warrant or validation sees this in an *inferential* light. It takes the view that the paradigmatic justification of accepted theses proceeds with reference to other warrantedly accepted theses from which they can be derived by appropriate argumentation (be this of inductive or deductive character). Acceptable theses are thus justified by means of further acceptable theses, even as in a deductive argument conclusions are justified with reference to premises. To be sure, this approach requires a starter-set of nonstandardly (i.e., immediately or non-discursively) warranted theses to serve in the axiomatic role of ultimate premises. But this special category aside, the justification of thesis-acceptance is seen as a matter of their system-internal derivation from others which have, as it were, already proven themselves as warrantedly acceptable.

There is, however, a significant alternative to this *intra-systematic* mode of justification, namely one which seeks to justify a thesis not by reference to some further supporting thesis or theses, but rather by reference to the (system-external) *method of inquiry* by whose means it is arrived at. When someone asks "Why do you hold that *P*?" one can respond either by proceeding (1) discursively, in indicating to him other accepted propositions

---

[3] Some of the key papers are given in the anthology *Knowing*, ed. by M. D. Roth and L. Galis (New York, 1970), where further references are given.

$Q_1, \ldots, Q_n$ that provide an adequate complex of reasons for holding P, or else by proceeding (2) methodologically, in taking him through the methodological steps of the procedure that warranted one's initial acceptance of P. These two modes of justification, the *discursive* and the *methodological*, are very different in their *modus operandi*.

Our knowledge, after all, is not just a matter of theses (of propositional *knowledge-that*), but also—and perhaps even more fundamentally—a matter of ways of doing things (of *how-to knowledge*). In the area of cognitive methods, these two seemingly divergent modes of knowledge draw together, since it is now a matter of *how-to-secure-knowledge-that*. But the methodological approach sees the how-to case as primary, approaching propositional knowledge from the direction of its methodological sources. Knowledge-that must be *obtained and secured*, and this demands how-to knowledge. By focusing upon *cognitive methods*— methods of inference, testing, checking, and other ways and means of task-accomplishment in the area of cognitive substantiation—we regard how-to knowledge as more fundamental than knowledge-that. The latter is held to be ultimately rooted in the former.

In the present context, this methodological perspective entails that instrumental/pragmatic considerations are deployed not upon *theses* at all (be they of particular or of generalized bearing), but rather upon the *methods* and procedures by which the acceptance of theses is validated. To be sure, such a method-pragmatism contrasts sharply with the thesis-pragmatism of the historical tradition launched by William James. But it is not out of tune with the inherent spirit of pragmatism. Pragmatism—so we insist —is naturally method-oriented: its standard of "success" represents what is the normal and natural criterion for the validation of methods, techniques, procedures, tools, and the like. The appropriateness of all such procedural instrumentalities is clearly a matter of the realization of their correlative ends, hinging on the extent to which the instrumentality is *effective* towards their realization.

An inquiry procedure is fundamentally *methodological* in character: it seeks to provide a substantiate *method*, a logico-epistemological procedure for warranting acceptance of certain propositions. Now working well—that is, manifesting effectiveness and efficiency in discharging the tasks for which it is designed —is the key standard for the rational evaluation of methods. The justification of the cognitive *modus operandi* represented by an inquiry procedure is thus seen in standardly instrumental—i.e., purposive—terms. The methodologically pragmatic approach treats an inquiry-procedure as determinative of thesis-acceptance subject to a complex teleology which prominently includes the issue of action-guidance in practically successful directions.

On this approach, then, the linkage between pragmatic utility and the truth of theses is broken apart, and *methods* are inserted into the gap that opens up. Pragmatic considerations are never brought to bear on theses directly. The relationship becomes indirect and mediated: a specific knowledge claim is supported by reference to a method, which in its turn is supported on pragmatist lines. This mediation of methods between pragmatic considerations and thesis-acceptance is central to, and indeed definitive of, the specifically *methodological* pragmatism at issue here.

It is helpful to consider our line of approach in the light of an analogy. The pragmatic theory of truth comes close to being the epistemological counterpart to ethical utilitarianism. Now it is well known that utilitarianism can take two forms:

(1) *Act utilitarianism*, which asserts that an act is to be done (i.e., qualifies as morally right) if its performance is maximally benefit-producing.

(2) *Rule utilitarianism*, which asserts that an act is morally right if it conforms to ethically warranted rules, and that a rule is warranted if its general adoption as a principle of action is maximally benefit-producing.

Correspondingly, pragmatism can take two forms:

(1) *Propositional or thesis pragmatism*, which asserts that a proposition is to be accepted (i.e., qualifies as true) if its adoption is maximally success-promoting (=benefit-producing).

(2) *Criterial or methodological pragmatism*, which asserts that a proposition is to be accepted (i.e, qualifies as true) if it conforms to an epistemically warranted criterion, and that a criterion is warranted if *its adoption as a generic principle for propositional acceptance* is maximally success-promoting (=benefit-producing).

When one considers *acceptance-as-true* as an act and construes—as it is natural enough to do—"classing a proposition as true" as a type of *action* (though, to be sure, a *cognitive* not a *physical* action), then the result of applying the utilitarian approach (in one or another of its two forms) is tantamount to pragmatism (in one or another of its two forms). And even as one can, in principle, be an act-utilitarian and not a rule-utilitarian (or vice versa), so one can be a thesis pragmatist and not a methodological pragmatist (or vice versa).

This analogy with the duality of utilitarianisms in ethics—though imperfect in the manner of all analogies—nevertheless helps to clarify the presently operative duality of pragmatisms in epistemology.

3. THE INHERENT GENERALITY OF THE METHODOLOGICAL APPROACH

As we have seen, thesis pragmatism is subject to the disability that on its basis little if any assurance of logical coherence and consistency can be available. As we saw in the preceding chapter, it cannot guarantee the absence of logical anomalies. (One might, for example, be brought to the unhappy pass of having to maintain P & Q as true, but not P alone—with the disastrous result that one's purported truth will not comport itself in line with the principles of logic.) More pertinently for present purposes, we might encounter the anomaly that one person succeeds when acting on the acceptance of a thesis, but another not. The question thus arises: Does this mean that it is to be proper for one person to accept the thesis but the other not? William James at one point skated dangerously near the thin ice on this issue. Replying to an opponent who held that pragmatism has the consequence that belief in the existence of a nonexistent thing might be true, he wrote:

When you say the idea is true—does that mean true for *you*, the critic, or true for the believer whom you are describing? The critic's trouble over this seems to come from his taking the word "true" irrelatively, whereas the pragmatist always means "true for him who experiences the workings."[4]

The point, of course, is the unacceptability *as a theory of TRUTH* of a theory that operates with a concept of "truth" that is person-relative or even group-relative.

All such difficulties are removed at a stroke when the focus of concern is shifted from theses to methods. Considerations of the *suitability* and *effectiveness* of methods introduce an inherently rational orientation which serves to assure the logical properties. Moreover, methods are intrinsically public, interpersonal, and communal. A method is not a successful *method* unless its employment is *generally* effective—otherwise we are talking about a knack or skill rather than a method. A skill can only be *shown*, it cannot be *explained*. A method can be codified and taught as a collection of procedures defined in terms of instructions and rules. This line of thought indicates the fundamentally social dimension of methods. They must be transmissible from one person to another, and, above all, they must be transmissible across generations (otherwise we could not get a sufficiently diversified test of a method's success!). Accordingly, methods possess an inherent objectivity and freedom from any sort of personal dependence. They can be examined and evaluated *in abstracto*, without any dependency on particular practitioners. Thus the problem of possible person-to-person variation cannot arise. Methodological efficacy must be systematic—it must obtain *semper et ubique*. (We are brought back at this point to Peirce's stress on the long run and the whole range of humanity.)

These considerations apply with special force to methods of inquiry. As was insisted above, their social transmissibility is crucial to their very nature. A cogntive method must be *teachable* —it is not even a method unless it can be codified as a canon of more or less explicit rules of a generally accessible sort. (The calculating prodigy has a *skill* but not a *method*.) Not only are the *results* of our cognitive inquiry methods (viz., the propositions or theses we substantiate by their means) possessed of an objective and interpersonal standing, but these methods themselves have

[4] *The Meaning of Truth* (New York, 1909), p. 177.

such a standing, both in their nature and in their warrant. Again, appeal to the inherent generality of inquiry procedures can remove as candidates certain artificially complex procedures, like using scientific method in relation to one range of predictions and astrological methods in relation to another.

Methods are inherently general and the systematic success of a method cannot by its nature plausibly be dismissed as a sheerly fortuitous piece of luck. Moreover, an *inquiry procedure* is by its very nature a method having a uniquely vast range and comprehensiveness: it represents an effectively *boundless* methodology for the verification of theses. These considerations lay bare a critically important aspect of the generality of the present approach—a generality which, as we shall see, is crucial to its capacity to overcome the shortcomings inherent in thesis-pragmatism. The traditional pragmatists could not afford to concede possible discrepancies between success and truthfulness. On the other hand, the success of a method is a factor whose *systematic* nature gives it great probative weight in spite of occasional failings.

4. THE ASPECT OF RATIONALITY

Someone might still object as follows to such a method-oriented pragmatism:

> The justification of a thesis-validating method in terms of its success is bound to be insufficient from the angle of its capacity to provide rational warrant. Surely nobody would be content to rest satisfied if such a proceeding were used to justify the "method" of *asking the oracle* (or the seer, or whatever).

Note that the factors of unrestrictedness and generality do not of themselves resolve matters—there clearly being no limit to the sorts of questions we can put to the oracle. But the crucial fact is this. The oracle's own procedure is presumably simply not a *method* in the sense at issue here, since it does not afford a teachable, codifiable, transmissible technique. It is crucial that the sort of method at issue in our considerations be correlative with technique! The oracle "method" is not, in fact, qualified to serve as an inquiry procedure: though general in one sense it lacks *the right sort* of generality. (It is not limited on the side of the questioner and what he can ask, but limited on the side of its potential practitioners.)

The sort of "method" that concerns us here has to represent an *inquiry procedure* in the most authentic sense of the term. The methods at issue are, broadly speaking, ones of rational argumentation and substantiation. This indicates that the generality at issue has special ramifications, since rationality must also enter in. We are not dealing with the pragmatic success of a method *in abstracto*, but with the pragmatic success consequent upon use of a very special sort of method, a *cognitive* method: an inquiry procedure. This is not just a black box of some sort that issues assertions (à la the oracle), but an essentially rational methodology of verification and validation—a codifiable procedure with a perspicuous rationale of its own, an internal structure of intelligibility and rationality.[5] It deserves stress that our methodological pragmatism is concerned with cognitive methodologies at the level of verification procedures, and so with cognitive instrumentalities that encompass a mechanism of substantiation and validation, an architectonic of supportive reasoning.

We thus need not trouble ourselves much with the complaint that pragmatic success might well attend the use of occult thesis-validating methods of the black box type. Black box procedures run afoul not of *generality* but of *publicity*: they cannot be unpacked into teachable and learnable processes. We are not concerned simply with a device for answering questions, but with that certain very special sort of cognitive method for securing such answers, viz., an inquiry procedure. Of course, if we had such a black box method and it worked we would have pragmatic grounds that support our continued reliance on its deliverances. We would have, if you like, a *decision procedure*. But we would not have an *inquiry procedure*, and consequently, would not be dealing with the sort of cognitive methodology that is at issue throughout these deliberations. (We shall eventually

---

[5] Compare William James: "Pragmatism has in fact no prejudices whatever, no obstructive dogmas, no rigid canons of what shall count as proof. She is completely genial. She will entertain any hypothesis, she will consider any evidence." (*Pragmatism* [New York, 1907], p. 61.) Thesis-pragmatism has a *laisser faire* amorphousness on the side of logical standards that methodological pragmatism can happily avoid.

explore these ramifications in greater detail—principally in the subsequent chapter on self-supportiveness and self-sustainingness.)

All of these aspects of rationality are crucial to the over-all argument. Its main components are: (1) that we are dealing with a publicly available *method* (one which is general and teachable), (2) that we are dealing with a *method of inquiry* with its internal rational structure of grounds, ampliative arguments, evidence, etc., and (3) that *this methodology is objectively warrantable*, that is, it is not only rationally self-sustaining on its own grounds, but is also legitimated from an external perspective (viz., from a pragmatic one).

The dimension of rationality thus introduces an important facet of quality-control, one coordinate in its importance with that of pragmatic efficacy, Moreover, rationality and pragmatic efficacy are interlocked. This factor is sometimes overlooked. Thus in his semi-conventionalist approach, P. F. Strawson maintains that:

> the rationality of induction, unlike its "successfulness" is not a fact about the constitution of the world; it is a matter of what we mean by the word "rational" in its application to any procedure for forming opinions about what lies outside our observation.[6]

But this endeavor to drive a neat wedge between the *success* and the *rationality* of our inductive practices—with the former as a factual and the latter as a conceptual feature of them—is ill-advised. Given the role of the concept of rationality—the work that is cut out for it in our thought and speech—the success of induction becomes a crucial facet of its own rationality: playing "by the rules of the inductive game" would not be the unproblematically rational thing it in fact is, were that element of "successfulness" absent. To be sure, its presence is an empirical element that hinges on "the constitution of the world." But that does not block the conceptual aspect—it merely reflects the fact that our concepts are attuned (through the evolutionary process of their development) to the realities of the world we live in.[7]

[6] *Introduction to Logical Theory* (London, 1952), pp. 261–2.
[7] For a fuller development of this theme of the fact-ladenness of our concepts see Chapter VI, ("A Critique of Pure Analysis") of the author's *The Primacy of Practice* (Oxford, 1973).

5. HOW THE PRESENT METHODOLOGICAL APPROACH
   CONTRASTS WITH THAT OF PEIRCE

It is of some interest to raise the historical question of just how the present methodological pragmatism squares with the analogous teachings of Peirce. Defining inquiry as the generic process by which we move from doubt to belief, Peirce recognized a plurality of methods of inquiry: not only the *scientific* method, but also the *traditionary* ("method of tenacity"), the *dogmatic* ("method of authority"), and the *metaphysico-speculative* ("*a priori* method"). The scientific method is the most superior of these—so Peirce argues—for two connected reasons: (1) it is *self-corrective*: if it leads us into missteps it will itself discover these and put them to rights in the long run, and (2) it is *stabilitarian*: it alone leads to the establishment of stable beliefs—beliefs that will stand up over the long run. Thus Peirce too takes an approach that is methodological in spirit.

But while Peirce is both a pragmatist (in his theory of meaning) and a methodologist (in his theory of methods of inquiry), he is not a methodological pragmatist in his theory of knowledge. This is so because for Peirce the decisive consideration in truth-determination is stability—or "fixity" as Peirce himself characterizes it—and *not* pragmatic efficacy.[8] According to him, the mark of a true belief—one constrained by an external and independent reality—is implicit in its destiny as fated to be underwritten by the operation of scientific method.[9]

This stabilitarian approach gives Peirce's epistemological theory a conceptual structure quite different from that of our methodological pragmatism. The crucial difference is that Peirce's

[8] In the essay "What Pragmatism Is" (*Collected Papers*, Vol. V: 5.416–434), Peirce proposes "to define the 'truth' as that to which belief would lead if it were to tend indefinitely toward absolute fixity."

[9] Thus Bertrand Russell is—as regards Peirce—quite wrong in saying that the crucial difference between the pragmatist's theory and his own is that he defines truth in terms of the *causes* and they in terms of the *effects* of beliefs. (*An Inquiry into Meaning and Truth* [London, 1940], Penguin reprint 1963; see p. 308.) Peirce's conception of truth is realistic and correspondistic; true beliefs are "satisfactory" in virtue of their consonance with reality, and in no danger of subsequent overthrow once arrived at.

approach is still oriented to theses: their truth-claims are to be assessed in terms of stability. For Peirce, the whole issue of the adequacy of methods is subsequent and secondary: a method is adequate if it produces true (i.e., stable) beliefs. Our own approach reverses this seemingly more natural order. It treats methods as basic, and it does *not* propose to evaluate the adequacy-claims of cognitive methods in terms of the claims to truth of the theses they validate. Instead, we are to judge the adequacy of a method in terms of the pragmatic ramifications of its products. Our tactic is to settle on a good method first, and then determine truth in its terms. Clearly this approach *inverts* that of Peirce—and that of most traditional epistemologists— in regarding the truth-claims of theses as an issue *subsequent to and derivative from* rather than (as with Peirce) *prior to* that of the adequacy of the methods by which they are validated.

6. HEGELIAN RAMIFICATIONS

It is of particular interest to consider the justificatory process above sketched from a temporal perspective, looking at the process in terms of the format sketched in Figure. 2.

Figure 2

THE HISTORICAL PROCESS OF METHOD-DEVELOPMENT

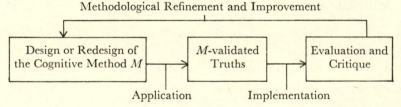

As one moves successively through the loops of this justificatory cycle, one arrives at a sequence of successively refined and improved methods:

$$M_1, M_2, M_3, \ldots$$

(Conceivably, a point of stabilization may be reacted after which all subsequent M_i differ only trivially if at all.) Particular interest attaches to those *theses* (M-validated truths) which eventually survive intact through the process of methodological refinement and sophistication. For the course of historical events has been a course of test and trial. (In this cognitively methodological context one can say, with Hegel, that *die Weltgeschichte ist das Weltgericht.*) But while the *content* of such theses remains (*ex hypothesi*) intact, their *epistemic status* clearly changes: they come to be placed on an increasingly firmer cognitive footing. In this case we return again and again to the same theses, but endow them with a successively deeper and firmer rationale. One knows the same thing one knew before, but the *manner* in which one knows it is different and more sophisticated. The process points towards the Hegelian idea of an ascending spiral where one repeatedly returns to the same place, but at a successively higher level of sophistication.

On this approach, the touchstone of acceptance-as-true of a thesis lies in its validation by a suitable sort of method which is itself in turn vindicated by a "rationale"—that is, a line of supporting argumentation capable of establishing its rational warrant. Thus reality-as-it-is-for-us—our picture of reality, as defined in terms of a complex of accepted-theses-about-the-real—must ultimately rest on a probatively effective body of rational considerations. These considerations "rationalize" at the methodological level those mechanisms of inquiry by which our picture of reality is constituted. The methodological approach thus commits us to a version of the Hegelian dictum that the real is rational—and it can indeed itself be helpfully illuminated by this dictum. For our strategy of legitimation ensures that "the real"—insofar as our epistemically warranted mapping of it can reach—must conform to the regulative canons of rationality. (We are here concerned not simply with pragmatic success *per se*, but with the pragmatic success of a certain kind of thing—viz., an *inquiry procedure* which must as such meet certain fundamental requisites of rationality.)

It is clear that one cannot *demonstrate* that any truth-claim based upon a superior methodological procedure will itself be correct or otherwise inherently superior. The Wheel Argument (*diallelus*) decisively precludes any such demonstration. (It even prevents our claiming that the statistical chances of being correct are greater in the case of a methodologically superior procedure!) No such *substantive* claim of superiority in truth-provision can be made out on behalf of our duly legitimated inquiry procedures. It remains *a rationally warranted presumption* that the truth-claims based on a superior inquiry procedure are themselves superior in their rational legitimation. Accordingly, the warrant at issue in the "warranted assertability" of the truth-claims validated by a duly legitimated inquiry procedure resides in a *regulative principle of rationality.*

But by just what justificatory rationale can such a regulative presumption be legitimated? Clearly, the key question remains: How is one to validate the linkage between the factor of methodological success on the one hand and that of thesis-truthfulness on the other? We must devote to this crucial issue the separate chapter it deserves.

Chapter VI

WHY RELATE SUCCESS AND TRUTHFULNESS?

1. THE BASIC PROBLEM

The methodologically pragmatic justification of inquiry procedures takes the capacity of such a procedure to validate theses for acceptance as truths to reside basically and ultimately in the *pragmatic success* of their implementation in practice. But how can success serve as in indicator of truthfulness? Why should the pragmatic success attending the utilization of its deliverances be taken to justify this criterion and allowed to count towards establishing its legitimacy as a *truth* criterion?

These questions are particularly problematic because "The factual thesis '*P*' is true" certainly does not *mean* "The factual thesis '*P*' is vouched for by pragmatically successful criterion of acceptance." The *meaning* of "true" must surely continue to be understood in orthodox, correspondentist terms: '*P*' is true iff *P*; that is, a true statement is one that affirms what is actually the case. How, then, can our claimed linkage between success and truthfulness be rationalized?

2. THE INHERENT GENERALITY OF METHODOLOGICAL SUCCESS

An obvious concession is at once in order. Action which proceeds on beliefs that are false and fail to capture "what is actually the case" can on occasion—or even frequently—eventuate as pragmatically successful, due to chance or good luck or kindly fate or whatever. However, the situation must be different when what is at issue is not an isolated action or a particular believed thesis (or even a cluster of them), but rather a general policy of acting based on alignment with a *methodologically universalized standard* of belief-validation. Individual theses may well manage to slip through the net of disconfirmation singly or in groups. But *methods* for factual inquiry operate across a very broad and extensive front, and this feature of across-the-board systematicity

D

renders them much more vulnerable. Their flaws and deficiencies are bound to manifest themselves in the vast multiplicity of their applications.

Methods function at a wholesale rather than retail level. As was stressed above, the success of a method must be construed in *systematic* terms: working on one occasion—or on some limited number of occasions—does not entail working in general, and failing on one or more occasions is not necessarily completely invalidating. Success hinges on how the method fares *in general* over the whole gamut of its applications. It is on such a generic and systematic plane that instrumental justification must be sought. These considerations, operative at the level of methodology-in-general, apply with special force to cognitive methodology in particular. The range and versatility of an inquiry procedure is too obvious to need much elaboration. Generality is here tantamount to openendedness; a methodology of *inquiry* has to operate across the board of an enormous variety of areas of application and a literally innumerable proliferation of particular instances. In its case, above all, success is strongly indicative of adequacy or appropriateness. Here all of the safeguards built into the statistical theory of the "design of experiments" come into play with respect to the probative significance of the number and variety of instances. It is inconceivable that a *systematic* success across so broad a range should be gratuitous. We cannot reasonably look on nature as a friendly collaborator in our human efforts, systematically crowning our cognitive endeavors with wholly undeserved successes.

3. GENERALITY BLUNTS SOME OBJECTIONS

Consider the traditional objection against pragmatism that it might well prove highly successful to act on some (quite incorrect) thesis—say, that one's superior is *competent* in his vocational role, a stance bound to please him and likely to lead to good results. This perfectly possible prospect makes one rightly hesitant to maintain that the successful implemetation of a thesis in practice is an adequate basis for holding it to be true. But if what were in view were, say, a *general procedure* by whose means one ruled universally in all sorts of cases—including all questions of vocational competence, in any and every sort of situation—then if application of this procedure proved highly successful, the issue of the rational warrant for accepting its rulings as true would clearly rest on a very different, infinitely more secure basis.

A. C. Ewing offered essentially the following objection to this line of thought:[1]

> Even the "success" of a generalized procedure need not provide a sound warrant for truth claims. For suppose that a railway bridge were built on odd and unsound engineering principles, but that this led to a train-crash in which Hitler was killed (near the outset of his career) and millions of lives saved.

It seems, however, that while this objection does have some degree of merit, it fails to tell damagingly against the present position. Its view of a "general procedure" for truth-determination is still far too narrow in its restrictive orientation. What is at issue in the present context is vastly more universalized, viz., an inquiry procedure for the determination of (presumptive) truth across the entire factual board, and not just in one narrow area (e.g., bridge-building).

Thus the sort of objection envisaged by Ewing is circumvented by the fact that our concern is with *the systematic methodology of inquiry* at a highly generalized level. Methodological systematicity is so comprehensive that probatively irrelevant side effects by way of fortuitious bonuses or disasters—even such a "success" as the removal of a Hitler—become cancelled out in the larger scheme of things. That a mistaken or unwarranted procedure might prove really successful at this level of generality is a prospect so far-fetched that it can be dimissed with confidence. Fundamental mistakes at *this* level would have repercussions across a limitless frontier and would be bound to prove ultimately catastrophic.

4. THE METAPHYSICAL RATIONALE: I

To move towards an explanation of why pragmatic success should count as *truth*-indicative, we must probe into the metaphysical foundations of our position. For what validates the pragmatic account is not a definitional revisionism concerning the *meaning*

---

[1] In a discussion in Geneva, Switzerland in March of 1973, not long before the death in June of that year of this charming septuagenarian (b. 1899) of spry intellect.

of "truth," but rather a certain *metaphysical* posture. The justificatory rationale which establishes the needed link between success and truth lies in a particular *Weltauschauung*—a metaphysical stance.

The linkage of success to truth is—on this view—neither immediate nor self-evident: it is the product of the operation of a nexus of metaphysical principles regarding the nature of man and the world. Most importantly, the fact that men are rational agents functioning in a highly reactive environment and are themselves sensitively responsive to its operation is crucial to the metaphysical stagesetting. For this fact of itself goes far towards providing the rationale of a methodologically pragmatic validation of man's cognitive methodology.

In delineating this metaphysical rationale, we may thus begin by considering three coordinated principles: activism, reasonableness, and interactionism.

(i) *Activism*

Man finds himself emplaced *in medias res* within a world-environment that presses in upon him from every side. He must constantly act upon his environment to ensue his own well-being and indeed survival. A substantial proportion of his actions are necessitated by requirements that sometimes represent merely *felt* needs, but for the most part perfectly *real* needs. To satisfy these needs he must not only act, but act appropriately. And this is so all the more once the range of *needs* is supplemented with that of *wants*. Moreover, these needs and wants are of a relatively constant sort that represent reasonably stable determinants of action.

Accordingly, man's theorizing is not just of interest in its own right (as part of a purely abstract quest for knowledge), but also in providing the essential foundations of his practical—and, indeed, survival-relevant—activity. Theory must be determinative of action. If men were systematically passive and did not implement their beliefs in action, the adequacy of their theorizing obviously could not be judged by its results. But the acceptance of factual theses generally has extensive and immediate implications for action, and these actions produce results that reverberate back to their initiating agent in one way or another.

(ii) *Reasonableness*

A thesis of rationality or reasonableness forms another important part of the foundations of the present line of justificatory reasoning. It is crucial that men not only hold beliefs as a kind of exercise in abstraction, but that their actions are in general guided by accepted beliefs. If men were inconsequent in acting in disregard of them, then the adequacy of their theorizing would again be irrelevant to its results.

Man is a rational animal: a being whose actions are kept in consonant alignment with his beliefs. Human convictions are practically efficacious, and human actions belief-determined. We cannot live without effective interaction with nature, and a *reasonable* man will generally coordinate his actions and expectations in the light of the best information he can secure regarding the course of events *in rerum naturae.* This factor of reasonableness has several key aspects: (1) Men are not and cannot in point of fact afford to be systematically *passive*: they must act and their acts are belief-determined: men *implement* their beliefs in action; (2) Men are not systematically *perverse*: they do not act counter to or in disregard of their beliefs; and (3) Men are not systematically *insane*: they do not act counter to, or without regard to their felt needs (those needs they believe themselves to have). All these conditions are necessary to assure that the adequacy of our theorizing can be judged by its results. If beliefs were dissociated from action in any of the indicated ways this could not be done.

The due coordination of beliefs, needs, and actions at issue in what we have called "reasonableness" is a crucial aspect of the pragmatic justification we have in view. A merely instrumental justification could in principle aim at *any* sort of goals; a pragmatic justification is committed to the specific family of welfare-oriented goals.

Thus under certain circumstances a perfectly good sort of instrumental justification could be developed for an inquiry procedure of *counterinductivist* purport. Put briefly, the counterinductivist acts on the predictive policy that generalizations that hold up to the time *t* will not hold thereafter. Now it is really conceivable that this predictive method would—in certain circumstances—prove to be a great "success." For take the man whose goal-structure is, as it were, suitably *perverse* who yearns for failure, for example, or else who is neurotically addicted to the theory that the world "is out to get him," that things are so arranged that there is one vast conspiracy to frustrate his plans and actions. For a person with this sort of goal-structure, a counterinductivist inquiry procedure would point a way to great success, because he would meet with the constant realization of his expectations. By effectively interchanging failure and success at the level of goals—i.e., by *counting* failure as a "success," it becomes possible to give an instrumental validation of a very odd sort of inquiry procedure indeed.

But, of course, *real* success lies in realizing the reasonable and rational goals of people. Objectives that are *pathological*—the courting of pain, privation, anxiety, harm, etc.—must be excluded. In the sense operative with respect to pragmatic justification, "success" must be taken to lie not in the realization of objectives as such, but in the realization of our orthodox affective objectives, i.e., those that have a positive bearing on human welfare. In its pragmatically relevant sense, "success" is oriented towards realizing the *real interests* of people in satisfying their recognized welfare needs.

(iii)   *Interactionism: Feedback, Sensitivity, Vulnerability*

Procedures which generate sets of beliefs that systematically support successful courses of action deserve *ipso facto* to be credited with a substantial measure of rational warrant. To be sure, if a bounteous nature satisfied our every whim spontaneously, without effort and striving on our part, the situation would be very different. For then the beliefs which guide and canalize our activities would not come into play—they would remain inoperative on the sidelines, never being "put to the test." There would then be no need for active (and thought-guided) intervention in "the natural course of things" within an uncooperative (at best indifferent, at worst hostile) environment. But *as things stand* we are constantly called upon to establish varying degrees of "control over nature" to satisfy even our most basic needs (to say nothing of our wants). The human condition is such that active intervention in the course of events is constantly required (and even the noninterventionist process of "letting things take their course"

becomes, in such a context, simply another mode of control).
Moreover, human agency produces a flow of consequences that
rebound back upon the agent, ultimately producing satisfaction
or frustration. This interactionism is a crucial part of the metaphysical background: the *sensitivity* of nature to human intervention (in the physics/engineering sense of this term), and the
vulnerability of man to the feedback effects of his acts. The
prospect of purpose-guided interaction with nature—of acting so
as to produce successfully the intended results of our efforts—is a
vital part of the cluster of metaphysical principles which establish
the cognitive relevance of pragmatic success. Effective control of
nature—ranging from prediction as minimal intervention (the
mere alignment of our own expectations) to more elaborate modificatory changes in the course of events—thus emerges as the
arbiter of cognitive adequacy in the factual realm.

5. THE METAPHYSICAL RATIONALE: II

The preceding agent-oriented factors are only part of the relevant
cluster of metaphysical principles: Certain conditions must also
be met by the ongoing *community* of inquirers. For one thing,
we must suppose a degree of *purposive constancy*. Obviously if
a method were deployed for one purpose on some occasions and
for other purposes on others, its success record in the former case
does not provide an adequate basis for judgment regarding the
latter. And, similarly, there must also be a continuity of methodological proceeding. Clearly, if the community of method-users
rapidly and drastically modified its *modus operandi*—doing so
frivolously and without substantial warrant—then a record of
success cannot count for, nor a record of failures against, a single
method.[2]

[2] Peirce already strongly emphasized this methodologically controlling role
of purposive constancy:

> If you really want to learn the truth, you will, by however devious a
> path, be surely led into the way of truth, at last. No matter how
> erroneous your ideas of the method may be at first, you will be forced
> at length to correct them so long as your activity is moved by that
> sincere desire. Nay, no matter if you only half desire it, at first, that
> desire would at length conquer all others, could experience continue
> long enough. (*Collected Papers*, Vol. V: 5.582; cf. *ibid.*, 2.781.)

Last but not least, certain conditions must also be laid down regarding the ways of the "external world." For one thing, it becomes necessary to invoke (perhaps merely as a regulative presupposition) a principle concerning the *uniformity of nature* to insure the right sort of uniformity on the side of methods. Suppose a method succeeded one day and failed the next simply because some fortuitous whim of nature had changed the ways of the world. Then clearly the past success of a method would become irrelevant to its general efficacy. More fundamentally, the very idea of a method as a *principled rule* for action implies a basic uniformity of circumstance and operation—of doing a given *sort* of thing in a given *sort* of (potentially repetitive) situation. (Of course we cannot block by any probatively feasible establishment of substantive theses the prospect that the world as we know it—with all its operative laws of nature—should come to an end or completely and fundamentally alter its ways. But this prospect is pragmatically irrelevant—we must simply lay it aside in the sphere of *praxis*, and proceed on a very different *regulative* basis in the conduct of our practical and cognitive affairs.)

Again, it must be presupposed that the world operates in a way which is at bottom *nonconspiratorial*, in both the positive and the negative directions. That is, one must hold nature to be indifferent to our cognitive endeavors: neither *angelic* in systematically crowning our wholly unmerited and rationally unwarranted successes, nor *demonic* in systematically frustrating the deserved successes of even our most shrewd and rationally warranted efforts. Again, nature must be in some degree *responsive* to human intervention, for clearly, if our actions never made an impact upon it, the success or failure of these efforts would fail to reveal anything about its workings.

In sum, our validation of the primacy of practice—in terms of the fundamental role of practical purposes as the controlling norms of theory in the epistemology of factual knowledge—rests ultimately on the metaphysical foundation of a complex composite of metaphysical theses. Only through the operation of a constellation of metaphysical principles of this sort can a proper probative linkage between success and truthfulness be established.

But the relevant metaphysic does not envisage a very sophisticated body of machinery. Its picture is that of a plurality of persons in intelligent contact with one another and in reciprocal interaction with their environment. Person and nature, purpose and action, impact and reactions, conscious striving for ends, limited control, success or disappointment—these are the principal categories at issue. It is a naive and simple picture of which even deep philosophers have not disdained to make much. (For example, the categories enumerated contain all the basic elements operative in Fichte's *Wissenschaftslehre*.) Its principal elements may be summarized as follows:

Inquirers	World

Individual
   reasonableness
   activism
   interactionism (with the
     "external world")
   sensitivity (to feedback)
	responsiveness of nature
	   (to human intervention)
	
	 nonconspiratoriality of nature
	   (neither on the angelic
	   nor the demonic side)

Communal
   methodological continuity
   purposive constancy
	uniformity of nature

6. PUTTING THE PIECES TOGETHER: THE METAPHYSICAL DEDUCTION

Let us now at last come to grips with the pivotal question:

> Why is the pragmatic success of its deliverances to be taken to *justify* a criterion—i.e., to count towards establishing its "correctness" or adequacy as a *truth* criterion?

We maintain that the adequacy of a suitable inquiry procedure is not a matter of the theoretical necessities of the situation, but rather hinges upon an appropriate complex of metaphysical principles. What validates the pragmatic account is thus—in the final analysis—a certain *metaphysical* posture. The leading idea is that while action on false beliefs (i.e., those which fail to capture "what is actually the case") can on occasion succeed—due to chance or good luck or kindly fate or whatever—it cannot do so *systematically*, the ways of the world being as they are. Isolated successes can be gratuitous and probatively impotent, but the situation will be otherwise when what is at issue is not isolated actions based on particular beliefs, but a general *policy* of acting, based on a generic and methodologically universalized standard of belief-validation. When one views man as a vulnerable creature in close interaction with a hostile (or at best neutral) environment, it is—to be sure—conceivable that action on a false belief or even set of beliefs might be successful, but it surpasses the bounds of credibility to suppose that this might occur systematically, on a wholesale rather than retail basis. Given a suitable framework of metaphysical assumptions, it is effectively impossible that success should crown the products of *systematically* error-producing cognitive procedures. (Perhaps ill luck might come in battalions rather than single spies, but good luck seems to prefer travelling alone.) In this methodological context, success indicates adequacy.

Inquiry procedures which systematically underwrite success-conducive theses thus deserve to be credited with a significant measure of rational warrant. Given the mooted cluster of metaphysical principles, a persuasive case can be made for the conclusion that an inquiry-methodology that underwrites pragmatically successful action is cognitively adequate (and, of course, conversely). It is thus *not* our view that pragmatic efficacy constitutes another mode of justification independent of truth. The whole point is that the pragmatic efficacy of an *inquiry*-procedure is inherently truth-correlative—not because of what *truth* means, but because of the metaphysical ramifications of success in this sphere.

One of the major components of this metaphysical framework is the principle we have characterized as *activism*. If man were not highly activistic in implementing his beliefs about the nature of things—or if the world were such that these implementing actions were pretty much irrelevant to the course of events and did not produce a host of consequences fraught with the aspect of success or failure—the situation would be altogether different. The discriminative "bite" of a policy of "awaiting nature's ruling" on the products of our methods of inquiry would be lost. The key presuppositions of the underlying justificatory process are reasonableness, activism, interactionism, and feedback. These represent the controlling parameters which yield a substantial discriminative capacity for testing our methods for underwriting factual beliefs. The present validation of the probative role of practice in the epistemology of factual knowledge rests on a metaphysical basis of this sort. That we men are rational agents functioning in the environment of a duly responsive nature, and sensitively responsive to its operation, is crucial to the rationale of this methodologically pragmatic validation.

To be sure, someone might say:

> Practice makes a very low demand on theory. Successful practice in general comes cheap. Only a very low degree of correctness or accuracy in our action-governing beliefs is needed to channel these actions into successful results.

But nothing could be further from the truth. In a complex and volatile environment wrong beliefs readily prove fatal. The man who believes he can cross a busy street without looking about him will soon learn the error of his ways, if, indeed, he survives to do so.

Accordingly, a Darwinian pragmatism of rational selectors is at work here.[3] Theory is evaluated in terms of the success of its guidance of action: theorizing canalizes our acts, leading to consequences of markedly practical implications in producing a feedback that substantially affects our weal and woe. The correctness of intellectual endeavors is presumptively reflected in its pragmatic success, preeminently in proving survival-conducive.

If success is to be the touchstone of their validity, our methods of inquiry must actually be put to trial by appealing to the court of experience with respect to the practical application of their deliverances. On this line of thought, our theorizing about matters of fact is open to supportive evidence only when failure is risked—only if it is prepared to stub its toes on the hard rock of reality. If intellectual theorizing about matters of fact is to lay claim to any element of truthfulness, then it must—on any ultimately tenable account—be viewed as constrained by an external and independent reality. And on our approach it is exactly *praxis* that pro-

---

[3] For further considerations regarding the theory of pragmatic Darwinism with respect to conceptual schemes see Chapter IX ("Idealist Philosophy of Nature") of the author's *Conceptual Idealism* (Oxford, 1973).

vides the crucial reality-principle for controlling the adequacy of cognition. (This, in the final analysis, is why the pragmatic validation of methods, though presumably effective in the sphere of our factual knowledge, is not comparably serviceable in the theological area—*pace* William James.)

The present analysis thus envisages an intricate interdependence or symbiosis between man's factual views and his practical objectives and thus between the practical and the theoretical sectors of rationality. Our thesis of the primacy of practice comes to this, that practical considerations serve to determine and to legitimate the methodological canons of our factual knowledge. To say this is not to deny that any reasoned pursuit of practical objectives must proceed with reference to claims validated as factual by such canons. To paraphrase Kant's dictum: Without some recourse to purposes, facts are unattainable; without some recourse to facts, purposes are futile. The complex dialectic of interaction and feedback between the practical and factual levels is the forge which generates the testing heat by which our cognitive tools are tempered.[4]

7. THE DESIRABILITY AND FEASIBILITY OF A METAPHYSICAL DEDUCTION

What we have found to be necessary to have—and have endeavored to provide—is a "deduction" (in Kant's sense) of the rational legitimacy of an inquiry procedure setting out from metaphysical principles regarding the nature of the objects and the agents of inquiry. The mission of such an enterprise is to ground epistemology in metaphysical considerations that provide our cognitive *modus operandi* (in the factual domain) with a justificatory basis in the nature of the world.[5] To be sure, this effort at rational validation goes against the grain of much current

---

[4] The discussion of this section draws upon material initially presented in the author's *The Primacy of Practice* (Oxford, 1973).

[5] It is this two-sided appeal to "the nature of reality"—as not just a product of man's cognitive quest, but part of its justificatory *basis* as well—that marks the present analysis as metaphysical. This way of posing the issue brings to the fore its circular aspect, a circularity whose harmlessness the next chapter will argue in detail.

opinion in the theory of knowledge "Don't worry about how we come by our knowledge—and above all leave metaphyisics out of it" is a common view. K. R. Popper puts this idea in the form of a self-denying injunction: "No theory of knowledge should attempt to explain why we are successful in our attempts to explain things."[6] This stance may perhaps provide a useful antidote to that cognitive hubris which endeavours to explain too much, but all the same it does not represent a rationally comfortable position. A theory of knowledge that cannot explain—nay deems *inexplicable*—why our ventures at knowledge-acquisition are as successful as to all appearances they seem to be is *ipso facto* seriously deficient.

It is thus so desirable as to be effectively necessary to give a *metaphysical deduction* to validate the operation of our inquiry procedures—along some such lines as those indicated in the present chapter. Such a metaphysical rationalization of our epistemological procedures must acknowledge that a methodology and technology of knowledge-acquisition demands certain conditions to be satisfied both on the side of the investigating *agents* and on the side of its investigated *objects* (viz., the world about us). That is, it must be possible to specify both certain features of the *modus operandi* of our factual inquiry, and certain features of the "external world," in virtue of which the capacity of our inquiry-methods to yield objectively valid knowledge can be cogently accounted for. Such conditions must be fulfilled if methods which provide our *vaunted* knowledge are justifiably to be acknowledged as providing genuine knowledge. (The fact that an account of this sort is *ex hypothesi* not forthcoming is one consideration among others that blocks the rational legitimation on grounds of pragmatic efficacy alone of the so-called "inquiry procedure" of an applicatively successful "black box.")

Such a Kant-reminiscent quest for the "conditions under which factual knowledge is possible" represents a promising and distinctive methodology for the conduct of metaphysical inquiry. Its approach is simple: Proposing to follow an epistemological route into the domain of metaphysics, it begins with the question:

What sort of evidence could *inquirers constituted and positioned as we are* possibly gather to *account for* the way in which the

[6] K. R. Popper, *Objective Knowledge* (Oxford, 1973), p. 23.

inquiry procedures they employ actually work and to *legiti-mate* their use?

This question provides the determinative guide to the issue: given the *de facto* workings-out of our methodology of inquiry, what sorts of *further* assumptions must be made regarding ourselves and our world to *explain and justify* the fact of its effective operation. We proceed via the question: Given that our *de facto* mode of operation in the cognitive sphere works—and works as it actually does—what conditions must reasonably be postulated regarding ourselves and the world to provide a plausible account for this circumstance?

The process of reasoning thus involves an inference from certain actual or presumed facts to a suitable explanatory ration-ale for them, a rationale that of itself may well transcend altogether our information-acquiring techniques in the empirical area. The argumentation calls for a presuppositional regress from the *de facto* realities of a certain practice into the fact-transcending regulative principles by which the workings of this practice are accounted for (i.e., explained and validated). It is in this way—by the route of a metaphysical deduction—that we propose to answer the very Kantian question of how natural science is possible, that is, how a limited and particularized experience of nature is able to provide an adequate basis for claims to generalized knowledge.

This metaphysical methodology envisages a Kantian program of analyzing the presuppositionally regulative rationale of our *praxis* in the sphere of factual inquiry. It does not adduce evidence of an empirical sort to establish the substantive con-clusion that certain facts obtain. Rather, it begins with refer-ence to a certain domain of human *praxis* (specifically the process of inquiry into matters of fact regarding the ways of the world), and it then inquires into its regulative foundations—the implicit suppositions needed to legitimate its employment and to explain its workings.

Someone might well object as follows:

You maintain that the "Wheel Argument" shows decisively that no satisfactory justification of a truth-criterion is possible along purely theoretical lines. Is this not inconsistent with the claim made on behalf of the "metaphysical deduction," as serving to provide such a theoretical justification?

But in fact there is no inconsistency here. The Wheel Argument does indeed show decisively that no purely "theoretical" course of truth-criterial justification can be *sufficient* to do the justificatory job. And the metaphysical deduction—though necessary as an element of our argument—is certainly not sufficient. It critically needs theory-external supplementation by a reality-principle of the sort the pragmatic cycle provides. This need for an entry into the domain of *praxis* is actually the crucial moral to emerge from the Wheel Argument's story, and its important lesson is nowise abrogated in resorting to a "metaphysical deduction" for truth-criterion.

A pivotal question is inevitably raised by such justificatory resort to metaphysical principles which—like interactionism, nonconspiratoriality, purposive constancy, and the like—are of a largely factual and empirical bearing: Does the "metaphysical deduction" of a linkage between the applicative success of an inquiry procedure and its cognitive adequacy establish this result as necessary or as merely contingent?

To resolve this question it will be helpful to step outside the conceptual confines of the all-to-familiar epistemic posture we occupy as members of the species *homo sapiens*. Accordingly, let us reintroduce for consideration a *Gedankenexperiment* suggested by Georg Simmel—that of approaching the problem of cognitive adequacy from the standpoint of an entirely different sort of cognitive being.[7] Imagine intelligent and actively inquiring creatures (animals, say, or beings from outer space) whose experiential modes are quite different from our own. Their senses are highly responsive to quite different physical parameters—relatively insensitive, say, to heat and light, but substantially sensitized to various electromagnetic phenomena. Accordingly, such intelligent creatures would have to be supposed to operate within a largely different framework of empirical concepts and categories. The problem now arises: How is one to conceive of *their* obtaining a rational warrant for the conclusion that their inquiry procedures function adequately and provide "a correct picture of how things work in the world"? Obviously we cannot take the parochial stance of requiring them to ascertain the

[7] Georg Simmel, "Ueber eine Beziehung der Selectionslehre zur Erkenntnistheorie," *Archiv für systematische Philosophie und Soziologie*, vol. 1 (1895), pp. 34–45 (see 40–1).

agreement of *their* conceptions of reality with *ours*. The only way in which we could reasonably expect them to validate their inquiry method is in terms of the predictive and manipulative control which its deliverances enable them to realize; in other words, by reference to the pragmatic success (in its affective and survivalistic dimensions) engendered in the implementation of the findings it underwrites. And there is no reason to refrain from generalizing this lesson by putting ourselves also into the position of the *Gedankenexperiment* creatures. In sum, we return to the upshot of our initial analysis of the Wheel Argument (*diallelus*): One is driven to construe the cognitive adequacy of an inquiry procedure to be determined along pragmatic lines. This eventuation is not a matter of contingent considerations but a necessary result built into the conceptual structure of the issue. But this necessity is a conditional one. Its format is as follows:

> *Given* that we are inquiring beings of a certain kind operating in a world-setting of a certain sort (both of which factors are throughout contingent), we *necessarily* find ourselves in a position where we can ascertain the adequacy of our cognitive methodology only in a certain way—one which involves reliance on the initially indicated contingent facts.

The "necessarily" of this argument is a rigid, conceptual necessity, yet a necessity that is not categorial or absolute, but hypothetical and conditioned—a merely *relative* necessity hinging upon the initial (themselves contingent) givens. Accordingly, the over-all position involves an intricate *mixture* of contingent and necessitarian elements: We *can only* validate our truth-claims on a certain basis (that's necessary),[8] but this basis which provides requisite warrant for our truth-claims itself remains contingent.

One thing very much needs to be said regarding this proposed metaphysical "deduction": It is *not* in fact to be regarded as providing anything approaching a demonstrative proof. For were this so, then, deductive logic being what it is, we would simply have to load into the premisses (in duly disguised form) the very con-

---

[8] Given this inevitability, it seems implausible to regard the conclusion that *our* truth is in a sense a *man-relative* truth as exciting as Simmel seems to have done.

clusion we are trying to extract. Rather, the inference at issue is essentially a *plausibility*-argument—one that builds a good case for its conclusion, providing it with a solid rational warrant which (admittedly) stops short of giving a logically airtight guarantee. The person who, in the face of such an argument, refuses to accept its conclusion (while yet granting the premises) is not being *inconsistent* but simply *unreasonable*.

The present strategy of epistemological justification thus rests on a framework of (fact-laden) metaphysical theses regarding the nature of man as inquirer, the world that is the object of this inquiry, and the relationship between these two. It must be granted freely that the principles appealed to (activism, sensitivity, interactionism, purposive constancy, the nonconspiratoriality of nature, and the like) constitute only a rather partial and one-sided metaphysic. They are very incomplete and perhaps also not very "interesting." (Certainly they bring no surprises!) But this is as it should be. It is not our task here to contruct a sophisticated and comprehensive metaphysic, but only to register those few principles needed for the limited work of validating a cognitive methodology for the factual realm. Nothing should thus be read —either favorably or unfavorably—into a silence regarding other matters. (And specifically, we have no intention whatever to restrict the sphere of legitimate human activity to the delimited area of knowledge-acquisition.)

Moreover, the theses that provide the materials for our "metaphysical deduction" do not come *ex nihilo*. Since they are fact-laden, their mere *postulation* would be a matter of seeking to obtain by theft what can be secured only through the expenditure of justificatory labor. The operative metaphysic is not itself unjustified, but needs in large measure to be based on our information regarding how things work in the world. Of course, the *results* of a duly justified truth-criterion must ultimately prove consonant with the system of justificatory assumptions and presuppositions on which its own validation rests. This demand is simply another aspect of our earlier insistence on the systematic coherence of the justificatory process as self-sustaining. (And in the present case there can be little question about the factual viability of the initial "metaphysical" stance on which the justificatory procedure rests.)

Does this resort to a truth-criterion to revalidate the metaphysical basis of its own justification not make the whole process circular? Here we are back to the old familiar vicious-circle line of objection. This spectre must be laid to rest once and for all.

Chapter VII

CLOSING THE CIRCLES

I. IS THE PROPOSED VALIDATION VICIOUSLY CIRCULAR?

The structure of the presently proposed process for justifying an inquiry procedure can now be seen in a clearer perspective. To begin with, it warrants stress that the line of justificatory argument envisaged here in effect calls for the closing of a "great circle" of the form sketched in Figure 1.

Figure 1

THE "GREAT CIRCLE" LEGITIMATION OF AN INQUIRY PROCEDURE

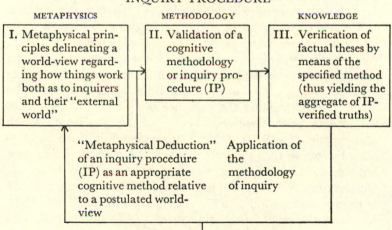

METAPHYSICS   METHODOLOGY   KNOWLEDGE

I. Metaphysical principles delineating a world-view regarding how things work both as to inquirers and their "external world"

II. Validation of a cognitive methodology or inquiry procedure (IP)

III. Verification of factual theses by means of the specified method (thus yielding the aggregate of IP-verified truths)

"Metaphysical Deduction" of an inquiry procedure (IP) as an appropriate cognitive method relative to a postulated world-view

Application of the methodology of inquiry

Assessment of the metaphysical world-view in terms of the IP-validated world picture which (hopefully) provides it with empirical and *a posteriori* support. (This amounts to a retrospective *ex post facto* revalidation of the adequacy of the basic metaphysic.)

On such an approach, the truth-claims of the products of our inquiry procedure are not direct and immediate, but, rather, are mediated through a family of metaphysical theses about the nature of man and the world. The keystone of the arch of systematic unification is provided by a metaphysical position which furnishes the basis for a "deduction" (in the Kantian sense) of the appropriateness of the inquiry-methodology at issue. The metaphysic, the process of inquiry, and the fruits of its application must all fit smoothly with one another in a careful dovetailing. The closing of this "great circle" of justificatory argumentation—one which relies on the support that our methodology-consequent factual findings are able to lend our methodology-antecedent metaphysical suppositions—constitutes the core of the justificatory program envisaged here.

William James himself portrayed the rationalization of a pragmatic approach in terms of an appeal to metaphysical principles ultimately revalidated by itself:

> Truth absolute, he [the pragmatist] says, means an ideal set of formulations towards which all opinions may in the long run of experience be expected to converge. In this definition of absolute truth he not only postulates that there is a tendency to such convergence of opinions, to such ultimate consensus, but he postulates the other factors of his definition equally, borrowing them by anticipation from the true conclusions expected to be reached. He postulates the existence of opinions, he postulates the experience that will sift them, and the consistency which that experience will show. He justifies himself in these assumptions by saying that they are not postulates in the strict sense but simple inductions from the past extended to the future by analogy; and he insists that human opinion has already reached a pretty stable equilibrium regarding them, and that if its future development fails to alter them, the definition itself, with all its terms included, will be part of the very absolute truth which it defines. The hypothesis will, in short, have worked successfully all round the circle and proved self-corroborative, and the circle will be closed.[1]

To his everlasting credit William James perceived clearly this

[1] *The Meaning of Truth* (New York, 1909), pp. 266–8.

aspect of pragmatic procedure as crucially involving a self-supportive circle.

It is necessary, however, to face the problems engendered by the circular nature the justificatory process thus envisaged. The metaphysical principles which it invokes (activism, rationality, interactionism, and the rest) are all in large measure themselves contingent and factual in orientation. Since they are to serve to legitimate the inquiry procedure, and the inquiry procedure is one for determining factual truths, their own factuality clearly poses problems. In particular, we must deal with the following line of objection:

> This entire methodological approach to justification fails to accomplish its intended objective because of its circular mode of argumentation. For it legitimates cognitive methods in terms of their producing acceptable (because applicatively successful) theses, and theses are then warranted as acceptable because they are produced by duly legitimated methods. This process is surely viciously circular.

The proper response to the objection is to concede the circularity while denying its harmfulness. For what is basically at issue is not a vitiating circle, but a recognition of the fundamentally symbiotic relationship of two interdependent elements. The warranting at issue is *not* successive and sequential. If this *were* the case—if the course of justificatory argumentation were strictly linear—then the circle would indeed be vicious, but this is emphatically *not* the case. It is not simply a matter of first setting this and then that, advancing ever further in a fixed direction. Rather, the argumentation is *comprehensively systematic*, placing its several elements into a coordinative framework which unites them within one over-all nexus of mutual substantiation.[2]

Despite its stress on the fundamentality of method, our justificatory reasoning thus does not envisage a unidirectional progress

[2] One contemporary writer who takes roughly this same pragmatic line—justifying scientific inference in terms of factual considerations and treating the resulting circularity as nonvicious because of the ultimate corrigibility of the theory as a whole—is Abner Shimony. See his essay "Scientific Inference" in R. G. Colodny (ed.), *The Nature and Function of Scientific Theories* (Pittsburgh, 1970), pp. 79–172 (see especially pp. 158–9).

from method to thesis, but rather a systematic union of the two—specifically in the manner set out in the diagram of Figure 2.

Figure 2

THE INTERACTION OF FACTUAL AND METAPHYSICAL
ELEMENTS IN INQUIRY

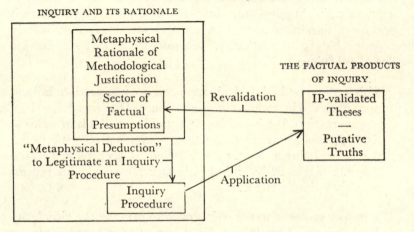

The critical facet of this process as a rationally satisfactory course of justification is once again the effective closing of the over-all circle. The symbiotic and mutually supportive nature of the enterprise is fundamental: its structure must afford a systematic union in which *both* methods and theses are appropriately interlinked.

These considerations also indicate the neo-Hegelian aspect of systematic coherence throughout the cognitive enterprise. When inquiry works along properly, there must be a kind of systematic unity in which output ("factual theses") is duly consonant with input (the "world-view"). The theses that represent the *results* of our duly justified truth-criterion must be such as ultimately to revalidate the system of these justificatory assumptions and presuppositions on which its own validation rests. This demand is simply another aspect of our insistence upon the systematic coherence of the justificatory process as ultimately self-sustaining. (And as the detailed considerations of Chapter VI have shown, there is, in this present case, little question about the factual viability of the initial "metaphysical" stance on which the justificatory procedure rests.)

Consider an analogy. Imagine a society of blind scientists with radiation scanning devices on the basis of whose (tactually monitored) performance they theorize about the phenomenal color of objects as perceived by others—a sphere with respect to which any *direct* check is (*ex hypothesi*) impossible for them, though they occasionally hear discourse about the matter from strangers. Theses scientists, we will suppose, have at their disposal a *background theory* (physics and especially optics), an *inquiry method* (the scanners) and certain *factual theses* (a body of claims regarding the colors of objects). When all these are brought into due mutual coordination with one another, our scientists can rest assured that sheer intelligence has done what it can under the restrictive conditions at issue.

This circular-structured process of validation conforms to the performance-monitoring *modus operandi* of a self-evaluating servomechanism, since it provides for a quality-control feedback loop that leads from the *product* ("factual theses") back to the *process* (the deployment of a method) which generated it. Just this retrospective character ultimately assures the adequate functioning of the whole machinery. The mechanism is equipped with a warning buzzer, as it were, that sounds when something is badly amiss with its workings. There is thus no reason to concede that the circle at issue is vicious or otherwise vitiating, for what is actually involved is simply a feedback process of a type nowadays familiar from the study of self-regulatory systems.

This cyclic process is reminiscent of what Wilhelm Dilthey called "the hermeneutic circle":[3] the problem inherent in the (surely correct) observation that the whole of a cultural product (be it a literary or philosophical opus, or the entire work of a thinker or of a period) can only be understood if one understands its component parts, while these parts in their turn can be understood only by understanding the whole. Dilthey's hermeneutic problem is a special instance of a far wider issue. For example, in the case of probative argumentation we also face "the evidential circle" arising from the consideration that the evidence must itself ultimately be evaluated in the light of the factual theses for

[3] On Dilthey see O. F. Bollnow, *Dilthey: Eine Einführung in seine Philosophie* (Leipzig and Berlin, 1936).

whose substantiation it is invoked. And in our present case we have "the justificatory circle" arising because the performance of a cognitive method must be judged in terms of its products, while these products must themselves be judged by means of the method. All these structurally analogous problems have a structurally analogous solution—viz., that the paradox arises from taking a strictly static point of view, and that these difficulties vanish when regards the issue from the dynamic perspective of a cyclic feedback process. All of the "circles" are instances of one basic model—the *epistemic* circle, which results from the reciprocal interdependence of parts and wholes in the constitution of our knowledge.

To illustrate the workings of systematic coherence and self-substantiation, let us consider the contrast-case of an admittedly artificial (and even perverse) inquiry procedure, that of *counterinductivism*.

The counterinductivist adapts the following policy of validation for empirical generalizations:

> If a generalization has been applied *un*successfully (sic) in prior applications, one is to infer its (probable) success in the application presently in hand; and if it has been applied successfully in prior applications, one is to infer its (probable) failure in the case in hand. (Cf. p. 67 above.)

There can be no doubt that—given the realities of our actual experience—this inquiry procedure *appears* to be thoroughly self-sustaining. That is to say, given its manifest failures in the past we would be led—by the standards of the principle itself—also to apply this method in present cases. Any fact-oriented inquiry procedure of a sufficiently broad scope can always be turned upon itself and its performance evaluated from its own point of view. For if it is capable of serving as a test of general factual theses, then general claims about *its own* performance will also fall within its scope. Counterinductivism too seems successful in this regard. The counterinductivist is concerned to achieve "normal ends"—namely to validate the rational claims of his method—only his warrant for believing that he achieves this goal is based on perverse standards.

Yet in a somewhat deeper sense this method is *not* self-sustaining. For our interest in any *method* is always clearly systematic: we care not simply about *this* application (or the next or the next two or three), but at least about the whole sequence of applications in the near term—if not more ambitiously about the long run as well. (A procedure to be applied in one certain special case hardly qualifies as a *method*.) And from *this* perspective, the method of counterinduction does not really qualify as self-sustaining. For consider the question: "What would lead the counter-inductivist to feel increased confidence—by the standards of his own method—that this method is effective in its future application beyond the next two or three cases?" The obvious answer is its *failure* in the near term cases—specifically including its *present* application. We thus reach the paradoxical result that the best support this "method" can provide for itself lies in its failure to provide any support at all. For if the counterinductivist is to have warrant—by his own standard—for the continued use of his method in cases beyond the horizons of the present moment, then he must *refrain* from using his method in the present case (*any* present case!) because its actual effectiveness in this case would only count against its effectiveness in further applications. On finding that the application of this method in a present case has been effective the counterinductivist will thus have to admit that he was not, after all, justified in applying the method in that case. Indeed, it is precisely the *lack* of warrant in the present case which provides (in part) the counterinductivist his "warrant" for future cases. (Consequently, if the method *were* warranted in the present case in terms of the objectives of the counterinducti-vist, it would to that extent provide counterinductivistic warrant *against* its future applications.) The very fact that this method realizes his goals in some cases counts *against* its future employ-ment. Thus, the counterinductivist method fails to acheive self-sustainingness in the *systematic* sense and so emerges as ultimately incoherent.[4]

But, of course, the systematic coherence at the level of cognitive-theoretical considerations is not enough to insure adequate quality-control. The issue is not one of simply fitting bits of theorizing to one another: the theoretico-ideational framework must somehow be grounded in an independent reality, and some

---

[4] Compare also A. Öfsti, "Some Problems of Counter-Inductive Policy as Opposed to Inductive," *Inquiry*, vol. 5 (1962), pp. 267–83.

sort of contact be made with "the real world." It is just this desideratum that is met by an appeal to pragmatic success. This line of consideration brings our analysis of cognitive justification to its next and crucial stage.

2. THE FIGURE-EIGHT STRUCTURE OF THE RATIONALE OF LEGITIMATION

The circular structure of the rationale of cognitive legitimation is even more complex than the preceding section suggests. What is actually at issue is a *double* circle, a process of figure-eight configuration. To see this, let us first return to an earlier stage of the discussion. We began by applying to *cognitive* methodology the general approach of instrumental evaluation, recognizing that the relevant purposive teleology lies in the pragmatic domain. This produced a picture of the systematic situation as shown in Figure 3 (cf. Figure 1 on p. 25):

Figure 3

THE PRAGMATIC EVALUATION OF AN
INQUIRY PROCEDURE

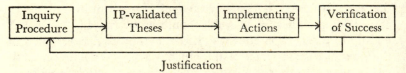

The burden of validation is thus borne by the systematic success of an inquiry procedure in underwriting theses whose implementation leads to successful results in the practical/affective sector.

But as the last chapter indicated, this is not the end of the matter. It was maintained there that a suitable justificatory rationale links the success engendered by use of an inquiry procedure and the presumptive truthfulness of its deliverances. This linkage is not, however, self-evident. Rather, it resides in the operation of a certain metaphysical principles and is underwritten by a series of complex (and largely factual) assumptions about the nature of the world and of man's place in it—assumptions we have signalized with such labels as *rationality, activism, inter-activism, feedback* and *sensitivity.*

Putting all these pieces together, it emerges that the over-all justification of an inquiry procedure lies in the closing of two cycles which constitute a double circle of the figure-eight pattern shown in Figure 4.

Figure 4

THE DOUBLE CIRCLE OF PRAGMATIC JUSTIFICATION

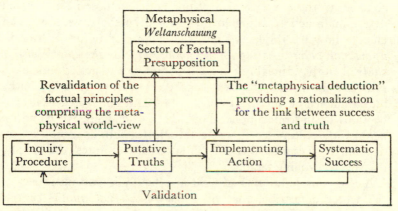

As this diagram clearly shows, the over-all justification is doubly self-sustaining. Two interlocked "cycles" are involved: the "truths" generated by the inquiry procedure must be sustained in implementing action, and they must themselves undergird the *Weltanschauung* by which the linkage of successful implementation and truthfulness can be validated. The central requisite of the whole process of justification is that this complex interlocking dual-cycle should be properly closed and connected. The present theory of cognitive validation is literally a matter of "wheels within wheels." Only when everything is adjusted and readjusted so that *all* the pieces fit in a smooth dovetailing, will we obtain a workable pragmatic methodological justification for an inquiry procedure.

3. PRAGMATIC EFFICACY AFFORDS A "REALITY PRINCIPLE"

One important consideration has, however, been left out of view in this picture. The diagram shows merely *how* various elements are connected, but does not indicate which of these elements lie within the range of our manipulative control, and which ones merely react to variations in those determining variables which, so to speak, hold the reins in their hands. In this regard it is clear that: (1) we can alter and readjust our *Weltanschauung*. (2) We can change our inquiry procedure (and hence, mediately, the range of "truths" that result from its application). (3) We can modify and reorient our actions. But the one thing that we cannot control are the *consequences* of our actions: those results which determinate actions bring in their wake. In short, while we can change how we think and act, *the success or failure attendant upon such changes is something wholly outside the sphere of our control*. In this crucial respect, our cognitive and active endeavors propose, and nature disposes—and does so in presumably blithe independence of our wishes and hopes, and our beliefs and conceptions or misconceptions about the world. Here we come up against the ultimate, theory-external, thought-exogenously independent variable. Pragmatic success consitutes the finally decisive controlling factor.

These considerations highlight a critically important aspect of the whole enterprise, that of a *theory-external quality-control* upon theoretical performance. The over-all process of justification thus involves the proper closing of two interlocked cycles, the one theoretical/cognitive and the other practical/applicative in orientation. We can see this most clearly by reconsidering the elements of the preceding double circle from the variant point of view presented in Figure 5.

As long as one remains in the confines of box I—in the domain of "theory"—one moves about in the realm of one's own views and beliefs. At this level nothing precludes the whole process from being a pure idealism, confined to the realm of mind alone; the pragmatic element of action and reaction is still absent. And even when one moves on to box II, the domain of action, one still remains within an area where we ourselves are masters, the realm of thought and action whose elements lie within our own control. Only with box III does one move from a secure, man-dominated realm to encounter the harsh realities of the external world whose workings lie in predominant measure beyond the reach of our control.

Figure 5

THE PRAGMATIC CONTROLS OF COGNITIVE ADEQUACY

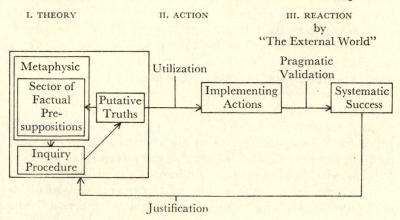

The process at issue is thus a complex of two distinct but interlocked cycles—the *theoretical* cycle of cognitive coherence and the *pragmatic* cycle of applicative effectiveness. Only if both of these cycles dovetail properly—in both the theoretical and the applicative sectors—can the whole process be construed as providing a suitable rational legitimation for the inquiry procedure at issue.

Everyone is familiar with the occasional surfacing even today of some occult or pseudo-scientific views of the world which substantiate fact-purporting theses of the strangest sort. It is always striking here how beautifully everything meshes at the theoretical level—one bit of strangeness being supported by others. The crunch comes only with the tough question: Does this world-view enable its proponents to navigate more successfully through the rocks and shoals of this world? The proof of such a theoretical pudding is its applicative eating.

The pivotal element of action *and reaction* thus provides for the operation of a "*reality principle*." And this is vital to the justificatory capacities of the whole process, because it blocks the prospect of a futile spinning around in reality-detached cycles of purely theoretical gyrations. Someplace along the line of justification there must be provision for a corrective contact with the bedrock of an uncooperative and largely unmanipulable reality—

a brute force independent of the whims of our theorizing. This crucial reality-principle is provided for in the framework of the present theory by the factor of the reactive success consequent upon implementing action.

However, it needs to be stressed that this factor of pragmatic success, though predominantly important, is only one part of a complex picture. It is helpful at this point to return briefly to the idea of a "black-box" decision-procedure for factual theses (as mooted above (at pp. 74–6). While this essentially occult procedure might (in theory) possibly score heavily on the side of pragmatic efficacy, we saw that its lack of an inherent probative rationale prevented it from counting as an inquiry procedure *of the right sort*. We can now see why this condition is no matter of arbitrary terminological fiat but plays a significant role of principle. Only a suitably ramified rationale of inquiry can receive the sort of in-depth support we have called a "metaphysical deduction." The existence of such a metaphysically grounded linkage of success and truthfulness is crucial, for this alone can secure the warrant of rationality on the basis of which *confidence* in the procedure becomes rationally certified. (The only reason for placing trust in the black box is its success in *some other* cases, and how could this ever provide a sound basis for it in this present case? Clearly only an appeal to principles—e.g., uniformity of operation—for which the black box itself could never provide the necessary substantiation.)

Accordingly, the process of legitimation of a methodology for the substantiation of our factual beliefs must unite two distinctive elements: (1) an apparatus of systematic coherence at the theoretical level (a coherence in which factual presumptions and metaphysical presuppositions both play a crucial part), and (2) a controlling monitor of considerations of pragmatic efficacy at the practical level. Both of these ingredients are essential for the legitimating power of the whole, and neither can be dismissed for the sake of an exclusive reliance on the other.

4. THE PROBLEM OF UNDERDETERMINATION

A significant question remains: Is it not possible that the pragmatic strategy of justification might fail to validate a unique result—that it might underwrite equally well several different, distinct and discordant inquiry procedures?

Any *instrumental* process for assessing the legitimacy of a method is inherently unable to provide a theoretical guarantee that there is a uniquely determinate solution. The instrumental strategy for assessing methods accordingly remains potentially *underdeterminative*. By its very nature it can yield no general reason of principle why the means-to-ends appraisal of methods should issue in a single result: it is quite possible that different and distinct methods should be equally effective in realizing specified purposes. William James, for one, faced this prospect with equanimity. "Common sense," he wrote, "is *better* for one sphere of life, science for another, philosophic criticism for a third; but whether either be true absolutely, Heaven only knows."[5]

In grappling with this problem of pragmatic underdetermination we must begin by inquiring into the sort of "distinctness" that is to be at issue. For it is clear that there are *alternatives* here. Inquiry procedures may be distinct *merely procedurally*, while necessarily consonant in their results, agreeing altogether on which theses are true and which are not. In our present context we may dismiss *this* sort of distinctness. These merely procedural differences are uninteresting because altogether harmless. On the other hand, there is a more significant and radical mode of methodological distinctness, that of leading to actually different results. In our present case, this would involve a plurality of inquiry procedures leading to discordant and conflicting findings as to what is true.

The theoretical possibility of this prospect must be admitted at the very outset. It represents a case that cannot be ruled out *a priori* on any logico-theoretical grounds of abstract general principle. But the question remains whether this theoretical prospect need actually concern us in the case in hand. Perhaps the specific circumstances of our problem-area are such that a unique result can be expected *in this case* thanks to particular characteristics of the specific application at issue. Against this background it is worth noting that the particular application of instrumental validation that has concerned us here—viz., the pragmatic justification of procedures for validating the acceptance-as-true of factual theses —is indeed such as to militate towards a definiteness of result.

[5] *Pragmatism* (New York, 1907), p. 125.

Consider the situation if the purely speculative prospect of a failure of uniqueness were in fact realized. This would produce a situation of methodological schizophrenia: *discordant* inquiry methods (methods that open-endedly validate *incompatible* factual claims) would *systematically* produce results which are nevertheless equally successful in point of practical implementation. There would, in this case, have to be at least two equally meritorious inquiry procedures yielding discordant results over the same range of applications in a systematic and general way. And it would have to be the case that: (1) both procedures are *internally* self-sustaining *vis-à-vis* the metaphysical rationale their application generates to provide for their substantiation, and (2) *externally* both procedures are pragmatically adequate in the sense that the regular implementation of their respective results would *systematically* yield a high measure of success. In short, the procedures would have to yield discordant factual claims whose implementation—either way—would issue in equally satisfactory results. Given the wide-ranging open-endedness of an inquiry procedure, this prospect is "inconceivable"—it is so far-fetched that it can be dismissed out of hand. It is astronomically more implausible than the prospect that two decyphering procedures should systematically translate encoded messages (across a vast range of texts) into discordant but equally tenable English versions. But, of course, what rules this prospect out is not a matter of purely theoretical logico-conceptual considerations: no actual self-contradiction is involved. Rather, what rules it out is a matter of metaphysics—viz., our recognition that the basic natural processes being what they are, this sort of prospect can be excluded from the realm of "practical politics."

It is important to the preceding line of argument that the conflict of the two postulated inquiry procedures will exhibit itself diffusedly throughout the entire range of inquiry and is not confined to separable compartments. One can, of course, readily envisage the case of procedures P_1 and P_2 where P_1 outperforms P_2 with respect to subject-matter area A_1 and P_2 outperforms P_1 with respect to A_2, but where in point of *over-all success*—with *everything* taken into account—P_1 and P_2 are evenly matched. However, in this event the obviously apposite course is to resort to the *mixed* methodology which would, in effect, be based on the precept: "Within area A_1 use P_1, and within A_2 use P_2." It is this fact—that the disagreement between competing procedures must be pervasive rather than localized, and that, despite of this, they must be equally balanced as regards success in application—which renders the failure of uniqueness as an effectively eliminable prospect. The rationale of the metaphysical deduction operates to eliminate any prospect of a discordant pluralism or inquiry procedures.[6]

In the case of a plurality of diverse inquiry procedures we must envisage a process of sequential revision unfolding so as to bring them closer in mutual conformation and approximation to one another as regards the results of their application. The temporal course of revision must move them along convergent paths. The "must" here is not, however, that of logico-conceptual *necessity* inherent in the very structure of the conceptions at issue, but that of *relative* necessitation with respect to a metaphysical *Weltanschauung*.

5. EPISTEMIC STRATIFICATION

But when all is said and done, is there not still something untoward, even *fishy*, about using facts in justifying a fact-validating procedure—using as *inputs* to justify an inquiry procedure theses of the very sort which this procedure is designed to establish?

To meet this objection we must enter once more upon the theme of *epistemic stratification*. It becomes essential to recognize the fact that a claim which is "one and the same thesis" insofar as its *substance* or *content* is concerned may enter into the cognitive sphere of knowledge or information at very different levels. At the outset, its status can be that of a mere assumption (whose sole initial basis is that of a regulative postulate or conjecture). It may then gradually come to be raised to the status of a reasonably well substantiated contention (a well-confirmed hypothesis).

---

[6] The case of "methodological schizophrenia" contrasts sharply with a methodological pluralism which calls for using significantly different methods of substantiation in different subject-matter areas (e.g., the human and the natural sciences). This consideration points towards the doctrine of "the methodological unity of science" and its ramifications. The issues here are subtle and complex and it seems possible to make out a reasonably good case for a methodological pluralism at *this* level.

E

Thereafter it may become a firmly-established thesis and finally even a known fact. Such a cyclic revalidation or cognitive up-grading of theses is by now a familiar aspect of our approach. Its consideration drives home the point that in epistemology (unlike logic) we must reckon not only with the assertive content of a thesis, but also with its *cognitive status:* its standing or status within the over-all epistemic structure of what we are pleased to call "the information at our disposal." The conception of cognitive levels or strata is a fundamental component of our theory.

Most philosophical theorists of knowledge beginning with Descartes—and continuing throughout the whole mainstream of modern tradition, from the classical rationalists (like Spinoza) and empiricists (like Hume), on via Brentano, to Chisholm and our contemporaries—have been concerned primarily with knowledge in the sense of what we *know for certain.* They have been obsessed with the realm of the (supposedly) certain and indubitable, to the almost total neglect of the less definitive forms of our "know-ledge." To a large extent, the philosophical theorists of knowledge abandoned the latter domain to students of scientific method and probable inference (in the tradition of Mill, Venn, Keynes, and Carnap). In consequence, the epistemology of what might be called the lesser degrees of cognitive warrant remains a relatively underdeveloped area. But just this domain of the "inferior" (and so spurned) grades of knowledge is pivotal for our present pur-poses. In particular, we must deal with those low-grade data which may be characterized as *presumptions.*

6. PRESUMPTIONS

Apart from forays into the domain of probability, modern epistem-ology has almost wholly neglected the range of conceptions in the neighborhood of presumption: that grey area of concepts having a tentative impetus towards truth, without accomplishing any decisive steps in this direction. And the quest for certainty has continued to exercise a virtually hypnotic fascination on contemporary epistemologists, who have, accordingly, tended to neglect cognitive claims which stop short of pretentions to ab-soluteness. In classical antiquity, however, the conception of presumption played a large part in the theory of knowledge. The concept of *prolepsis* (generally translated "preconception," but tantamount to a "natural presumption") was introduced by Epicurus and played a prominent part in the epistemological controversies between the Epicurean and Stoic schools.[7]

A *presumption* is a thesis that is avowedly not *known* (i.e., known *to be true*), but having some claim—however tentative or imperfect—to be regarded as a truth. The idea of "presumption" invokes the obvious difference between "buying" a thesis and "taking it on approval" to be returned marked *REJECTED* if found wanting. Presumption thus moots a low-level cognitive status. A presumed thesis falls far short of outright *acceptance*, but has provisional—tentative albeit not unencumbered—claims to acceptability. Presumptions thus do not qualify as knowledge proper: they are cognitive stuff of low grade: the mere "raw material" for the production of knowledge, so to speak.

The *acceptance* of a thesis is, to be sure, a decisive act. But like other decisive acts (marriage, for example) one can take tentative and indecisive steps in its direction. Taken initially on some slight provisional and probatively insufficient basis, a thesis can build up increasing trust. A fundamentally economic analogy holds good here: a thesis, like a person, can only acquire a solid credit rating by being *given* credit (i.e., *some* credit) in the first place—provisionally and without any very solid basis. (A fuller treatment of this idea is given in Chapter XII below.)

The particular conception of presumption which is to play a pivotal role in the ensuing considerations is something of a technical innovation. A presumption is a *truth-candidate*, a proposition to be taken not as true, but as potentially true. It is a proposition that one is to class as true *if one can*, that is, if doing so generates no difficulties or inconsistencies. A presumption is not *established* as true, it is backed only by a rationally warranted expectation that it may turn out true "if all goes well." It is a *prima facie* truth in exactly the sense in which one speaks of *prima facie* duties in ethics. A *prima facie* "duty" amounts to *an actual duty* only provided that no countervailing conditions are operative. Similarly, a presumption is a *prima facie* "truth" in that we

[7] One useful recent discussion is F. H. Sandbach "Ennoia and Prolepsis in the Stoic Theory of Knowledge," in A. A. Long (ed.), *Problems in Stoicism* (London, 1971), pp. 22–37.

should under the circumstances be prepared to class it as *actually true* provided that no countervailing considerations are operative. It lays a claim to truth, but it may not be able to make good this claim in the final analysis.

Unlike *established* (or even *probable*) truths, presumptions belong to a very inferior cognitive stratum, a low-grade subsoil. They are, of course, not altogether without probative weight (for then they could not serve the sort of truth-supportive purposes that constitute their *raison d'être*). But the weight they can carry is relatively small.

Presumptive truths generally do not stand alone. They come in clusters or families. The ancient theorists of knowledge usually construed these groupings in terms of the epistemic *sources* from which the theses at issue have their provenience. The "data of memory" and the "deliverances of the senses" were the paradigmatic cases then envisaged. Such an approach seems perfectly reasonable—presumptions should be understood as forthcoming systematically and diffusedly in terms of some general policy, method, or procedure. This systematic status is correlative with a generalized role in the regulative guidance of inquiry. The appropriateness of such a basis is ultimately subject to the controls of revalidation operative in the cyclic validating process in which its correlative presumptions are utilized. This aspect of the matter needs closer scrutiny.

7. PRESUMPTIONS IMPLICIT IN REGULATIVE PRINCIPLES

Regulative principles generally contain implicit correlative presumptions in just the way the *procedural injunction* "Treat people as innocent until proven guilty" embodies the *presumption* of innocence-in-the-absence-of-proven-guilt. Just this is the case with the various principles comprising the basis for the "metaphysical deduction" of our inquiry-methodology. To be sure, these were set out in the preceding chapter as theses rather than overtly regulative principles, but this should not disguise their true nature beyond recognition. They are at bottom of regulative and presumptive standing. (For example: "activism"—"Conceive of people actively involved in dealings within the setting of their environment!", "uniformity of nature"—"Extrapolate uniformly from accessible data!",[8] etc.) The *theses* correlative with such regulative principles are not (necessarily) certified truths that hold without exception "across the board"; they are mere presumptions: propositions provisionally accepted in the context of a purposive venture (viz., the validation of an inquiry method), and conceivably subject to correction or abandonment in the light of further considerations.

The diagram of Figure 6 sets out the patterns of justification for the presumptions implicit in these regulative principles.

Figure 6

THE REVALIDATION OF PRESUMPTIONS

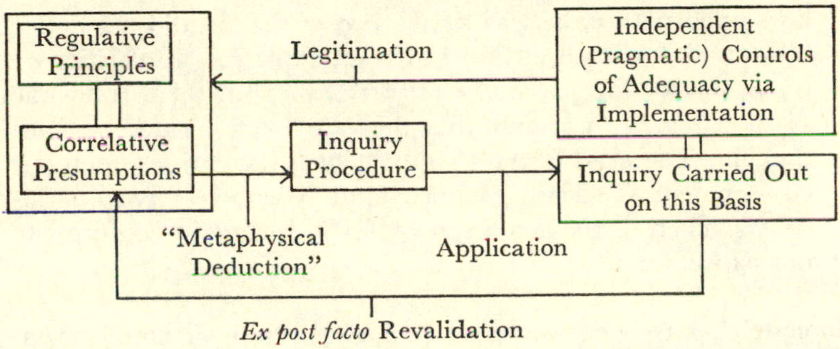

In the usual way envisaged throughout these pages, presumptions receive their rational validation through the workings of a self-substantiating cycle which is also subject to pragmatic controls. Presumptions of this sort open up a very useful middle ground between the security of actually established theses on the one hand and on the other a merely psychological and rationally unwarranted penchant-to-accept.

[8] C. S. Peirce insisted—perhaps more emphatically than any other philosopher of science—that the "uniformity of nature" (which he construed as the complex of two principles: that the whole is as the observed sample, and that similarity in discerned respects is an indicator of similarity in others) is not a law of nature but a condition of factual knowledge in general—a part of the "formal conditions of all knowledge." (*Collected Papers*, Vol. VII: 7.138. Cf. 7.581.) Regarding this sector of Peirce's thought see C. F. Delaney, "Peirce on Induction and the Uniformity of Nature," *The Philosophical Forum*, vol. 4 (1973), pp. 438–448.

The tendency of philosophers to neglect the instrumentality of rationally warranted presumptions can be illustrated by reference to K. R. Popper's interesting discussion of the uniformity-of-nature principle. He writes:

> It was first in animals and children, but later also in adults, that I observed the immensely powerful *need for regularity*—the need which makes them seek for regularities; which makes them sometimes experience regularities even where there are none: which makes them cling to their expectations dogmatically; and which makes them unhappy and may drive them to despair and to the verge of madness if certain assumed regularities break down. When Kant said that our intellect imposes its laws upon nature, he was right—except that he did not notice how often our intellect fails in the attempt: the regularities we try to impose are *psychologically a priori*, but there is not the slightest reason to assume that they are *a priori valid*, as Kant thought. The need to try to impose such regularities upon our environment is, clearly, inborn, and based on drives, or instincts. There is the general need for a world that conforms to our expectations. . . .[9]

One striking aspect of this passage is its emphatic disjunctiveness: the principle of regularity-subsumption is *either* a stipulated thesis (in which case it lacks adequately supportive warrant) *or else* a mere psychological penchant (in which case it is probatively irrelevant). From our standpoint, this dichotomy is deficient. The concept of a rationally warranted presumption provides a third alternative that opens up new epistemic vistas.

8. THE NEED FOR PRESUMPTIONS

Presumption represents a crucial epistemological resource which one would have to make room for in any case—quite apart from its utility in explicating the epistemic status of the metaphysical bases of cognitive justification. This is clear once one turns to the question of the *inputs* essential to the workings of an inquiry

[9] K. R. Popper, *Objective Knowledge* (Oxford, 1972), pp. 23–4.

procedure in the factual domain. If *their* status were that of established truths, then we could never get off the ground.

This problem of inputs is an inevitable facet of any concern with *inquiry procedures* in the area of contingent fact. If any "ordinary process of inferential reasoning" were at issue here, we would be in deep trouble at this stage. For an ordinary process of inference can only extract truths *from truths*. So if the inputs themselves had to be established truths, the whole process would be vitiated at the outset. Happily this is not so. An inquiry procedure is clearly *not* an "ordinary process of inference": It must constitute an *originative* mechanism, capable of yielding an output of (putative) truths without demanding an initial input of previously established (putative) truths. But what of the inputs indispensable to the extraction of factual truths? If we hewed to the line that rationally discursive procedures can only extract truths from truths, we would be offered the unattractive choice between (1) accepting a "starter set" of nondiscursively self-evident or self-validating truths, or (2) a scepticism that admits defeat, and gives up the whole project of a rational validation of truth-acceptance. This is the dilemma we propose to resolve by recourse to the special category of *presumptions*.

By using presumptions as inputs, our inquiry procedure serves as component of an input-output process of the type pictured in Figure 7.

Figure 7

INQUIRY AS AN INPUT-OUTPUT PROCESS

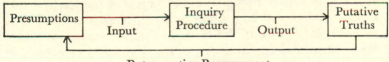

Retrospective Reassessment

An inquiry procedure having this over-all structure escapes the vitiating cycle of basing truth-claims solely upon prior truth-claims, and does so without appeal to a problematic category of self-certifying truths.

One simply cannot validate a methodology of inquiry in terms of its yielding "the real truth." The point of the Wheel Argument (*diallelus*) is precisely that this would be viciously circular, since we have no independent access to "the truth" as such. What we must do is pull ourselves up by our own bootstraps. We begin by provisionally accepting certain theses whose initial status is not that of certified truths at all, but merely that of plausible postulations, whose role in inquiry is (at this stage) one of regulative facilitation. Eventually these are retrospectively revalidated (*ex post facto*) by the results of that inquiry. At *that* stage their epistemic status—though not their *content*—changes. *In the first instance* these presumptions have a merely provisional and regulative standing, though in the final instance they attain a suitable degree of factual/constitutive substantiation.

The logical structure of this justificatory process incorporates a feedback loop leading from the truths validated by the inquiry procedure back to the initial "merely presumptive" truths, so that the appropriateness of these initial, tentative, merely plausible presumptions can be reassessed.

This points towards a cyclic process of revalidation and cognitive upgrading in the course of which presumptive theses used as inputs for the inquiry procedure come to acquire by gradual stages an enhanced epistemic status. The structure of this retrospective revalidation of *inputs* is precisely the same as that already considered for the revalidation of the metaphysical basis of cognitive legitimation as set out in the preceding discussion.

This line of approach abandons the foundationalist penchant of much of the epistemological tradition of modern philosophy. Already Francis Bacon wrote:

> It is idle to expect any great advancement in science from the superimposing and engrafting of new things upon old. We must begin anew from the very foundations, unless we would revolve forever in a circle of mean and virtually contemptible progress (*nisi libeat perpetuo circumvolvi in orbem, cum exili et quasi contemnendo progressu*). (*Novum Organon*, Bk. I, sect. xxxi.)

Just this prospect of progressing in a cyclic sequence of small steps —individually perhaps "mean and virtually contemptible" but potentially massive in their evolutionary aggregate—is accepted on the present theory. For it abandons the project—dear to Bacon and Descartes—of rebuilding from the very foundations, and rests content with the prospect of a gradual stepwise refinement ascending from one epistemic level to the next, always accepting for what it is the position in which we in fact find ourselves, but endeavoring to improve upon it.

Of course, matters need not always go smoothly. For one thing, this process clearly makes retrospective re-evaluation possible: the outputs can bite the input-providing hand that feeds them, and eventually dismiss some inputs as false. An initial presumption may well drop by the wayside in the long run. It is only normal and to be expected that this should happen, given the merely tentative probative nature of presumptions. But if it happens systematically rather than sporadically—if presumptions generally turned out false in this light of hindsight—then something would have gone seriously amiss. (But one could, without problems, invalidate an entire source that has provided a basis of presumptions, as is shown by the example of abandonment of the longstanding practice of giving probative weight to dreams, omens, signs, portents, etc.)

It is clear, in the light of these considerations, that the idea of *presumption* figures critically at two distinct stages of our epistemic theory—on the one hand in relation to the *inputs* needed as materials for the workings of an inquiry procedure, and on the other hand in relation to the principles of the *metaphysical rationale* of justification. Thus this particular piece of conceptual machinery achieves two indispensible tasks within the framework of the present approach.

The reasonableness of the over-all process again rests on the internal coherence and mutual support its various stages lend to one another. The justificatory rationale must be coherent as a whole. The entire process must function in a self-sustaining way, and it is a key aspect of this self-sustainingness that derived truths must revalidate, at least by and large, the claims built into input assumptions.

9. PRESUMPTIONS AND THE AVOIDANCE OF CIRCULARITY

On the present systems approach to cognitive justification, there is no denying that the over-all process is circular. Its structure is as pictured in Figure 8.

Figure 8

THE CYCLIC REVALIDATION OF PRESUMPTIONS

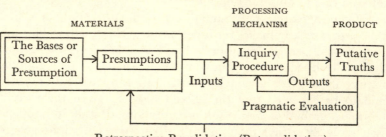

Retrospective Revalidation (Retrovalidation)

The circle here, while only too apparent, is *not* vicious or vitiating. If the circles close in the right way—so that the rationale of justification meshes properly—then our return to the same place will always be *at a different cognitive level.* What is at issue is thus a pair of distinct but connected cycles (the *theoretical* cycle of cognitive coherence and the *pragmatic* cycle of apparent effectiveness) which both move upwards in interlocked coordination—a pair of interlocked ascending spirals. The present approach to epistemic validation finds a "double helix" configuration to lie at the core of human cognition even as it lies at the core of human life itself. The cycle of revalidation moves in a figure 8 configuration. But when we return to "the same place" it is at another epistemic level altogether.[10]

Presumptions play an absolutely crucial role here. Some such warrant "prior" to justification-as-true as is built into the concept

---

[10] There is a question whether we need to take the view that the cyclic process of revalidation and epistemic upgrading issues in "the real truth" by some Peircean process of ultimate convergence. To issue such a guarantee we would either (1) have to redefine truth in the manner of Peirce; or else, (2) adopt a suitably powerful substantive principle to provide an *ad hoc* guarantee (e.g., a Principle of Limited Variety à la Mill). There is no need for any such desperate remedies, however. One does not have to give any such *constitutive* guarantee of the ultimate effectiveness of our inquiry efforts; it suffices to proceed on the strictly *regulative* basis of a reasonable assurance that in proceeding as we do we are doing as well as beings cognitively circumstanced as we are possibly can.

of a presumption is clearly needed to avoid vitiating circularity in the justificatory argument under consideration. But nothing vicious ensues if it turns out from the *post-justificatory* standpoint —as indeed if all goes well it must, at least by-and-large—that the thesis whose *antecedent* status is a mere presumption should ultimately acquire the *consequent* status of a truth. And there is nothing fatal if in some instances matters so turn out that the consequent status of a "presumptive truth" is acually that of falsehood. A rational presumption—unlike an established truth— is defeasible and can, in the final analysis, turn out to be untrue without thereby undoing its initial status as rationally warranted. Its *regulative* acceptance does not render it incorrigible at the *constitutive* level.[11]

Circularity is thus circumvented through the operation of a crucial difference in the utilization of "the same" thesis at different stages—though, to be sure, this difference pertains not to the *assertive content* of the theses used, but to their *epistemic status*.

The present theory of knowledge may thus be characterized as a "dialectical idealism." It is *dialectical* because of the nature of the feedback mechanism operative in the justificatory process that provides its fundamental *modus operandi*. And it is an *idealism* because of the crucial role of mind-contributed presumptions which are not only mind-contributed but (like simplicity, regularity, reasonableness, etc.) are also mind-patterned.[12]

10. THE PRECEDENT OF PEIRCE

After Kant, C. S. Peirce must certainly be reckoned as the principal pioneer of the presuppositions-of-inquiry approach. Peirce held that knowledge has its "foundations" not in the traditional *axiomatic* manner of an indubitable basis for derivative inference, but rather in the sense of background propositions which set out the presuppositions requisite for justifying the *modus operandi* of inquiry. Peirce formulated his position as follows:

[11] The considerations of this section are set out in somewhat fuller detail in Chapter II of the author's *The Primacy of Practice* (Oxford, 1973).
[12] For a fuller development of the relevant idealistic themes see the author's *Conceptual Idealism* (Oxford, 1973).

... inquiry must proceed upon the virtual assumption of sundry logical and metaphysical beliefs; and it is rational to settle the validity of those before undertaking an operation that supposes their truth. Now whether the truth of them be explicitly laid down on critical [i.e., Kantian] grounds, or the doctrine of Common-Sense prevent our pretending to doubt it [is immaterial]. . . . [These] beliefs that appear to be indubitable have the same sort of basis as scientific results have. That is to say, they rest on experience—on the total everyday experience of many generations of multitudinous populations. Such experience is worthless for distinctively scientific purposes, because it does not make the minute distinctions with which science is chiefly concerned . . . although all science, without being aware of it, virtually supposes the truth of the vague results of uncontrolled thought upon such experiences, cannot help doing so, and would have to shut up shop if she should manage to escape accepting them. . . . [T]he instinctive result of human experience ought to have so vastly more weight than any scientific result, that to make laboratory experiments to ascertain, for example, whether there be any uniformity in nature or no, would vie with adding a teaspoonful of saccharine to the ocean in order to sweeten it.[13]

Peirce thus treats the justificatory footing of "sundry logical and metaphysical beliefs" as based upon "the instinctive result of human experience." Our own position differs in this regard. We regard the metaphysical background as a matter of *regulative presuppositions having a partially experiential basis*, and thus as indeed partially endowed with "the same sort of basis scientific results have." But their postulational and presumptive character renders them more readily modifiable than anything as glacial as "the instinctive result of human experience." It is the regulative and presumptive aspect we emphasize, rather than that of experiential or inductive entrenchment. On the present approach, the metaphysical rationale is a potentially changeable theoretical structure whose justification lies not so much in whatever deep roots it may have in the course of human habituation, but in its functional capacity to accomplish its tasks in the framework of

[13] Collected Papers, Vol. V: 5.521–5.522.

legitimation. (Our "metaphysic" is thus vastly more amenable to rational readjustment than that envisaged by Peirce.)

Nonetheless, the present enterprise, like Peirce's, is rigorously empiricistic and experientialistic. The invocation of a justificatory metaphysic should not obscure the fact that the present theory envisages a thoroughly empirico-scientific approach to epistemology. Three steps are at issue: (1) empirical inquiry is seen as providing a factual, scientific picture of man, his *modus operandi* in inquiry, and his environing world, (2) this world-picture provides a factual basis for projecting a wider metaphysical view of the man-world situation, (3) the resultant metaphysic is in its turn deployed to legitimate the *modus operandi* of inquiry. The theoretical aspect of *coherence* plays a central methodological role throughout this cyclic process (though it must be stressed that what is at issue is coherence with respect to a set of factors among which empirical elements play a key role). But, pressing beyond this "internal" aspect of self-substantiation, it is the "external" and experiential issue of pragmatic success that provides the crucial mechanism of quality-control.

Chapter VIII

EVOLUTIONARY EPISTEMOLOGY

I. BACKGROUND

From one point of view it is not particularly surprising that men should succeed in acquiring knowledge. This is something only natural and to be expected because *if we did not succeed in this cognitive venture we wouldn't be here.* The rationale for this is fundamentally Darwinian: rational guidance is necessary for successful action; successful action is crucial for the survival of creatures constituted as we are; accordingly, our survival is indicative of cognitive competence.

The conception of knowledge as a tool for survival—cognitive Darwinism—is as old as biological Darwinism. The master himself put forward the idea that man's abilities in the area of language, reasoning, and theorizing are part and parcel of his biological endowment because these competences were biologically advantageous in the struggle for survival.[1] And after Darwin this idea burst like a Roman candle across the firmament of 19th century thought. The concept of evolution was applied to validate explanatory recourse to various intellectual resources not only by various of the major philosophers of the day—Schopenhauer, Herbert Spencer, C. S. Peirce—but a host of later and lesser thinkers of variant persuasions also followed suit.[2] And it seems

[1] "The small strength and speed of man, his want of natural weapons, etc., are more than counterbalanced, firstly, by his intellectual powers, through which he has formed for himself weapons, tools, etc., though still remaining in a barbarous state, and, secondly, by his social qualities which lead him to give and recieve aid from his fellow men. . . ." (*The Origin of Species* [New York: Modern Library, n.d.], pp. 443–4).

[2] Among the many older writers that deserve recognition here are J. M. Baldwin, Ludwig Boltzmann, H. S. Jennings, Ernst Mach, C. Lloyd Morgan, Georg Simmel, and Hans Vaihinger. James Mark Baldwin, in particular, espoused a combination of Darwinism and instrumentalism—as affording what he termed "a control upon knowledge and action"—which is closely akin in its spirit to the theory espoused here. See especially his *Darwin and the Humanities* (Baltimore, 1909).

obvious enough that since men transmit to their offspring not only genetic traits, but concepts, beliefs, tools, and methods, natural selection operates on *homo sapiens* also at the aphysical, paragenetic, ideational level, and serves to favor survival of those groups that propagate the most serviceable ideas.[3] William James, for example, defended a theory of cognitive instinct according to which the mind is governed by innate predispositions which, like Darwinian variations, owe their survival to adaptive facilitation.[4]

However, one important refinement is of somewhat later vintage, namely the development of a Darwinian approach to the very *content* of knowledge. This was implicit in the transition from an evolutionary concern with generic intellectual capabilities to one operating at the level of specific beliefs. On a position of this sort one has to do not with the advantageousness for human survival of the gamut of cognitive capabilities *in abstracto*, but with the advantageousness of certain substantive features of our cognitions *for their own cognitive survival*—that is, for their continued acceptance in the community of knowledge-seeking inquirers. This line of approach was initiated by C. S. Peirce in the closing decades of the century. From this standpoint, a Darwinian "survival of the fittest" does not merely operate as regards the survival of the group holding certain beliefs, but also as regards the survival of those beliefs themselves. This casts survival in the role of an index of truth. It is *this* sort of evolutionary epistemology that is the most relevant for our present concerns.[5]

[3] An interesting recent study of evolutionary aspects of cognition is J. W. S. Pringle, "On the Parallel Between Learning and Evolution," *Behavior*, vol. 3 (1951), pp. 174–215. The ideas of evolutionary espistemology are also exploited in a most suggestive, programatic way in D. T. Campbell, "Methodological Suggestions From a Comparative Psychology of Knowledge Processes," *Inquiry*, vol. 21 (1959), pp. 152–82, and this is further developed in his chapter on "Evolutionary Epistemology" in P. A. Schilpp (ed.), *The Philosophy of K. R. Popper* (La Salle, 1974), 2 Vols.

[4] William James, *Psychology*, 2 Vols. (New York, 1891). See especially the final chapter "Necessary Truths and the Effects of Experience," and also his essay "On the Function of Cognition" in *The Meaning of Truth* (New York, 1912).

[5] Peirce apart, the historic figure who came closest to holding a position akin to that developed here is Georg Simmel (though, to be sure, he is still a thesis-pragmatist of sorts). See his masterly and concise paper "Ueber eine Beziehung der Selectionslehre zur Erkenntnistheorie," *Archiv*

We must stress that this exploitation of the Darwinian aspect of cognition moves in a special and somewhat non-standard direction. As mentioned above, it was held from the very dawn of evolutionist theorizing that man's intelligence played a biologically significant role: human thought was viewed as survival-conducive and thus cast in a biologically positive role in the process of natural selection. But this survival-conducive role in biological evolution of man's generic capacity for thought is *not* at issue here. Rather, we shall deal with the role of biology-analogous selection phenomena in the development of the materials of human thinking. This epistemological approach envisages the operation of evolution-like processes in the historical development of the *substantive content* of man's thinking, and does not limit its perspective to the positive role of the *capability* of thought in biological evolution. The evolution of *thoughts* rather than that of *thinkers* is the issue. The program of "evolutionary epistemology" as standardly conceived envisages the development and transmission of man's beliefs, ideas, and theories as itself representing an evolution-like process.[6] Our present theory endeavors to give a methodological twist to this idea.

---

für systematische Philosophie und Soziologie, vol. 1 (1895), pp. 34–45. Simmel's stock in the market-place of philosophy deserves to stand far higher than it does: he merits a prominent place in the history of pragmatism.

[6] Current writers who maintain some version of evolutionary epistemology include: Jean Piaget, *The Language and Thought of the Child* (London and New York, 1959); Herbert Feigl, "Some Major Issues in the Philosophy of Science of Logical Positivism," *Minnesota Studies in the Philosophy of Science*, Vol. 1 (Minneapolis, 1956), pp. 3–37; Stephen C. Pepper, *The Sources of Value* (Berkeley and Los Angeles, 1958); Donald T. Campbell, "Methodological Suggestions for a Comparative Psychology of Knowledge Processes," *Inquiry*, vol. 2 (1959), pp. 152–82; Max Black, "Induction" in *The Encyclopedia of Philosophy*, ed. by P. Edwards, Vol. IV (New York, 1967), pp. 169–81; W. V. Quine, "Epistemology Naturalized" in *Ontological Relativity and Other Essays* (New York and London, 1969), pp. 69–90; K. R. Popper, *Objective Knowledge* (Oxford, 1972); Stephen Toulmin, *Human Understanding*, Vol. 1 (Oxford, 1972). The very interesting essay by Donald T. Campbell on "Evolutionary Epistemology" (in P. A. Schilpp [ed.], *The Philosophy of Karl Popper, op. cit.*), gives a fuller bibliography of the subject.

2. A METAPHYSICAL RATIONALIZATION OF THE LINK BETWEEN DARWINIAN SURVIVAL AND PRAGMATIC ADEQUACY

Given the reasonable man's well-advised predilection for *success* in his ventures, the fact that the methods we employ have a good record of demonstrated effectiveness is not surprising but only to be expected. The successfulness of our cognitive methodology is thus readily accounted for on an evolutionary perspective. At the most basic level the method may relate to the production of results essential to the very survival of the community itself. But in any case, continued resort to a method will, under the specified conditions, constitute a significant token of its effectiveness. In short, the methods of science would *not* be the methods of science if they were not successful: the community of rational inquirers would have given them up long ago.

Once we posit the rationality of the method-using community, only a short step separates the pragmatist issue of the applicative success of a method of *any* sort from the Darwinian issue of its survival. However, this short step leads across the rocky terrain of a metaphysical rationale—one in which rationality plays a central role.

This metaphysical rationale first of all incorporates certain fundamental assumptions regarding the character of the social community by which the method is adopted. Various essentially sociological theses regarding this community will be presupposed: purposive constancy, activism, reasonableness (realism, normality, etc.), interactionism, etc. (These were canvassed in Chapter VI.) The conjoining of principles of this sort—duly emplaced in a wider metaphysical context—yields the result that the *survival* of a method—its continued adoption among the community of rational practitioners—is a probatively weighty indicator of its *effectiveness*. For men are self-interested. They do not maintain an "ideological" commitment to unsuccessful methods, stubbornly clinging to them in the face of manifest failure. At the most basic level the method may relate to the production of results essential to the very survival of the community. But in less drastic cases, continued resort to a method will, under the specified conditions, constitute a significant token of its effectiveness. Under such conditions, the survival of relatively successful methods in place of relatively unsuccessful ones is a foregone conclusion. In the context of our metaphysical framework, success and survival become coordinated.

Moreover, the issue has another, deeper aspect—deeper because the preceding perspective lies wholly on the side of the inquirers and presupposes nothing whatever about the object of inquiry, the world, so that one crucial sector of the metaphysical scaffolding is left wholly out of view. The lawfulness of nature is perhaps the most significant of these omissions. This is especially untoward, since any Darwinian approach is based on a fundamental presumption of order, regularity, and persistence. We are often told that "if our actions and reactions were badly adjusted to our environment, we should not survive."[7] But the whole idea of good (or non-bad) *adjustment* is shot through with regularity; it calls for reacting to situations of a generic type in a constant and predictable way. If snow were sometimes cold to near absolute zero and other times hotter than the center of the sun, if it sometimes nourished and sometimes poisoned, if it sometimes melted to water and sometimes hardened to iron, etc.—and if a like irregularity affected things in general throughout the world—the idea of "adjusting to the environment" would become a shambles. There can be no adjustment to a grossly unstable environment. Moreover, without orderly species, orderly processes of transmission and variation, orderly processes of reproduction that stay true to type (at least in some basic respects), and the like, the whole Darwinian account of historical process would come apart at the seams. If the world is not a stable cosmos ordered by perduring laws, the entire enterprise of evolutionary explanation is vain. We cannot have it both ways,[8] that is, one cannot combine an evolutionary account of knowledge with a rejection of anything approaching a principle of the regularity of nature. (However, it bears repeating that such principles may have—initially—a presumptively *regulative* rather than substantively *constitutive* standing.)

The indicated line of reasoning thus does not envisage any direct and immediate linkage between the historical survival of a method and its functional effectiveness. Rather, the argument

---

[7] K. R. Popper, *Objective Knowledge, op. cit.*, p. 69.
[8] As, for example, Karl Popper wants to do in *Objective Knowledge, op. cit.*

connecting these two factors sees their linkage as indirect, and crucially *mediated* by various metaphysical principles laden with factual commitments as to how things work in the world. The two key stages of the argument are: that the historically realized success of a method in providing for the attainment of its correlative purposes is strong evidence for its being *in principle* effective and adequate, and that the historical survival in actual use of a method (within a community of active, realistic, normal rational agents) affords strong evidence for its being successful in realizing its correlative purposes. Putting together these two principles— viz., that success is an index of the effectiveness of a method and that survival is an index of success—we arrive at the sought-for link between historical survival and functional effectiveness.

Yet this Darwinian aspect of a survival of the "fittest" is a derivative rather than basic factor in the legitimation of methods: *success* is the prime indicator of adequacy; survival is adequacy-indicative *only* because it represents (under suitable conditions) an index of success. Thus the transition from method-survival to method-effectiveness is operative only in a context where certain factual presuppositions regarding the *modus operandi* of the method-utilizing community are met. What is at issue is not a necessary link of abstract principle, but a contingently conditioned link which rests upon certain metaphysical (and fact-laden) presuppositions.

It is useful to stress one consequence that ensues when these general considerations regarding methods *in abstracto* are applied in the cognitive realm. Philosophers since Kant have repeatedly sought to give a "Transcendental Deduction" of our cognitive mechanisms (for reasoning, describing, communicating, etc.). That is, they have sought to argue that such intellectual processes must be accepted as legitimate/adequate/"correct" *for us,* because their *modus operandi* is somehow inherent in the faculty structure of our mind, so that a being of our type *must inevitably* proceed by the processes at issue in attempting to realize their correlative ends (reasoning, describing, communicating, or whatever). Now at first sight it might seem that nothing could be further removed from this sort of absolutistic and inevitabilistic approach than an instrumental validation on the basis of considerations of relative efficiency, effectiveness, etc. But in fact the gap between these two approaches is drastically narrowed by an evolutionary theory that envisages the development of our cognitive tools through rational selection. For if those cognitive instrumentalities we men in fact have—the only ones with which *we* can work, since they alone are at our disposal—are the products of a selection process itself based on considerations of instrumental efficiency and effectiveness, then the convergence and concordance of these two seemingly opposed approaches is assured.[9] (But, of course, our approach mitigates the element of absolutism of a "transcendental" argument by relativizing its operation to a contingent methodological basis.[10])

[9] The idea of a recourse to evolutionary considerations as the basis for a priori categories of thought and perception in man is a set piece in the repertoire of the evolutionary epistemology tradition. It is clearly present in Georg Simmel in 1895 (*op. cit.*). But it has older antecedents in Herbert Spencer and his followers. J. M. Baldwin attributes it to Spencer in the following terms:

> It is here that Herbert Spencer's most valuable intuition appears—a conception to be placed beside that of Darwin.... The most absolute and universal-seeming principles of knowledge, viewed racially, are 'practical postulates' which have been woven into human thought as presuppositions of consistent and trustworthy experience. They were 'original ideas' at some time, found to be useful for the organization of knowledge and for the conduct of life; and, now, by processses of reflective abstraction, they are set up as schemes or forms divorced from the concrete contents which alone gave them their justification and value, and called 'the categories.' (*Darwin and the Humanities* [Baltimore, 1909], p. 70; Baldwin offers a most interesting development of these themes.)

Perhaps the most elaborate modern articulation of the idea is in Konrad Lorenz, "Die angeborenen Formen möglicher Erfahrung," *Zeitschrift für Tierpsychologie*, vol. 5 (1943), pp. 235–409. Interesting elaborations of this project are mooted in D. T. Campbell, "Evolutionary Epistemology" in P. A. Schilpp (ed.), *The Philosophy of Karl Popper* (2 vols., La Salle, 1974), pp 413–63 (pp. 460–3 of this essay give further references to a wide range of relevant literature).

[10] The present appeal to "transcendental" validation thus meets the objection of modern critics that the argumentation in its traditional form is unwarrantedly absolutistic. See, for example, Stephan Körner, "The Impossibility of Transcendental Deductions," *The Monist*, vol. 51 (1967), pp. 317–31; and also his "Transcendental Tendencies in Recent Philosophy," *The Journal of Philosophy*, vol. 63 (1966), pp. 551–61. For an attempted defense of this mode of argumentation against this line of criticism see my essay "Kant and the 'Special Constitution' of Man's Mind" in *Studies in Modality* (Oxford, 1974), pp. 72–83.

3. RATIONAL SELECTION

Natural selection is often thought of as a matter of killing off the less "fit" organisms. But this is too crude. The basic factor is not existential elimination but reproductive incapacitation: an impedence of cross-generation transmission. Any failure to reproduce will do—annihilation obviously, but also much subtler means such as Darwin's "sexual selection." Broadly speaking, then, the selection process is simply one that blocks transmission across successive generations (be it of biological items like genes or cognitive items like ideas, theses, or methods). It is in this sense that our cognitive Darwinism must be understood.

To be sure, a rigorously classical Darwinian model for methodological evolution goes too far. For what is basically at issue in this domain is *rational* rather than *natural* selection. Rational selection is a matter not of *biological* but of *rationally preferential* elimination—of historical transmission owing to a reasoned preference on the basis of purposive considerations, in the present case considerations oriented towards welfare and affective well-being. These affective factors relate to (i) the negative avoidance of (physical) unpleasantness over the whole spectrum from minor annoyance to rude shocks, and (ii) the positive pursuit of (physical) pleasantness, comfort, security, etc. What is at issue is not just the life-and-death matter of *existence*, but also issues relating simply to the *desiderata* rather than the *necessities* of life. For the most part, the determinative factors lie much more on the affective surface of experience; they pertain to a *favoring* of certain alternatives in the transmission process because these lead more readily to preferred results. This whole approach presupposes the picture of intelligent beings acting rationally with reference to ends-in-view.

Rational selection is a process of fundamentally the same *sort* as natural selection—both are simply devices for elimination from transmission. But their actual workings differ, since elimination by rational selection is not telically blind and bio-physical, but rather preferential/teleological and overtly rational. In this sense, rational selection is essentially Lamarckian: survival favors certain "preferred" conditions, with preferability determined in an explicitly purposive way.[11] Standard neo-Darwinism is in effect a way of *removing* teleology; it provides a way of accounting for *seeming* purposiveness in purpose-free terms, by deploying the mechanism of a *blindly eliminative* annihilation of certain forms in place of any recourse to preferential considerations. But our present rationally-oriented neo-Darwinism can only operate with respect to beings endowed with intelligence and action, with reasoning and purposes—its mechanism being the *deliberately rejective* annihilation of forms that are not purpose-serving.

Because of this difference, there is no danger of obscurantism in saying that while *biological* evolution is indeed rigidly Darwinian, *cognitive* evolution bears a Lamarckian aspect. Perhaps the most decisive difference between biological and ideational selection is that in the latter the mechanism of *rational* selection clearly envisages the "hereditary" transmission of acquired characteristics. The standard objection to Lamarckianism—viz., that it is essentially anthropomorphic—can be turned to its advantage here: it is obviously no disability to find anthropomor-

---

[11] Some evolutionary theorists have sought to superimpose explicitly telic considerations upon a Darwinian framework. Teilhard de Chardin is doubtless the best known of these. Already the American neo-Hegelian George H. Howison proposed (in his book on *The Limits of Evolution* [New York and London, 1901]) a conception of cosmic and biological evolution that had a heavy teleological emphasis, relying heavily on the use of rational fitness as an explanatory principle (in a manner reminiscent of Leibniz but extracted from Hegel). For present purposes, the critical point is that, however plausible a rationally teleological approach may or may not be at the cosmic and biological levels, it is eminently and unproblematically so in relation to the *modus operandi* of intelligent and rational beings, specifically in explaining the development and maintenance of a methodology of inquiry. For in methodological evolution the factor of survival operates in a double aspect of two distinct but critically interrelated factors. On the one hand is the physical survival *of* the method-using community itself—the evolutionary standard of the biologists. On the other hand lies the sociological issue of the survival of methods *in* the community through continued adaption and transmission. This second rule of survival clearly does not proceed through *biological* inheritance (which is telically blind), but through the social process of cultural transmission (which is telically guided). This second aspect of evolution was clearly recognized by Darwin himself, but is sometimes neglected by his successors. It is, however, very emphatically stressed by students of technological development. (See, for example, Tadeusz Kotarbinski, *Praxiology* [Oxford, 1965], esp. p. 195.)

hisms in a theory dealing with human capabilities and performances.

Rationality emerges as a key element in this picture. The survival of effective methods is not inevitable and automatic ("natural") and assured by some inexorable agency of nature. Rather, the crucial link between "success" and "survival" obtains because the rational man places his bets in theory *and* practice in consonance with those methods that prove themselves successful, tending to adopt those that succeed and to abandon—or readjust —those that fail.

Some might well object as follows:

> Evolutionary epistemology commits a mode of *genetic fallacy*. The "genetic fallacy" confuses the course of historical development with one of probative justification, for example, by arguing from the fact that a doctrine has a somehow reputable (or disreputable) origin that it must be tenable (or untenable). The Darwinian epistemologist in effect argues in just this way, moving from historical survival to the presumptive correctness of methods. Surely no such *transcategorial* inference from the *factual* issue of historical considerations to conclusions regarding the issue of the *normative* validation of a method can possibly be valid. One cannot move from the historical order of temporal development to the logical order of probative concatenation.[12]

Now whatever can be said against the "genetic fallacy" in *other* contexts, in the present context it is surely *not* fallacious. For our present line of thought rests *explicitly* on the premiss that the historical process is merit-indicative for methods because methodological survival in a rational community indicates a continued adoption that betokens "fitness," where fitness reflects a rationally warranted preference on grounds of demonstrated adequacy.

4. THE SPECIAL CASE OF COGNITIVE METHODOLOGY

By and large, the preceding considerations about rational selection

---

[12] For the "Genetic Fallacy" see M. R. Cohen and E. Nagel, *An Introduction to Logic and Scientific Method* (New York, 1934), pp. 388–90.

have been altogether general, bearing abstractly upon methodologies of any shape or description. They apply to methods across the board, and hold of methods for peeling apples as much as of methods for substantiating knowledge-claims. But let us now focus more closely on *cognitive* methods.

There is no reason to exempt cognitive methodology from the range of the role of rational selection in the evolution of methodologies. Quite to the contrary: this applies with full or increased force. As argued above, the probatively relevant mode of "success" in the legitimation of an inquiry procedure is its capacity to facilitate the welfare interests of people by effective guidance in practical affairs. Inquiry is as inquiry does—i.e., as it yields a view of the world which can guide our actions (including those relating to further inquiry itself) along practically successful lines.

The cognitive methods and substantive procedures we deploy for structuring our view of reality evolve selectively by an historic, evolutionary process of "trial and error"—analogous to the mutations affecting the bodily mechanisms by which we comport ourselves in the physical world. Accordingly, cognitive methods develop subject to revision in response to the element of "success and failure" in terms of the teleology of the practice of rational inquiry. The central issue is a matter of "survival of the fittest" with *fitness* assessed in terms of the practical objectives of the rational enterprise—particularly in the guidance of man's practical affairs. Their evolutionary development proceeds by explicitly *rational selection*, rather than by some purpose-indifferent process analogous to the natural selection of the standard biological case.[13] As changes are entertained (under the pressure of necessitating circumstance), one methodological instrument may eventuate as more fit to survive than another, because it answers better to the range of relevant purposes. An inquiry procedure is an instrument for organizing our experience into a systematized view of reality. And as with any tool or method or instrument, the question of evaluation here takes the instrumentalistic form: Does

---

[13] Of course even in the most orthodox and rigoristic of biological evolutionisms one cannot but recognize that with the historical emergence of man the purposive aspect must be given a role upon the evolutionary stage, since purpose and final causation here overshadow efficient causation and introduce a "Lamarckian" aspect into evolution. See G. G. Simpson, *The Meaning of Evolution* (New Haven, 1949), pp. 289ff.

it work? Does it produce the desired result? Is it successful in practice? Legitimation along these lines is found in substantial part in
the fact of survival through historical vicissitudes in the context of
such questions. The pivotal issue is that of "working out best."
Just what does "best" mean here? This once again leads back to
the Darwinian perspective of the preceding discussion. A Darwinian legitimation in terms of "survival of the fittest" clearly
requires a standard of "fitness."

There are a *variety* of approaches to the problem of determining "how things work in the world." The examples of such
occult cognitive frameworks as those of numerology (with its
benign ratios), astrology (with its astral influences), and black
magic (with its mystic forces) indicate that alternative explanatory
frameworks exist, and that these can have very diverse degrees of
merit. Now in the Western tradition the governing standards of
human rationality are implicit in the goals of *explanation, prediction*, and preeminently *control.* (And thus the crucial factor is
not, for example, sentimental "at-oneness with nature"—think
of the magician vs. the mystic vs. the sage as cultural ideals.) These
standards revolve about considerations of *practice* and are implicit in the use to which our conceptual resources are put in the
management of our affairs in the conduct of life. In the Western,
Faustian[14] intellectual tradition, the ultimate arbiter of rationality
is represented by a very basic concept of knowledge-wed-to-
practice, and the ultimate validation of our beliefs lies in the
combination of theoretical and practical *success*, with "practice"
construed in its pragmatic and affective sense.

William James wrote:

> Were we lobsters, or bees, it might be that our organization
> would have led to our using quite different modes from these
> [actual ones] of apprehending our experiences. It *might* be too
> (we cannot dogmatically deny this) that such categories, un-
> imaginable by us to-day, would have proved on the whole as
> serviceable for handling our experiences mentally as those we
> actually use.[15]

[14] *Im Anfang war die Tat* as Goethe's *Faust* puts it.
[15] *Pragmatism* (New York, 1907), p. 171. (Compare the discussion of Georg
Simmel's comparable thought-experiment on pp. 95–6 above. James is
presumably indebted to Simmel here.) Unlike most philosophers since

Now the premiss of the first sentence is true enough. But the implication present in the "our" of the second sentence goes badly awry. The prospect that beings constituted as *we* are should function more effectively with the experiential modes of creatures constituted on different lines can be dismissed as simply untenable on Darwinian grounds. The serviceable handling of *our* experiences by *our* cognitive instruments is guaranteed—not by a preestablished harmony but by the processes of evolution.

To be sure, the orthodox, scientific approach to factual inquiry is simply one alternative among others, and it does not have an irrevocably absolute foothold on the very constitution of the human intellect, nor indeed any sort of abstract justification by purely "general principles." Its legitimation is not *a priori* and absolute, but *a posteriori* and relative. The merit of entrenched cognitive tools lies in their (presumably) having established themselves in open competition with their rivals. It has come to be shown before the tribunal of bitter experience—through the historical vagaries of a Darwinian process of selection—that the accepted methods work out most effectively in actual practice *vis-à-vis* other tried alternatives. Such a legitimation is not absolute, but only presumptive—the product rather of a democratic struggle among rival candidates than of the divine right of a seventeenth-century absolute monarch. But it does, in its Darwinian aspect, give justificatory weight to the historical factor of being in *de facto* possession of the field.

It is not difficult to give examples of the operation of Darwinian processes in the cognitive area. The intellectual landscape of human history is littered with the skeletal remains of the extinct dinosaurs of this sphere. Examples of such defunct methods for the acquisition and explanatory utilization of information include astrology, numerology, oracles, dream-interpretation, the reading of tea leaves or the entrails of birds, animism, the teleological physics of the Presocratics, and so on. There is nothing intrinsically absurd or contemptible about such unorthodox cognitive programs, even the most occult of them have a long and not wholly unsuccessful history. (Think, for example, of the

---

Kant, James was prepared to consider the prospect of radically different conceptual schemes which dispense with the familiar concepts of space, time, causality, the self, etc.

prominent role of numerological explanation from Pythagoreanism, through Platonism, to the medieval Arabs, down to Kepler in the Renaissance.) Distinctly different scientific methodologies and programs have been mooted: Ptolemaic "saving the phenomena" vs. the hypothetico-deductive method, or again, Baconian collectionism vs. the post-Newtonian theory of experimental science, etc. The development of the means of inquiry and explanation invites a Darwinian account.

There can be little question that the history of science encompasses the development of scientific methods and explanatory mechanisms as well as the development of theories and explanatory models. The history of such investigative methods and explanatory procedures in science is a relatively recent study.[16] The labor is unfinished. A fascinating survey could be made of the development of scientific method from an evolutionary point of view, but this task remains to be achieved. However, it can be said with reasonable confidence—even with the rudimentary information at our disposal—that such an evolutionary approach to the growth of science (one not oriented towards the atomistic level of specific theories and hypotheses, but towards the generic level of cognitive methodologies and generic procedures of explanation) holds considerable promise of giving not only an interesting but also a relatively adequate account of the historical phenomena.[17]

Be this as it may, the evolutionary approach to methodological validation has an interesting ramification that deserves comment. For it views the *historical, developmental* process of methodological refinement as isomorphic with a certain line of *systematically justificatory* argumentation.[18] From its standpoint, *methodological*

[16] It might be said to begin in a serious way with Pierre Duhem's masterly ten-volume study of *Le Système du monde*, which commenced publication in Paris in 1913.

[17] From this perspective, what justifies inclusion of the Presocratics in works on the history of science is not merely that they are dealing with some of the same questions we still ask today, but—more importantly—that their efforts figure prominently in the evolutionary process by which our own methods for dealing with these questions has developed.

[18] Philosophers of science during the 1940's and 1950's tended to adopt the position that a sharp line of distinction must be maintained between the *context of discovery* of interest to historians of science and the *context of justification* of interest to philosophers of science. They insisted

evolution replicates a course of probative substantiation. This circumstance has far-reaching implications for the relationship between the history of science and the epistemology of science to which we can do no more than allude here.

5. THESIS DARWINISM VS. METHOD DARWINISM

From the very inception of epistemological Darwinism, various writers have argued against this line of approach. They have maintained the cognitive irrelevancy of pragmatic and Darwinian success, arguing along such lines as these:

> A wide gap separates the efficient pursuit of man's *practical* interests from the domain of his *cognitive* endeavors. False beliefs can be practically or survivalistically efficacious, true beliefs can be counterproductive in these ways. No amount of theoretical argumentation can paper over the lack of a strict correlation between the truth-status of our opinions and the success or failure of actions predicated on them.

The sort of argumentation that might be developed to support this objection can readily be envisaged, *mutatis mutandis*, in terms of the previous critique of "thesis pragmatism" (Chapter IV). And the appropriate reply to the objection is also discernible on this basis, for it suffices once again to point out the discrepancy between the thesis-oriented and method-oriented versions of pragmatism. A cognitive methodology is so general and so open-ended in its orientation that gratuitous success on a *systematic* basis can be ruled out as a genuine prospect.

---

that historical considerations are without probative weight. See, for example, Hans Reichenbach's *Experience and Prediction* (Chicago, 1938), K. R. Popper's *Logik der Forschung* (Vienna, 1935), and C. G. Hempel's *Philosophy of Natural Science* (Englewood Cliffs, 1966). Whatever merit there may be to such a doctrine as regards scientific hypotheses and theories—and the issue is still hotly contested—it is at any rate untenable on the side of *methodology*, where, as we have argued, the sequence of evolutionary developments decisively reflects considerations of probative justification. (For an interesting discussion of relevant issues see Kenneth Schaffner, "Logic of Discovery and Justification in Regulating Genetics," *Studies in History and Philosophy of Science*, vol. 4 (1974), pp. 349–85.)

The major criticisms of evolutionary theories of epistemic validation all have a common core and purport. All proceed by dwelling heavily on the distinction between the cognitive/intellectual side of human affairs and their affective/physical side. They insist that there is no decisive reason of theoretical principle why conceptions and beliefs conducive to the welfare of man must be theoretically valid.[19] The question is pressed: How—in the face of counterexamples of the sort readily constructed—can one validly maintain a necessary linkage between practical advantage and theoretical truth?[20] Survival-conducive beliefs are surely not *invariably* (and perhaps not even *generally*) correct; nor need correct beliefs necessarily prove survival-conducive. This objection poses a serious difficulty for any program of evolutionary epistemology.

Such considerations have a by now familiar ring. They mount an attack against linking the survival-conduciveness of beliefs and their correctness in a way which parallels exactly the usual attacks

[19] The fundamentals of this line of thought go back to Plato's myth of the cave (in Bk. II of the *Republic*) with its moral that too close a heed of the realities and practicalities of this world will impede those unconstrained excursions of intellect through which alone an insight into theoretic truth can be obtained. Henri Bergson developed at length this theme that only by separating the mind from the restraints of quotidian action-directedness can man achieve a proper understanding of reality, as there is no reason to think that a cognitive apparatus which has evolved for *survival* purposes should provide a handle on *theoretical* truth. (See his *Essai sur les données immédials de la conscience* [8th ed., Paris, 1889], as well as his *Introduction à la métaphysique* in the *Revue de la métaphysique et de morale*, vol. 2 [1903], pp. 1–183.) In recent days this position—that the aims of survival-promotion and knowledge-enhancement may even be antithetical—has been vigorously argued by Herman Tennessen.(See his essay "Knowledge versus Survival," *Inquiry*, vol. 16 [1973], pp. 407–14; and also "On Knowing What One Knows Not," in J. Royce and W. Rozeboom (eds), *The Psychology of Knowing* [New York, 1972], pp. 111–60.)

[20] Bertrand Russell's criticisms of the pragmatists gives many quaint examples, among them this: "Dr. Dewey and I were once in the town of Changsha during an eclipse of the moon; following immemorial custom, blind men were beating gongs to frighten the heavenly dog, whose attempt to swallow the moon is the cause of the eclipses. Throughout thousands of years, this practice of beating gongs has never failed to be successful; every eclipse has come to an end after a sufficient prolongation of the din." "Dewey's New Logic," in P. Schilpp (ed.), *The Philosophy of John Dewey* (New York, 1939), pp. 143–56.

against linking the practical utility of beliefs and their theoretical truth (as with the thesis pragmatism of William James). And essentially the same weakness indeed affects both these doctrines: their orientation towards *theses*.

But the telling force of such criticisms of evolutionary epistemology is blunted once we take the methodological turn. For then considerations of survival-conduciveness are no longer asked to militate for the adequacy (i.e., truthfulness) of specific beliefs or belief-systems, but for the adequacy of *methods* of inquiry. And a good case can be made for their capacity to accomplish this particular job by means of a "metaphysical deduction" of inquiry methods as set out in Chapter VI.

The methodological turn thus becomes crucial here, thanks to the fundamental difference between methods and theses as regards the proper modes of justificatory argumentation. For the argument rests on the presence of a cogent link between pragmatic success and theoretical adequacy (truthfulness), a linkage which is forthcoming in the case of methods, but not in the case of theses (as per our earlier argument). Accordingly, the presently envisaged strategy of legitimation resorts to a *method* Darwinism and not a *thesis* Darwinism.

Consider again J. S. Mill's contention (advanced in his famous essay *On Liberty*) that the competition among schools of thought is akin to that between biological varieties: the rivalry among ideas for acceptance amounts to a struggle for existence (i.e., perpetuation or *continued existence*), a struggle in which those beliefs which are the fittest—viz., those that represent "the truth" —must finally prevail. The survival of beliefs within an intellectual community is viewed as parallel with biological survival. (C. S. Peirce's theory of truth can be seen as a systematic development of this line of thought.)

It is perhaps unnecessary to dwell, at this stage, on the shortcomings of this unduly optimistic view. Acceptance of theses is all too often governed by extra-rational factors: mere entrenchment, faddism, social pressures, bandwagons, propaganda ("thought control"), etc. And there can be no secure assurance that such perturbations will inevitably or even usually be eliminated in the course of time. The view that the inherent attractions of the truth assure its ultimate victory in a struggle for acceptance among the beliefs of imperfect humans is thus overly hopeful. However, its most serious shortcomings stem from its operation *at the thesis level.* An evolutionary approach seems to have substantially greater promise at the more general level of *methods* where the force of the above-mentioned disabilities is removed or attenuated. The generality and open-endedness of an inquiry-method furnish it with a capacity to wash out the influence of these fortuitous and extraneous factors. To be sure, the survival of a thesis in continued espousal is only weakly and obliquely truth-indicative; but method-survival (in a group of active *inquirers* who are rational and realistic) is a cogent and powerful indication of adequacy.[21]

To say all this is not to deny that *some* degree of truth-indicativeness attaches to the survival of a thesis in a community of rational inquirers. But the link is relatively tenuous and oblique —not direct, but mediated through the argument that thesis survival over a considerable period is presumptively indicative of adequacy subject to the refinement of a validating method during this course of time. Method Darwinism does not carry any very strong or emphatic thesis Darwinism in its wake, and is relatively secure against the sorts of objections applicable to it.

The process of rational selection implements an evolutionary model which renders pragmatic efficacy correlative with historical survival. But, of course, people are not all that rational—they have their moments of aberration and self-indulgence. Might not such tendencies selectively favor the survival of the fallacious rather than the true, and slant the process of evolution in deteriorating directions? Peirce certainly recognized this prospect:

> Logicality in regard to practical matters . . . is the most useful quality an animal can possess, and might, therefore, result from the action of natural selection; but outside of these it is probably of more advantage to the animal to have his mind filled with pleasing and encouraging visions, independently of their truth; and thus, upon unpractical subjects, natural selection might occasion a fallacious tendency of thought.[22]

[21] It is perfectly conceivable that in the course of intellectual history a quite untenable *thesis* may long prevail, lodged securely in its peculiar ecological niche simply because no one has found it worthwhile to dislodge it with some rival. One need not reckon with this sort of aberration in the methodological case under the conditions basic to our "metaphysical deduction."

[22] *Collected Papers*, vol. V: 5.366. On the broader aspects of Peirce's views

However, the methodological orientation of our approach again provides a safeguard against an unwarranted penchant for such fallacious tendencies. At the level of individual beliefs "pleasing and encouraging visions" might indeed receive a survival-favoring impetus. But this unpleasant prospect is effectively removed where a *systematic* method of inquiry is concerned—a method which must by its very synoptic nature press deeply into the sphere of the pragmatically effective.

Yet another line of objection runs as follows:

The possibility of a pragmatically successful exploitation of the instrumentalities afforded us by nature is surely compatible with the most profound ignorance of the workings of things. Think of an analogy: One can learn to drive a car or operate a cyclotron most successfully, and yet maintain a profound ignorance as to the workings of these devices. Successful manipulation requires only the most superficial sort of knowledge: what happens when we pull which levers, so to speak. Successful action may thus be compatible with massive cognitive inadequacy.

This objection is sound enough in its own way, but its way is not that of our methodological pragmatism. For the objection is rendered ineffective by the vast range and extent, the tremendous *generality* of the pragmatic success at issue with an inquiry procedure. Such success is not just a matter of a manipulative control of the surface of things; it is something that cuts through to the innermost internals. If someone controls effective practice at the superficial level—if he knows merely how to start and drive and stop the car—he may indeed know precious little of what makes it tick. But what is needed for the analogy to hold is a practical mastery that is totally comprehensive and systematic—one that includes the ability to repair all manner of breakdowns and malfunctions, a capacity to design, assemble, and maintain it and its components and their components, the ability to modify and improve it for more effective and efficient operation, and so on—in

on evolution see Thomas A. Goudge, "Peirce's Evolutionism—After Half a Century" in E. C. Moore and R. S. Robin (eds), *Studies in the Philosophy of Charles Sanders Peirce*, Second Series (Amherst, 1964), pp. 323–41.

short a capacity for pragmatically effective action in virtually endless comprehensiveness and detail. That all this should be afforded by a belief-underwriting inquiry procedure which would not on this basis be cognitively adequate is a circumstance that boggles belief. The standard objections to epistemic Darwinism all come to grief on the specifically *methodological* ground upon which our present approach takes its stand.

This line of thought points towards what is in fact one of the greatest merits of the present approach. It is surely an obvious desideratum to meet the profoundly *sceptical* objection that human cognition is fundamentally inadequate to the attainment of *theoretical* truth because it is the product of an evolutionary process attuned to the needs of *practice*. Darwin is himself the father of this thought, raising the question "Can the mind of man, descended, as I believe, from the lowest animals, be trusted when it draws such grand conclusions?"[23] One commentator observes that "Darwin's 'horrid doubt' as to whether the convictions of man's evolved mind could be trusted applies as much to abstract truth as to ethics."[24] And another goes on to draw the inference that "there is surely something wrong with a theory which, at its very root, invalidates itself."[25] A whole host of variations have been played on this theme of the possible or probable theoretical inadequacy of practice-oriented cognition.[26] A theory that casts pragmatic efficacy in the role of *arbiter* of cognition leaves no room for neurotic fears that the intellectual resources of *praxis* may be found wanting before the tribunal of *theoria*.

[23] Charles Darwin *Autobiography* (London, 1929), p. 93. Various post-Darwinian writers developed this theme at length. See, for example, G. H. Howison, *The Limits of Evolution* (New York and London, 1901).
[24] David Lack, *Evolutionary Theory and Christian Belief* (London, 1957), p. 104.
[25] Marjorie Grene, *The Knower and the Known* (New York, 1966), p. 200.
[26] See, for example, Herman Tennessen, "Knowledge versus Survival," *op. cit.* This develops in epistemic terms "the Bergsonian position that a language with a conceptual frame. . . .fashioned to fit a *survival* project, or other practical or quotidian objectives, is bound to fail when it comes to unpractical, 'useless,' antibiological, transquotidian contemplations of what there is and what we can know" (p. 113).

F

Chapter IX

A CRITIQUE OF THESIS DARWINISM

1. POPPER'S EVOLUTIONARY EPISTEMOLOGY

One of the most fully developed and influential versions of epistemological Darwinism is the evolutionary model of scientific progress presented in K. R. Popper's *Objective Knowledge* (Oxford, 1972). Popper's cognitive Darwinism addresses itself specifically to *theories and hypotheses* from the standpoint of their "fitness to survive by standing up to tests" (p. 19). Hypotheses arise as variant answers in the context posed by problem-questions. The testing of these hypotheses with a view to their falsification provides a process of "selection" among them. The basic idea of Popperian hypothesis-evolution calls for such a mechanism of cognitive variation and selection by "the method of trial and the elimination of errors" (p. 70).[1]

The dynamics of this evolutionary process involve a cyclic pattern of movement: initial problem to tentative theory to error-elimination to refined problem to refined tentative theory, and so

[1] This resort to the mechanism of trial and error as a basic model for the theory of scientific method is not confined to Popperians. Stephen C. Pepper, for example, also maintained that "the inductive methods of experimental science are essentially systematized trial and error," and he based on this idea a rather sophisticated Darwinian model of knowledge (as well as of value). See his book, *The Sources of Value* (Berkeley and Los Angeles, 1958), whence the preceding quote (from p. 106). The stress on *blindness* in lieu of *randomness* is eminently well-advised. One knows from information theory that, for example, if the game of Twenty Questions were played perfectly—so that each yes or no yields the contestant one bit of information—then twenty bits would suffice to identify 2^{20} candidate-objects. (i.e., one out of more than a million). But this prospect means that there must be nothing random about these questions—they require vast "background knowledge" for the careful partitioning of the information-space at every stage. For "blind" inquiry to prove efficient, this blindness must pertain only to one small part of the cognitive field. Efficiency here demands the demonically shrewd deployment of an "inductive talent" of the kind which Popper finds unpalatable. (See footnote 5 on p. 151 below.)

on. "The neo-Darwinist theory of evolution is assumed; but, it is restated by pointing out that its 'mutations' may be interpreted as more or less accidental trial-and-error gambits, and 'natural selection' as one way of controlling them by error elimination" (p. 242). The trial-and-error search procedure at issue here is blind and virtually random. According to Popper, the difference between Einstein and an amoeba is—from the epistemological standpoint—a matter of degree rather than kind, since "their methods of almost random or cloud-like trial and error movements are fundamentally not very different" (p. 247). Rather, the crucial difference between them lies in the sphere of reactions to solutions, because unlike the amoeba, Einstein "approached his own solutions *critically*" (p. 247) and subjected them to deliberate falsifying tests. As a result of this eliminative selection of hypotheses, "our knowledge consists, at every moment, of those hypotheses which have shown their (comparative) fitness by surviving so far on their struggle for existence; a competitive struggle which eliminates those hypotheses which are unfit" (p. 261).

A comparison and contrast with Popper's 1972 position will prove helpful in elucidating our present approach.[2] Just as the earlier critique of a Jamesian thesis pragmatism highlighted certain strengths in the present methodological pragmatism, it will transpire that a critique of Popperian thesis-evolutionism can serve to reinforce the claims of a method-oriented Darwinism.

The model of scientific inquiry presented by Popper rests on a combination of its three basic commitments:

(1) With respect to any given scientific issue the number of alternative hypotheses is always in principle infinite

(2) Science proceeds by the trial-and-error elimination of hypotheses

(3) This elimination process is inductively blind: Man has no inductive capability for discriminating good from bad

[2] In Popper's book there is a stress on mutation-reminiscent randomness or near randomness ("more or less accidental trial-and-error gambits," "almost random or cloud-like trial-and-error movements") that is revoked in Popper's Schilpp essay (*The Philosophy of Karl Popper*, ed. by P. A. Schilpp [2 vols., La Salle, 1974].) "I regard this idea of the 'blindness' of the trials in a trial-and-error movement as an important step beyond the mistaken idea of random trials" (p. 1062).

hypotheses—of separating the promising from the un-
promising, the inherently more plausible from the
inherently less plausible, and there is never any reason
to think that those hypotheses that have been proposed
or considered are somehow more advantageous than those
that have not. At every stage, our search among the
alternatives must be a matter of blind groping.

But now unfortunate consequences loom up. 'The moment we
put these premisses together, we destroy any prospect of understanding the success of man's cognitive efforts. The whole achievement of science—its historically demonstrated ability to do its
work well and to produce results which, if not true, are in some
way satisfying and creditable—becomes altogether unintelligible. Indeed, this is now an accident of virtually miraculous
proportions, every bit as fortuitous as someone's correctly guessing
at random the telephone numbers of someone else's friends.

Popper is deeply (and apparently proudly) committed to this
consequence of his theory. For him the success of science is
something fortuitous, accidental, literally *miraculous* (p. 204),
and totally unintelligible:

> However, even on the assumption (which I share) that our
> quest for knowledge has been very successful so far, and that
> we now know something of our universe, this success becomes
> miraculously improbable, and therefore inexplicable; for an
> appeal to an endless series of improbable accidents is not an
> explanation. (The best we can do, I suppose, is to investigate
> the almost incredible evolutionary history of these accidents,
> from the making of the elements to the making of the
> organisms.)[3]

There is no doubt that on the premisses of Popper's theory of
science, the question of an explanation of the success of science—
i.e., the question of an account of the nature of the world and
the nature of man's cognitive technology that can *explain* why
our endeavors to acquire knowledge are as successful as they are
—is met with blank *ignorabimus* of intrinsic mystery.

[3] *Objective Knowledge* (Oxford, 1972), p. 28.

As Popper himself stresses, discovery of truth is the regulative ideal of the enterprise of inquiry (pp. 29–30). But how can the process of Popperian error elimination ever provide us with any sort of warrant for the conviction that the actual course of our efforts at inquiry involves a movement—however slow or hesitating—towards this ideal of truth? "We test for truth," so Popper maintains, "by eliminating falsehood." But clearly this would work only in the context of a theory of limited possibilities. (One can eliminate endless possibilities as solutions to a problem—say all the odd integers as answers to a Diophantine problem whose real answer is eight—without thereby moving significantly closer to the truth.) Once we grant (as Popper time and again insists) that any hypotheses we might actually entertain are but a few fish drawn from an infinite ocean—are only isolated instances of those infinitely many available hypotheses we have not even entertained, none of which are *prima facie* less meritorious than those we have[4]—then the whole idea of *seeking truth* by error elimination becomes pointless. If infinitely many distinct roads issue from the present spot, there is no reason to think that, by elimination one or two (or *n*) of these, we have come one jot closer to finding the one that leads to the desired destination.

All this, of course, holds only on the quixotically "democratic" view that all the possible hypotheses stand on an equal footing, that our process of selection is nowise shrewd but virtually random—that we are not to take the stance that those hypotheses we propose to treat seriously can reasonably be supposed to be more promising candidates than the rest. In short, we are to insist on refusing to credit the human intellect with any *inductive skill*, any capacity to single out those alternative hypotheses that are (likely to prove) more promising candidates than the rest. But if one is not entitled to regard hypothesis-elimination as narrowing the field of the *real* possibilities, then this entire eliminative process becomes probatively pointless. The technique of error elimination is capable of serving the Popperian desideratum of leading closer to the truth only if one is willing to take the Popper-repugnant step of crediting man's inquiring intelligence with a capacity for

---

[4] Here there is a substantial disanalogy with the evolutionary case. Darwin did not need to include unicorns in the purview of the theory and explain their non-existence by some process akin to an account for the extinction of dinosaurs.

doing reasonably well in the selection of hypotheses for testing—and thus as *not* constrained to operate by blind trial and error.

Popper explicitly and emphatically insists that "no theory of knowledge should attempt to explain why we are successful in our attempt to explain things" (p. 23). And yet this self-denying ordinance is nowhere defended on the basis of an inexorable inevitability in the nature of things—the only sort of defense, surely, that could force the acceptance of so unpalatable and counterintuitive a doctrine. It is difficult to exaggerate the unsatisfactory nature of this position. It fails the basic and rudimentary task of any adequate explanatory theory, that of "saving the phenomena" by providing some promising account for them.

An adequate philosophical theory of the rationale of our scientific knowledge of the world must combine a theory of nature and a theory of inquiry in such a way that an account of the success of science is a straightforward and natural result when once they are conjoined together. But the very best Popper can offer is the thought that our efforts to acquire information about the world by our investigative processes *may possibly* succeed: "That we cannot give a justification ... for our guesses [i.e., scientific hypotheses and theories] does not mean we may not have guessed the truth; some our our hypotheses may well be true" (p. 30). As regards the capacity of scientific inquiry to afford a true picture of reality, "it is not irrational to hope as long as we live—and actions and decisions are constantly forced on us" (p. 101). In the search for truth, the finding of something that "may well be true" deserves no celebration; it smacks of failure rather than success. Clearly *a not irrational hope* in the adequacy of science is not good enough: what is wanted is a *rationally based expectation*—not, to be sure, an airtight *guarantee*, but at least a *reasonable assurance* that in taking the scientific route to the solution of cognitive problems in the factual area we have done as well as one can.

The model of the growth of scientific knowledge along Popperian lines—through the falsification of hypotheses arrived at by blind trial-and-error groping—is thus crucially deficient in being admittedly unable to account for the *reality*, let alone the *rate* of scientific progress. Yet this very issue of the *rate and structure of scientific progress* is certainly among the basic phenomena which any adequate account of scientific knowledge must be able to account for. A theory that insists that it is necessary to hide this away behind a veil of ignorance blazons forth the clear marks of its own inadequacy.

The vitalistic opponents of a rigoristic Darwinism have traditionally objected that evolution has proceeded too quickly and unerringly in devising such highly survival-efficient instrumentalities as, e.g., the human eye, for the developmental process to have been wholly the result of natural selection working on random variation. Accordingly, beginning with the "creative evolutionism" of Bergson, vitalists have always objected that the random-variation-cum-natural selection model of the evolutionary process does not provide an explanatory basis adequate to account for the rapidity of evolution. They have maintained that the operation of some sort of vital principle is needed to pull the evolutionary process in the right direction and at the right speed. Now in the case of biological evolution this objection is doubtless untenable— all the evidence indicates the available timespan is large, and large enough for the neo-Darwinian mechanisms of mutation and genetic selection to do their work. But genetic mutations are of limited variety—unlike the possibilities for hypothesis formation where literally endless variations are available. In the cognitive case the timespan is just too short to account for the phenomenon of progress in terms of a blind trial-and-error groping amidst infinite possibilities.[5]

[5] Popper is by no means wholly unaware that this problem of the rate of scientific progress involves difficulties for his theory. His discussion (on pp. 281–4) of the large-scale evolutionary leaps represented by the theory of "hopeful monsters" of R. B. Goldschmidt (*The Material Basis of Evolution* [New Haven, 1940]) seems to recognize that a piecemeal progress advancing, so to speak, thesis by thesis may not be able to account for the speedy efficiency of scientific advance, and his treatment of the issue ends on the hopeful note of the claim: "It will be seen that this Darwinian theory of hopeful behavioral monsters 'simulates' not only Lamarckism but Bergsonian vitalism as well" (p. 284; cf. also p. 270). But it emerges from whole tenor of the discussion that the machinery of "hopeful monsters" is itself just that—a hopeful monster, a *deus ex machina* introduced to save the theory from inherent difficulties which the resources of its fundamental commitments have been unable to avert. Again, at one stage Popper seems to withdraw (in a footnote) from the reliance on the methodology of purely random trial and error which predominates throughout the body of his theory as developed in the main text. This footnote reads as follows:

It is not difficult to discern the root of the problem. Popper's evolutionary theory of knowledge envisages a Darwinism based on a mechanism of selection by trial and error *with respect to theses.*[6] This microscopic concern with individual claims and theses is its weak-spot. For Popper factual theses are not somehow linked by inherent interrelationships of natural necessity—true empiricist that he is, he dismisses this sort of thing out of hand as obscurantist and illegitimate nonsense. Popper agrees with Hume that all factual theses are wholly independent—save insofar as their mode of formulation may embody strictly logical interconnections. The result is a fundamentally Humean position to the effect that—logical overlaps apart—factual theses stand atomistically disconnected from one another.

This poses a problem of how the cohesive generality, orderli-

---

The method of trial and error-elimination *does not operate with completely chance-like or random trials* (as has been sometimes suggested), even though the trials may look pretty random; there must be at least an "after-effect" (in the sense of my *The Logic of Scientific Discovery,* pp. 162 ff.). For the organism is constantly learning from its mistakes, that is, it establishes *controls* which suppress or eliminate, or at least reduce the frequency of, certain *possible* trials (which were perhaps *actual* ones in its evolutionary past). (*Objective Knowledge, op. cit.,* p. 245, note 55.)

It it easy enough to see why Popper *wants* to take this line, but a difficult dilemma remains with regard to his ability to do so: (1) If the only ones among *possible* trials that can be bypassed are *actual past tests* and perhaps their very close cognates (in the manner of an "after-effect"), this cannot cut deeply enough into this immense multitude of available alternatives to do much good. (2) But if one concedes the existence of a (rationally cogent and unwarranted) learning process that can make really massively effective reductions in the range of alternatives that need consideration, then this resort to an "inductive talent" runs counter to the whole tenor of Popper's anti-inductivist program, which renders us impotent to carry the case-inductive strategy over from one situation to another. If *this* sort of device is needed to make the program work, then it effectively self-destructs.

[6] The casual reader of Popper's book might seek to counter this contention with the claim that Popper is concerned with the evolutionary development of scientific *problems*, rather than theses. (See, example for pp. 176–7.) But this will not do because, for Popper, a scientific problem simply *is* the circumstance that obtains when a theory encounters difficulties. Thus the evolution of theories and that of problems in science are simply seen as perspectively different aspects of one selfsame issue.

ness, and systematicity of our scientific macroknowledge could ever emerge from the scattered minutiae of thesis-microinformation within the very limited *span of time* that science has had at its disposal. There are *just too many* imaginable hypotheses to be gone through in an inductively blind trial-and-error search. If indeed our only investigative resource were of this character, then it would have required something verging on a preestablished harmony between scientific guesswork and the ways of nature to come as far as we have managed to do over so short a course of human history.[7]

Note how very different a situation faces the historian and the methodologist of science. The historian can without difficulty resort to a thesis-oriented evolutionism: alternatives crop up, the "fittest" tend to survive, and that's that. But it is incumbent upon the methodologist to go further and to consider how science *should* proceed if it is to make proper headway in the accomplishment of its aims. If one considers the scale of movement towards an ideal of adequacy, there is no reason for the *historian*

$$\xrightarrow{\hspace{3cm}}$$

nil   increasing adequacy   maximal

—once he has learned about limited sequences—to worry about the prospect that whole process of conjecture and replacement should play itself out within the left-hand quarter of the scale. But the *methodologist* must fret over this prospect. He must probe into the theoretical conditions for making real headway. He must come to grips with the issue of *the requisites of absolute progress* (as well as *relative* progress). And to account for the reality of absolute progress he will have to postulate either that the intrinsically

---

[7] This "too little time" complaint is reminiscent of the objections William Thomson, Lord Kelvin at one time offered against Darwinian Evolution on the grounds that—as he put it in his Presidential Address to the British Association in 1871—its mechanism of natural selection is "too like the Laputan method for making books, and that it did not sufficiently take into account a continually guiding and controlling intelligence...." However inappropriate this objection might be deemed in the case of *biological* evolution, the situation would be quite otherwise in the case of *cognitive* evolution. For an interesting account of the time-availability dispute between physicists on the one side and biologists and geologists on the other see Stephen G. Brush, "Thermodynamics and History" in *The Graduate Journal*, vol. 2 (1969), pp. 477–565.

superior alternatives *must* enter the contest (by envisaging the range of the theoretically available rather than actually proposed alternatives), or he must concede an "inductive talent" to assure that the superior alternatives figure among those actually proposed. At this stage we encounter a deep and fundamental drawback of the use of a theory-evolutionistic approach for epistemological (rather than historical) purposes. In and of itself, evolutionary variation and retention *at the level of theory* can account for *relative* progress towards adequacy, but it is *in principle impotent* in itself (in the absence of further special assumptions of a sort unpalatable to theoreticians of empiricist inclinations) to account for *absolute* progress.[8] This is perhaps the most crucial reason for redirecting evolutionary epistemology from theses towards methods, since the relative adequacy of thesis-validating methods has implications for the absolute merits of the theses it justifies.

Popper's theory thus faces a vitiating dilemma: he must choose between having the Darwinian selection process operate between all *conceivable* (i.e., theoretically available) theories or between all *proposed* (i.e., actually espoused) theories. If he opts for the second course—taking the (intrinsically surely more attractive and plausible) line that Darwinian selection operates with respect to the *actually* proposed and genuinely espoused alternatives—then the difficulty of accounting for substantial progress within a limited timespan becomes pressing. And it can be solved only if one grants man a capacity for efficiency in hypothesis-conjecture— a kind of inductive skill—so that those hypotheses actually conjectured are in fact likely to prove among the intrinsically superior alternatives. (As the example of cryptanalysis shows, a shrewd insight into principles of regulative regularity can cut down to reasonable proportions search-times that would require astronomical periods of time on a random trial-and-error basis.) But Popper is, of course, emphatically unwilling to concede any such inductive talent for superior hypothesis-conjecture, given his well-known antipathy to anything of inductive-confirmationist tendencies. And consequently, he is driven onto the other horn of the dilemma: his trial-and-error mechanism is saddled with

---

[8] It seems a not implausible conjecture that a functional equivalent to this disparity lay at the bottom of the dispute between "vitalists" and others who argued against blind Darwinian evolution in the biological sphere.

having to grapple with the whole gamut of conceivable alternatives, and so becomes trapped in the problem of time-availability and unrationalizable rates of progress.

To be sure, any epistemological Darwinism is in a position to exploit the fact that the rapidity of cognitive adaptation proceeds at a rate vastly faster than any genetic adaptation. The acceptance of factual claims can in principle arise and fade in their movement through human populations with a rapidity very much greater than the diffusion of genetic materials. For it is clear that the speed with which ideational adaptation can arise from the impact of selective forces far exceeds the possible rate of genetic adaptation. But even so, the range of *de facto* and actual genetic mutation is limited and presents only a small scope of variation at any given time, while the range of *possible* alternative theses that are in principle available is endlessly large. And it is at this possibilistic level that, so Popper insists, the selective mechanisms must do their work. The advantage of a gain in speed of a few orders of magnitiude in dealing with ideational rather than biological evolution is lost a myriad-fold over if we must there search randomly through the *logically possible* alternatives, rather than grappling merely with the comparatively small handful of those *physically presented*. In the face of this discrepancy, we face the fact that a workable thesis-evolutionism—one that can provide adequately for the astounding efficiency of scientific progress —demands some sort of process-internal *conatus* impelling the course of events in the right direction. This demand is familiar —and rationally anathema—from the history of Lamarckianism and its intensified revival in Bergsonian vitalism.

The force of these general considerations bears with particular impetus on Popper's theory. For the only route to efficiency open to a thesis-directed Darwinism is to orient it towards theses of very high generality—those which subsume a great multiplicity of special cases within their scope. But since the *falsification* of general theses lies in the determination of counter-instances, the greater the scope of a thesis the less the cognitive progress made— other things being equal—by its falsification—i.e., by finding some counterexample to it. The model of selection by error-determination is thus of the least cognitive utility and minimally information-providing at the very point which is focal for the interests of scientific progress.

2. COMPARISON WITH METHODOLOGICAL DARWINISM

All these difficulties are cut off at the root once we make the shift from a Darwinism of *theses* to a Darwinism of *methods*. For now we can suppose a trial-and-error model that operates not with respect to *possible* theses but with respect to *actual* methods of thesis-substantiation. On such a model, the course of evolution, however slow in the initial stages, is able to provide for very rapid eventual progress when once *any* headway at all is made. Only a cognitive evolutionism which—like our methodological approach —is inherently oriented towards generalized instrumentalities can successfully pull its way out of the quicksands in which a thesis-oriented evolutionary theory becomes enmired.[9]

A spectrum of theses is just too broad for a trial-and-error mechanism to work adequately. Plausibility considerations can serve to avert a need for random groping. Only if we have good reason to believe that the process of elimination proceeds with respect to the really optimal alternatives can this process produce any truth-presumptive results.

Cardano, a sixteenth-century mathematician with a Rennaissance penchant for boasting, maintained that a monalphabetic cipher of his own invention was unbreakable because of the large number of possible solutions that must be tested. (A monalphabetic cipher is the simplest kind; each letter of the original message is replaced by one and and only one cipher letter consistently throughout the whole message.) Since there are 26 letters, there are 26 factorial different ways of pairing plaintext letters with cipher letters, or approximately 1.1×10^{28} different possible solutions, a consideration that led Cardano to feel the safety of numbers. Yet with a few hours' instruction in frequency analysis and anagramming, most amateurs can solve these ciphers in a

---

[9] In his Schlipp volume essay (*op. cit.*) Popper seems to have reached much the same conclusion:

> But although the blind man who searches for a black hat may *bring* some order into his trials, the order is not *given* to him; he may choose or invent one order (method) first, and a different order later; and these choices will be trials too—even though on a higher level. (They may, but need not, be influenced by his earlier experience in somewhat similar or in very different situations.) (P. 1061.)

matter of minutes. Such is the potency of method. One leading authority on cryptology, commenting on amateur inventors of cipher systems, has said:

> Many inventors also invoke the vast number of combinations of keys afforded by their system as proof of its invulnerability. To exhaust the possible solutions would take eons, they contend, unwittingly using the same argument . . . as Cardano. . .—and with the same lack of validity. For, as Shannon has shown, the cryptanalyst does not go after these possibilities one by one. He eliminates millions at a time. Moreover, the trials progress from the more probable to the less probable hypotheses, increasing the cryptanalyst's chance of striking the right one early.[10]

It is thus important, even when we recognize the utility of a trial-and-error technique, that this be thought of not as a blind groping amongst *all conceivable* alternatives, but as a carefully guided search among the *really promising* alternatives.[11] Inquiry is not a process of setting a random generator to work to produce hypotheses for testing. Hypotheses emerge not from random combinations but from the detection of patterns in the empirical data.

Three methodological inputs are crucial in such inquiries: (1) the mechanisms for obtaining the presumptively relevant data,

[10] David Kahn, *The Codebreakers* (New York, 1967), p. 766.

[11] This represents a crucial disanalogy between biological and cognitive evolution indicative of the quasi-"vitalistic" character of the latter. In biological evolution the mutations that actually arise fall across the entire spectrum of possible alternatives with equal probability, and so the direction of evolution is not determined by the direction of mutation: "It is emphatically selection, not mutation, that determines the direction of evolution," and if this were not so, then "it would be necessary to suppose that such mutations must be predominantly favourable." (Sir Gavin de Beer, "The Darwin-Wallace Centenary," *Endeavour*, vol. 17 [1958], pp. 61–76; see p. 68.) In the case of cognitive evolution *viewed from the standpoint of thesis-acceptance*, the case is exactly opposite: the actualization of possible mutant alternatives is probabilistically skewed, favourable mutations predominate, and the direction of evolution is governed as much by the inherent selectivity of mutation as by selection proper. But, as we shall see, in the cognitive case—unlike the biological—there is nothing occult about any of this, because one can imbed the "vitalistic" features of epistemological evolution at the thesis level within an orthodoxly randomized and blindly unguided evolutionary model at the methodological level.

(2) the (presumably apposite) conceptions of "pattern," and (3) the procedures for eliciting these structures. Hypotheses are not created *ex nihilo* by random groping, they are *constructed* upon a suitable methodological foundation. Without such methodological guidance we are driven to a "method" that is in effect tantamount to the absence of method, that "method of last resort," as it were, a merely random search through the possibilities. It is just at this point that methodological, regulative, and procedural considerations can come into effective operation.[12] One cannot at each stage of inquiry place the whole spectrum of logically possible alternative hypotheses on equal footing. Of course, we cannot eliminate the "implausible" candidates on the basis of *certain* knowledge since the operative principles of analogy and coherence are only *presumptive* in their force. Such a cognitively *constitutive* stance is not appropriate. But we can take the cognitively *regulative* approach that certain sorts of alternatives ("plausible" on the basis of preserving analogies) can be taken as more worthy of serious considerations.

As long as the principles of generality at issue are simply *general theses*—as long as they are *constitutive* generalizations of a factually substantive import that "transcends the evidence"— the problem of their validating justification remains. We are left with all the old Humean puzzles. But when we take the step from theses to methods these difficulties vanish. Methods, as we have insisted time and again, are inherently general. Their function is *regulative* and their role is thus quite different from that of cognitively *constitutive* general theses. Moreover, they have an

---

[12] The issues of this problem-area have perhaps been pursued more effectively by Herbert A. Simon than by any other cognitive theoretician. See his essay "Does Scientific Discovery Have a Logic?" *Philosophy of Science*, vol. 40 (1973), pp. 471–80 where further references to his work are given. One key summary runs thus: "The more difficult and novel the problem, the greater is likely to be the amount of trial and error required to find a solution. At the same time, the trial and error is not completely random or blind; it is, in fact, highly selective." (*The Sciences of the Artificial* [Cambridge, Mass., 1969], p. 95.) Exploration of the computer simulation of the processes of human learning and discovery brings clearly to light the operation of a heuristic of an essentially regulative/methodological kind. It is based on principles (such as the priority of "similarity"-augmenting transformations in problem-solving) which *qua* theses are clearly false (are heuristic "fictions" in the sense of Vaihinger), but which prove methodologically effective.

entirely different (and theoretically more tractable) manner of justification since their legitimation lies in the *practical* sector, where ground-rules different from those of the *theoretical* sector come into play.[13] All of the characteristic difficulties of an evolutionary epistemology based on thesis Darwinism are consequently obviated when we make the shift to a method Darwinism.

The weaknesses of an evolutionary model of scientific inquiry based on thesis-oriented trial and error can thus be overcome by a cognitive Darwinism of the method-oriented sort mooted here, one which operates at a level of generality that is lacking when our attention focusses on particular theses. On such an approach, the process of trial-and-error mutation and rational selection is not seen as operative primarily and in the first instance in regard to theories or theses themselves, but in regard to the methodological principles and rule-of-thumb heuristics used in their substantiation. The human imagination is fertile enough that any given stage the range of theoretically envisageable hypotheses is "more plentiful than blackberries." But the range of human experience is such that where the solution of our cognitive problems is concerned, the range of available investigation and explanatory *methods* is emphatically limited. At this level, the prospects of a trial-and-error evolutionism are vastly improved.

In effect, the shift from *theses* to *methods* (viz., methods for thesis-substantiation) enables us "'to have it both ways." We avoid occultism by relying *at the methodological level* upon a strictly trial-and-error mechanism of learning. And we avoid the rational impotence of an inability to account for the actual course of scientific progress. The combination of a model of method-learning based on the blind groping of trial and error and of thesis-learning based on the use of methods makes it possible to have the best of both worlds.[14] It means that the venture of

[13] The supportive reasoning for this contention is set out in Chapters I-II of the author's *The Primacy of Practice* (Oxford, 1973).

[14] The methodological approach can thus lay claims to resolving the issue perceptively posed by D. T. Campbell in the following terms:

> Popper has, in fact, disparaged the common belief in "chance" discoveries in science as partaking of the inductivist belief in directly learning from experience....[T]hat issue, and the more general problem of spelling out in detail the way in which a natural selection of scientific *theories* is compatible with a dogmatic blind-variation-and-selective-retention epistemology remain high priority tasks for the

thesis-validation is not condemned to blind trial and error but is guided by *heuristic principles of method*, involving the use of methods that have proven their effectiveness in the past, and whose application in present conditions thus embodies a fundamentally inductive commitment.[15]

To be sure, the methodology itself rests on a basis of presumptions which themselves represent a generalized "knowledge" of the world, a knowledge arrived at on the basis of the "lessons" of past experience in whose make-up trial and error has played a prominent part. What is at issue is a "nested hierarchy" of heuristic processes that reflect the funded experience of the past. And, so, we need never confront the theoretically proliferated manifold of alternative hypotheses empty-handed, but can filter it through these basic methodological presumptions which in themselves represent a heuristic proto-model of the world by whose means yet further knowledge can be secured.

In taking this methodological line, one need not contend that a thesis-oriented trial-and-error process does not have its limited place within the framework of scientific method. A methodological approach need by no means exclude a significant role for the operation of the device of blind trial and error. What we deny is simply the essentially *imperialistic* thesis that this random trial-and-error model of inquiry with respect to *theses* is a tool so powerful and pervasive that the whole of scientific methodology can be reduced to its operation alone.

3. REMOVAL OF AN OBJECTION

Given the preceding critique of thesis Darwinism, someone may well object to the presently projected method Darwinism as follows:

Your argument against thesis Darwinism is (put roughly) that

---

future. (P. A. Schilpp [ed.], *The Philosophy of Karl Popper* [2 vols; La Salle, 1974], p. 436.)

The present theory provides a natural basis for combining a natural selection process at the level of *theories* with an epistemology of blind-variation-and-selective-retention at the level of *methods*.

[15] Albeit one of a regulative sort. See Section 5 of Chapter III above.

the *pace* of progress of science is too rapid to be plausibly accounted for by a process of trial-and-error selection among the available alternatives. But does this argument not hold against your own position? The success of science certainly indicates very substantial sophistication on the side of methodology, and is this not every bit as difficult to account for along the lines of a Darwinian trial-and-error theory as is progress on the side of accepted theses?

Clearly if this objection held it would be serious, but—fortunately —it is seriously flawed. For the argument that "not enough time" is available for the accretion of observed progress by more or less random improvements tells very differently as between theses and methods. For thesis Darwinism requires a tremendous number of successive improvements, given the immense range of the claims at issue in the build-up of the sciences. It is this enormous number of successive iterations of the selection-process that demands so much time on the Darwinian account, and that makes the rapid progress of science appear virtually miraculous from the Darwinian point of view. However, there is—by contrast—no reason why methodological improvement cannot proceed at a glacially sedate Darwinian pace. Then, when at last an even modestly effective method has finally been devised, any further development can clearly proceed with extreme rapidity. Think of an analogy: a vast long and stumbling process may have lain behind man's ultimately successful development of the technological method for human flight, but once the rudimentary beginnings of the venture were in hand, the further development of sophisticated aerial transport proceeded with astonishing speed, and yet in an almost routine way. There is no reason to believe that the case of cognitive rather than technically manipulative methods should be any different in this regard. Once an even partially adequate method for the testing of factual theses has been contrived, there is every reason to think that human ingenuity will devise suitable occasions for putting it to use—to the great advantage of the rapid progress of knowledge. At the level of theses—of envisageable alternative explanatory hypotheses— one faces an embarrassment of riches that makes effective progress through randomized selection-processes unintelligible on any basis that does not call for suppositions rationally unpalatable to any mind of empiricist inclinations. But the situation is very different in the methodological case. Once an even modestly satisfactory inquiry method is at hand, progress at the thesis level can be very swift because of the inherent power and generality of such a method. Moreover, thanks to the cyclically self-corrective aspect of such a method, further substantial progress in the methodological side itself becomes a real prospect.[16]

4. THE ROLE OF TRIAL AND ERROR

The present critique of Popperian evolutionism by a blindly groping trial-and-error development of theories was anticipated not only in its general tendency but in its details by C. S. Peirce. I cannot forebear quoting him at considerable length:

> But how is it that all this truth has ever been lit up by a process in which there is no compulsiveness nor tendency toward compulsiveness? Is it by chance? Consider the multitude of theories that might have been suggested. A physicist comes across some new phenomenon in his laboratory. How does he know but the conjunctions of the planets have something to do with it or that it is not perhaps because the dowager empress of China has at that same time a year ago chanced to pronounce some word of mystical power or some invisible jinnee may be present. Think of what trillions of trillions of hypotheses might be made of which one only is true; and yet after two or three or at the very most a dozen guesses, the physicist hits pretty nearly on the correct hypothesis. By chance he would not have been likely to do so in the whole time that has elapsed since the earth was solidified. You may tell me that astrological and magical hypotheses were resorted to at first and that it is only by degrees that we have learned certain general laws of nature in consequence of which the physicist seeks for the explanation of his phenomenon within the four walls of his laboratory. But when you look at the matter more narrowly, the matter is not to be accounted

---

[16] Although stated flatly and without much development here, this point is actually one of great importance. (Presumably the reader can work out its ramifications for himself, given the structure of the cyclic models of methodological reappraisal set out in Chapter VII above.)

for in any considerable measure in that way. Take a broad view of the matter. Man has not been engaged upon scientific problems for over twenty thousand years or so. But put it at ten times that if you like. But that is not a hundred thousandth part of the time that he might have been expected to have been searching for his first scientific theory.

You may produce this or that excellent psychological account of the matter. But let me tell you that all the psychology in the world will leave the logical problem just where it was. I might occupy hours in developing that point. I must pass it by.

You may say that evolution accounts for the thing. I don't doubt it is evolution. But as for explaining evolution by chance, there has not been time enough.

However man may have aquired his faculty of divining the ways of Nature, it has certainly not been by a self-controlled and critical logic. Even now he cannot give any exact reason for his best guesses. It appears to me that the clearest statement we can make of the logical situation—the freest from all questionable admixture—is to say that man has a certain Insight, not strong enough to be oftener right than wrong, but strong enough not to be overwhelmingly more often wrong than right, into . . . Nature. An Insight, I call it, because it is to be referred to the same general class of operations to which Perceptive Judgments belong. This Faculty is at the same time of the general nature of Instinct, resembling the instincts of the animals in its so far surpassing the general powers of our reason and for its directing us as if we were in possession of facts that are entirely beyond the reach of our senses. It resembles instinct too in its small liability to error; for though it goes wrong oftener than right, yet the relative frequency with which it is right is on the whole the most wonderful thing in our constitution.[17]

---

[17] *Collected Papers*, vol. V: 5.172–3. Compare the following passage:

> Nature is a far vaster and less clearly arranged repertory of facts than a census report; and if man had not come to it with special aptitudes for guessing right, it may well be doubted whether in the ten or twenty thousand years that they may have existed their greatest mind would have attained the amount of knowledge which is actually possessed by the lowest idiot. (*Ibid*, vol. II: 2.753)

With magisterial shrewdness Peirce puts his finger upon exactly the right point: An evolutionary model with respect to possible hypotheses just cannot operate adequately within the actual (or perhaps even any realistic) timespan.[18] The only point at which our present position parts company with Peirce is in its explicit and deliberate substitution of the *methodology* of inquiry and substantiation in place of an otherwise mysterious capacity of *insight* or *instinct*.

It is easy enough to see why a judicious theory of knowledge should favor recourse to the "method" of pure trial and error (of a "blind groping" among alternatives) as the prime mover of cognitive progress—the ultimate mechanism through which the whole process gets its initial impetus and in terms of which an account of its workings must ultimately be given. For any alternative to blind groping as *ultimate* mechanism requires either an unrationalizable supposition of pure luck and/or the favoring conspiratoriality of nature, or else calls for a somehow uncanny and inexplicable talent on the part of the inquirers for hitting near the truth of things. In either case, we are confronted with assumptions that are profoundly *occult:* inherently implausible and beyond rationalization. It is not as a matter of peculiar whim that learning theorists and cognitive psychologists uniformly presuppose an ultimate mechanism of blind trial and error.

In explaining the historical realities of cognitive progress one thus seems to be caught in a dilemma: *EITHER* one relies upon a model of the development of scientific theories by blind trial and error (in which case there is no way of getting a plausible account of the historical realities of the rapidity of scientific progress), *OR* one gives up reliance on pure trial and error and is then driven back to a reliance on an occult vitalism-reminiscent *deus-ex-machina* device.[19] This dilemma would make it seem that

---

[18] This point warrants emphasis. Most writers on induction who hold that man has (or develops) inductive skills do so to assure the nontrivial a priori probability of our conjectures for the purpose of Bayesian argumentation. Peirce sees that this is also needed to rationalize the relatively rapid rate of scientific progress. On this aspect of Peirce's thought compare Robert Sharpe, "Induction, Abduction, and the Evolution of Science," *Transactions of the Charles S. Peirce Society,* vol. 6 (1970), pp. 17–31.

[19] As one knowledgeable theoretician has said, "All existing learning theories contain explicit or implicit assumptions about some selective

on the one hand trial and error is of itself insufficient, while on the other hand what is different from trial and error is beyond rational legitimation.

But the presently envisaged approach slips between the horns of this dilemma. In taking the methodological turn we are able to have it both ways. We can accept a model of cognitive progress based on the mechanism of pure trial and error, but we reorient its applicability from *theses* (theories) towards *methods* for their substantiation. And we are able to account for the rapidity of scientific progress in straightforward methodological terms. Our approach thus proceeds by inserting the matter of methodology as a mediating link emplaced between the operation of a trial-and-error mechanism and the espousal of factual theses. An orientation towards methodology once again resolves the problems encountered on the orthodox thesis-oriented approaches.

Moreover, the above concession that methodological progress might proceed purely and solely by blind trial and error (i.e., by wholly random and rationally unguided variation) may well go too far. After all, even methodological innovation is not wholly haphazard. In any field, say woodworking or chess—and so even perhaps in the cognitive sphere of fact-substantiation— methodological innovation is itself to some extent guided by methodological considerations. It makes sense to conceive of the issue of methods for making methods on analogy with the enterprise of engineering machine-tools, i.e., machines for making machines. These considerations would also serve to foster the prospects of providing a reasonable account for the rapid pace of cognitive progress in terms of a Darwinian model oriented towards methods rather than theses.

Orthodox Darwinian evolutionary theory envisages no "coupling" between the sources of variation and selection; mutational variation is seen as a fundamentally blind process untouched by any "precognition" of ultimate selective outcomes. In this sense, the evolution of methods by a process of rational rather than natural selection departs from the orthodox picture: to be sure it calls for uncoupling in the *final* analysis, but in the first and second

principle operating on initially random responses." (Donald T. Campbell, "Adaptive Behavior From Random Response," *Behavioral Science*, vol. 1 [1956], pp. 105–10.)

(and third, etc.) analyses, it does not see a blind stumbling in the dark, but a groping in the dim half-light of the preestablished and *in some degree* prevalidated methodologies for handling analogous cases.

5. TRANSITION TO SCIENTIFIC METHOD

Our treatment of the legitimation of a methodology of inquiry regarding factual matters began with the factor of pragmatic success and subsequently transmuted this into the issue of Darwinian survival. What the analysis has done (or endeavored to do) is to exhibit how the historical issue of temporal development comes to be correlative with the probative issue of rational warrant. To this point, however, we have usually talked of the justification of thesis-verifying inquiry procedures on a very general and abstract plane. It yet remains to face the key question of just where the victory in this Darwinian struggle among inquiry procedures in the factual realm actually lies. To be sure, the appropriate answer here is a virtually foregone conclusion, one that is writ plain across the course of human experience in the cognitive domain. As the discussion has already foreshadowed at many points, it is clearly the *method of scientific inquiry* that carries the day. No elaborate argumentation is necessary to establish the all-too-evident fact that science has come out on top in the competition of rational selection with respect to alternative processes for the substantiation of factual claims. We can thus descend from the previous level of abstraction regarding the working of "inquiry procedures" in general, and focus specifically and concretely upon the *scientific* method. Here, then, is the natural transition-point for a fresh perspective of consideration—and for a fresh chapter.

Chapter X

AUTONOMY, SELF-CORRECTIVENESS, AND THE CREDENTIALS OF SCIENCE

1. DOES SCIENCE LEAD TO TRUTH?

Despite its appeal and persuasiveness, the claim that scientific inquiry is a route to truths about the ways of the world encounters various theoretical obstacles. For one thing, the Wheel Argument (*diallelus*) shows that, precisely insofar as one is serious in a commitment to science as a means to information about the world, it becomes the more difficult to substantiate this position, since one cannot then maintain without circularity that what science yields is presumably true. Moreover, science is an enhanced and systematized use of experience, and if experience has taught us anything, it has taught us that science goes wrong—that the science of today invariably contradicts the science of yesterday. We realize full well that the science of the future will regard as a tissue of errors much or all of what its present-day counterpart asserts. And in any case, it makes no sense to view scientific progress as a progression from actual or probable error to certified truth. There always remains the prospect—at least in principle— of a change-of-mind regarding the acceptability of scientific theses. (Accordingly one must not construe scientific progress along the lines of an accretional "geographical exploration" model that envisages the steady accumulative accretion of new items of firm information, constantly filling in the gaps of what was heretofore *terra incognita*, without any need for revising old findings.) Considerations of this sort indicate that—perhaps surprisingly—serious theoretical problems arise in establishing scientific inquiry as a satisfactory route to knowledge about the world.

Just where, then, do the merits of science as a cognitive instrument lie? This question is often answered by the contention that the cognitive credentials of science root in the fact (or alleged fact) that *science is self-corrective*—that even though it may not provide us with certified truths it exhibits a constantly progressive advance of "moving closer to the truth." But just how is this idea to be understood: how does the purported "self-correctiveness" in fact work? These issues define the problem-area of the present chapter.

2. THE SELF-CORRECTION THESIS AND THE AUTONOMY OF SCIENCE

The traditional background of the doctrine of the "self-correctiveness" of science goes back to several 18th century writers (especially David Hartley [1705–1757], Georges Le Sage [1724–1803], and Joseph Priestley [1733–1804]), who took as their model the various mathematical methods of successive approximation, exemplified by such procedures as the well-known processes for the determination of n-th roots.[1] These methods—the rule of false position for example—operate in such a way that, given an initial position based on guesswork (however wild) there is an *automatic* procedure for successively refining and developing this wrong answer into one that approximates stage by stage more closely to the correct answer.[2] As Priestley put it:

> Hypotheses, while they are considered merely as such, lead persons to try a variety of experiments, in order to ascertain them. These new facts serve to correct the hypothesis which gave occasion to them. The theory, thus corrected, serves to discover more new facts, which, as before, bring the theory still nearer to the truth. In this progressive state, or method of approximation, things continue. . . .[3]

Le Sage drew the analogy between the work of the scientist and

[1] For the historical background see Laurens Laudan, "Peirce and the Trivialization of the Self-Correcting Thesis" in Ronald N. Giere and Richard S. Westfall (eds), *Foundations of Scientific Method: The 19th Century* (Bloomington, 1973) pp. 275–306.

[2] It deserves emphasis, however, that *this* cook-book sort of a routine procedure for self-correctiveness was *not* operative in the ideas of C. S. Peirce.

[3] Joseph Priestley, *The History and Present State of Electricity* (London, 1767), p. 381.

that of an arithmetician working a problem in long-division, producing in the quotient at each stage a number more accurate than that of the preceding stage.[4] Implicit throughout this 18th century view is the conception that science possesses an *automatic, mechanically routine method* for improving in the future on its older incorrect theories. This thesis that science proceeds by way of routine steps of successive approximation in moving inexorably closer to the truth—that scientific progress is a matter of convergence upon "the correct answer"—is the initial form of the theory of self-correction.

This view of the self-correctiveness of science is, of course, untenable. When the progress of science indicates that an accepted hypothesis is no longer warranted, then neither "the scientific method" nor any other cognitive resource at man's disposal affords any *automatic* device for producing a new hypothesis that can more appropriately be put in its place.

But, of course, to say of the scientific method—with Peirce—that it renders science self-corrective in the long run, certainly does not commit one to the claim that this method affords some automatic procedure or a cook-book routine for ultimately determining "the correct solution" to scientific problems. When one says of the calculating prodigy that his genius affords him a means for solving arithmetical problems, one need not hold that it provides him with a routine *procedure* (capable of codification and transmission to others) for solving such problems. Or again, when someone maintains that the free market provides a mechanism for pricing commodities, he surely does not thereby imply that it provides some explicit routine procedure for determining the market price of commodities. Analogously, to maintain that the use of the methods of scientific inquiry will—or can—in the long run determine the truth-status of *proposed* answers to scientific questions, is *not* to say that science possesses a methodological routine (in the sense of anything approaching an automatically effective mechanical procedure) enabling it to ferret out the appropriate answers to its questions. A potential gap always remains between what is *proposed* and what is *appropriate*.

Moreover, the idea of the 18th century theorists (reflected also

[4] Georges Le Sage "Quelques opuscules relatifs à la méthode," published posthumously in Pierre Provost, *Essais de philosophie*, Vol. II (Paris, 1804), pp. 253–335.

in Peirce) that science proceeds by way of successive approxima-
tions to the truth—that scientific progress leads successively ever
closer to the truth by way of an asymptotic approach to "the final
answer"—has little rational appeal.[5] Apart from its internal
difficulties relating to the concept of successive aproximation,
it lies wholly beyond any prospect of plausible substantiation.[6] The
Wheel Argument or *diallelus* blocks any prospect of our being able
to implement the program of showing that our scientific claims
are somehow drawing nearer and nearer to "the real truth." The
Peircean theory that science is destined to reach "the truth of
things" in the long run suffers from a decisive disability at just
this point. For to hold this view, one must be prepared (as we are
not) to join Peirce in *redefining* "truth" so as to make this thesis
a guaranteed fact (by reconstructing truth in terms of the ultimate
deliverances of scientific method).[7] Unless this is done, the doctrine remains at the level of an unrationalized faith in the in-

---

[5] Note that ultimate arrival and successive approximation are quite
distinct. (For example in proceeding by elimination in a finite range of
cases, one is assured of ultimate arrival but by no means of successive
approximation.) But they are frequently run together. Thus Peirce writes:
"Induction is that mode of reasoning which adopts a conclusion as
approximative, because it results from a method of inference which must
generally lead to truth in the long run." (*Collected Papers*, vol. I: 1.67).
Peirce in fact knows better: "Quantitative induction," he writes, "always
makes a gradual approach to truth, though not a uniform approach"
(*ibid.*, vol. II 2.770). Ultimate convergence (possibly despite wild nearer-
term oscallations) is something very different from a monotonically uniform approach of asymptotic convergence.

[6] This position also encounters immediately the difficulty of how this ap-
proximation-concept can be made to work in the case of theories or hypotheses, in view of the consideration, urged by W. V. Quine, that "...there
is a faulty use of a mathematical analogy in speaking of a limit of
theories, since the notion of a limit depends on that of 'nearer than,'
which is defined for numbers and not for theories." (*Word and Object*
[New York, 1960], p. 23.) Presumably, then, the approach at issue would
have to deal with theories in some suitably oblique manner, in terms of
the numbers generated by the success statistics of their applications.

[7] Regarding the relevant aspects of Peirce's teaching see John W. Lenz,
"Induction as Self-Corrective" in E. C. Moore and R. S. Robin (eds),
Studies in the Philosophy of Charles Sanders Peirce, Second Series
(Amherst, 1964), pp. 151–62. Compare also David Savan, "Peirce's
Infallibilism," *ibid.*, pp. 190–211, for a useful exposition of Peirce's rele-
vant ideas. For an interesting critique of Peirce's position see L. Laudan,
op. cit.

herent ultimate adequacy of scientific methods, a basis which—while suited to the needs of the argument—has little rational appeal.

In any event, our own position moves in quite a different direction and does not view the self-correctiveness of science in terms of a Peircean assurance of its ultimate accuracy. We hold that "self-correctiveness" is best understood to lie—in the final analysis—simply in the fact that *science is autonomous:* it is not subject to *any external standard* of correctness. Scientific claims must—whenever corrected—be corrected by further scientific claims. A "science" viewed as falling subject to *external* standards of truthfulness is simply not deserving of this name: the truthfulness of scientific claims is a matter to be settled wholly at the level of considerations internal to the scientific enterprise. The correction of scientific findings can come only by way of other scientific findings. This fundamental fact is the rock-bottom on which the doctrine of the self-correctiveness of science must find its foothold.

3. THE TRUTHFULNESS OF SCIENTIFIC THESES AND THE NATURE OF SCIENTIFIC PROGRESS

Science—that is *theoretical,* rather than *applied* science—seeks to provide generalizations as to how things work in the world and to enunciate general truths regarding the eventuations of nature. Now we may take it as established by Hume—and consolidated by the recent tradition in the philosophy of science of which he is fountainhead—that a general thesis about the world, a *factual* generalization, can never be *decisively* established by the (of necessity finite) body of available evidence accumulated on its behalf. The empirical evidence in hand is *always in principle insufficient* to provide any absolute demonstration of a factual thesis about the world. Accordingly, we must always regard scientific claims as *defeasible.*

But even if science does not yield irrefragable truths, the question remains: Can scientific progress not be construed in essentially *probabilistic* terms, as involving an ongoing movement towards claims having an ever higher probability of truth? The answer is presumably *yes.* But this affirmative reply does not actually help much, because there remains the crucial issue of resolving just exactly what is the *nature* of the probability at issue here.

This certainly cannot be *objective* probability, with scientific progress understood as a move from less to ever more likely generalizations regarding the world. The issues that arise at this point are vast, but let it suffice here to say that all of the major current theories of scientific method—Carnapian inductivism, Popperian falsificationism, Peircean fallibilism, Feyerabendian anarchism, etc.—all agree that there is no workable way of speaking of the objectively probabilistic status of scientific theories. And in the background there always lurks the argument of the Wheel Argument (*diallelus*) which also precludes our construing the idea of "coming closer to the truth" in this area of scientific generalizations in probabilistic terms of arriving at results that are more likely to be true.

Even if *objective* probability is ruled out, there yet remains the recourse to *subjective* probability. Unhappily this prospect too proves unavailing. A recourse to subjective probability could do no more than show that humans in fact trust the later findings of science more than the earlier, an interesting psychosociological fact that does not bring us any closer to the issue of truthfulness.

But how is one to understand the concept of scientific progress if it is not feasible to implement the idea of "moving closer to the truth" in either categorical or probabilistic terms? Possibly one can approach the goal indirectly. Perhaps the task of "progress towards truth" can be implemented in terms of *moving further from error*, in that the later theories embody fewer mistakes, advancing the truthfulness of the body of our scientific beliefs by *reducing* the errors present in it.

Unfortunately this sort of "progress" is not very helpful, because error is endless, and error-avoidance is not really a very promising principle of cognition. Having mistakenly given 15 as a value of the solution of an equation, I may manage to avoid *this* particular error by moving on to 16, but what is to assure that such avoidance of an old error is not simply the embracing of a new one? Error-avoidance is a singularly ineffective principle, because the avoidance of erstwhile error is no assurance of any real improvement: the scope of potential error is endless, and we might simply be exchanging the mistakes we have come to recognize as such "for those we know not of." A step away from an identifiable error may lead to a position even more gravely erroneous.

Error-*avoidance* is not a sure means for moving in the direction of error-*reduction*, unless one is prepared to adopt some version of John Stuart Mill's rather far-fetched position on the issue. Espousing a version of the Principle of Limited Variety, Mill held that there are only a limited number of possible candidates rival to any proposed scientific law, so that a process of successive elimination (say by judicious deployment of the five "canons of induction") is increasingly more likely to lead to the correct result, and is, in any case, a step ahead in a movement towards this result. The doubtful basis on which this position is premissed makes rather implausible the theory that error elimination indicates a "progress towards the truth." It is, alas, unlikely that one could ever exhaust the stock of possible mistakes. The falsification of its rivals just does not indicate the truth of an hypothesis.

We have now surveyed—and rejected—various alternative conceptions of scientific progress in terms of "getting closer to the truth," specifically the following four:

(1) the "*ultimate arrival*" theory—that, as scientific change-of-mind continues over the ages, at some eventual stage the transition from error to truth is ultimately bound to be arrived at, finally issuing in a sort of scientific millenium. (This doctrine comes close to the Peircean view that science is destined to succeed in the long run.)

(2) the "*successive approximation*" theory—that with the advance of science we get closer and closer to the real truth by way of an asymptotic approach to "the final answer" as to how reality comports itself in this context.

(3) the "*probabilistic enhancement*" theory—that later stages of "scientific knowledge" are bound to be closer to "the real truth" *in probabilistic terms* than their predecessors at earlier stages: they are successively more likely to be correct.[8]

(4) the "*continuous correction*" theory of *error elimination*—that later stages of "scientific knowledge" will, by

---

[8] On the historical aspect of this theory see L. Laudan, *op. cit.*, pp. 285–6.

avoiding earlier errors, reduce the distance between our putative knowledge and the "real truth."

These conceptions of scientific progress are deficient in the same fundamental respect: all of them require for implementation the certification of an anchoring—direct or probabilistic—of our purported knowledge in the *terra firma* of "the real truth." When this condition is not fulfilled, the claim to progress cannot be justified. And this requirement simply cannot be met. With respect to all these approaches to the problem of progress we are simply not in a cognitive position to *implement* the claims to scientific progressivism articulated along the lines of drawing "nearer to the truth."

Little wonder, then, that virtually all contemporary schools of thought in the philosophy of science—Popperians, Carnapians, Pragmatists, etc.—have soured on attempts to establish *any direct relationship* of the products of scientific inquiry to "the truth." They refuse to see scientific claims as claims to "the actual truth of things" in some direct, non-Pickwickian sense. Unfortunately, however, the logical terminus of this approach is a cognitive scepticism that not only abandons the idea of scientific progress as such, but abolishes the very conception of science as a source of information about the world. Unhappily, a substantial sector of the contemporary epistemology of science has been moving in this very direction.

All this points towards the pivotal question: If one gives up the view that science somehow draws "closer to the truth" by way of cumulative addition or of successive approximation, does it then not become simply illegitimate—or question-begging—to speak of scientific or cognitive progress? Given our rejection of any of a whole host of seemingly plausible constructions of the "self-correctiveness" of science (ultimate arrival, successive approximation, continuous correction, probabilistic enhancement), the question arises: Can one salvage *any* aspect of the traditional thesis that science is "self-corrective" in some progressivistic sense?

Fortunately, the bleak prospect of a negative answer to this question can be averted. Notwithstanding the inadequacies of the preceding models of scientific progress, there yet remain good reasons for holding that science "draws nearer to the truth," and accordingly for maintaining the progressivist conception of scientific development. But the realization of this prospect requires a new point of departure.

4. THE SELF-CORRECTIVENESS OF SCIENCE AND THE FOUNDATIONS OF ITS CLAIMS TO COGNITIVE ADEQUACY

Let us begin by reconsidering the concept of "self-correctiveness." Think of this now as oriented not towards increased truthfulness, but rather simply as resting upon *increased refinement of the procedures and methods* used in the acceptability-screening processes for truth-candidates. And let us construe this in such a way that, at least in the first instance, the "improvement" at issue is not understood *directly*, in relation to the *truth of the theses* maintained by science, but *indirectly*, in relation simply to the *adequacy of its methods* for thesis-substantiation (say with reference to the comprehensiveness of the data or the sophistication of the procedures by which the *presumptive* truths at issue are validated).[9] On this view, the superior epistemic standing of a thesis does not reside (in the first instance) in the superiority of its content, but in the superiority of its probative method.

The implementation of this strategy takes the following form: the new methods adopted in the later stages of methodological evolution are (*ex hypothesi*) capable of accomplishing the work of the old (where the old were successful) and improving on it (by succeeding in some respect in which the old did not). Progress in the development of inquiry procedures thus arises when the new methods can encompass (and account for) strengths of the old, and add new ones off their own bat: when it can *dominate* the old ones at their own work, so to speak.

[9] Pascal was perhaps the first to view the progressiveness of science as residing in the first instance not in the enhanced truthfulness of its later claims, but in the constantly augmented data-base on which its later theses take their probative stand: "The experiments which give us an understanding of nature multiply continually. . .from whence it follows. . .that all men together make continual progress in them [sc. the sciences] as the universe grows older." (*Fragment d'un traité du vide,* quoted in Charles Frankel, "Progress, The Idea of" in *The Encylopedia of Philosophy,* ed. Paul Edwards, vol. 6, p. 484a).

With any inquiry procedure, "self-correctiveness" must be construed in a certain very special sense. As the Wheel Argument once more shows, one is not in a position to discover that the *results* (outputs) of using the procedure are wrong. At best we can be in a position to be put on our guard that there is "something amiss" because the inquiry procedure itself functions in such an anomalous way as to indicate this. Self-correctiveness thus comes down to a phenomenon of cyclic feedback—the capacity of an inquiry procedure to criticize at each given stage its workings at the earlier stages through which the present position was achieved. No inquiry procedure in the factual area can be such that when it produces a "wrong" result it will itself provide a means of finding this out and provide a "correct" (or "correcter"—i.e., *more* "correct") substitute. But *this sort of self-correctiveness* simply need not be at issue. Where inquiry procedures are concerned—and in particular defeasible ones—the issue need not be a matter or providing *truer* (or closer-to-truth) results, but a matter of providing *more adequately based* results.

But what is the nature of the "adequacy" at issue here? To be sure, systematic self-sustainingness and cyclic self-correctiveness are elements of adequacy that will have to be counted as merits in an inquiry procedure. Such aspects of internal coherence may be taken as *necessary* conditions of adequacy: one would certainly expect any satisfactory inquiry procedure to be self-sustaining and would view a failure in this regard as constituting a decisive defect. And various other purely theoretical factors also enter in—all of them in the sphere of theory-internal issues of systematic coherence (comprehensiveness, systematicity, simplicity, etc.). However, such theoretical factors, while undoubtedly representing positive assets of a method, are clearly not enough.

As we have seen, many very different inquiry procedures can readily prove adequate from *their own* standpoint. However, passing the muster of this sort of *self*-appraisal is clearly not enough to underwrite adequacy in the face of an externalized view of the realities of the matter. Apart from how it fares from its own *internal* standpoint, there remains the more "objective," duly externalized issue of the rational qualifications of the inquiry procedure. Room must be made for the operation of the *external* controls of a factor that is essentially disjoint from the realm of pure theory, viz., pragmatic efficacy.

We thus envisage a two-fold criteriology of cognitive adequacy (and *ergo* of scientific progress), namely the internal factor of systematization and the external factor of pragmatic efficacy. Yet while the theoretical factors of systematicity and comprehensiveness do figure indispensably as prime criteria of progress,[10] it must be said that the whole structure of our discussion underpins the claim that this second factor is no less crucial to rational legitimation. The two criteria are co-equal and coordinate in importance. (Both figure crucially in that "closing of the great circles of validation" of which we spoke in Chapter VII above.) It is here that we find the ultimate guarantors for the cognitive procedure we indeed employ in the factual domain—the scientific method.[11]

On this dualistic approach to cognitive legitimation, it appears that the superiority of the scientific framework does not revolve only—or even primarily— about theoretical considerations (such as that of explanatory adequacy, or—more broadly—considerations of coherence in general), but also and particularly about the pragmatic issues of *problem-solving* and *control*. It is ultimately in *this* regard—and thus not with respect to wholly theoretical considerations—that the scientific method is able to make good its claims to predominance. In the final analysis, the credentials of science derive from a suitable coordination of strictly practical with purely theoretical considerations. And any advance in adequacy in these regards on the part of methodology places the theses validated by these latter-day methods on a cognitively firmer basis of enhanced warrant.

[10] Underlying our present resort to a (never explicity articulated) concept of "the scientific method" as an inquiry procedure for the substantiation of factual claims is the position that this method is best articulated along the lines of a coherentist approach. A development and defense of this view is not needed for present purposes, since the position at issue at most rests implicit in the tacit background of our present deliberations and is never needed for the explicit development of the theory.

[11] It is almost (but not quite) needless to observe that in speaking of "the scientific method" of inquiry and thesis substantiation, we have no wish to deny the internal complexity of this methodology—that what is at issue is a diversified organon of methods and not one single all-enhancing method. The situation of mathematics provides an analogy. When one speaks of the probative method of mathematics as that of demonstrative proofs there is no wish to deny a pluralism of proof procedures (*reductio ad absurdum*, mathematical induction, etc., etc.).

5. THE COPERNICAN INVERSION AND THE ROLE OF PRESUMPTION

Any inquiry procedure whose operation is dependent upon the availability of *certified truths* as prior "givens" will, of course, inevitably be *incomplete*. For if the make-up of the inquiry procedure demands a prior basis of certified "givens" to yield materials for its own workings, then it is clearly not autonomous, but other-dependent in its reliance for exogenous inputs upon an external mechanism quite *outside* its own scope. An autonomous inquiry procedure cannot rely on extraneous "fixed points" to provide the fulcrum of an Archimedean lever. To be sure, a complete or autonomous inquiry procedure in the factual domain will also require "inputs" or "givens," but it must be in a position to criticize and question and reject them—they must fall *within* its scope rather than lie outside it. Only an inquiry procedure that views the status of its own inputs as provisional, acceptable merely *prima facie*—and so ultimately *defeasible*—can make claims to autonomy and systematic completeness. Such a procedure must be able to evaluate its inputs from its own resources. It must make room for *self*-criticism, since we must be able to turn the testing-processes of the inquiry procedure upon the starting-points of its own applications.

The autonomy of science means that it must be *self*-corrective —criticism and correction of scientific findings must come *from within*—through more scientific findings. The only viable reason for abandoning a view held on scientific grounds is going over to another one that is *also* held on scientific grounds. All "external" criticism is disqualified. Science is thus seen as "self-corrective" because it is autonomous: no *external* corrections can be accepted; any correction of scientific findings must (insofar as such correction is forthcoming at all) come as a result of further scientific inquiry. With an autonomous inquiry procedure such as the project of scientific inquiry—where external "quality control" (check on output) is impossible—one has to rest content with checks on systematic functioning (such as the controls of pragmatic efficacy at the methodological level). A cognitive methodology that is autonomous and defeasible will of its very nature be such that the "later" results *cannot be certified as truer* in some categorical or probabilistic manner.

This line of thought drives us towards a Kant-reminiscent "Copernican Inversion." Later findings do not rest on a superior methodological basis because they are "truer"; rather they must count as truer because they rest on a superior basis. In effect this Copernican Inversion proposes that we not judge a method of inquiry by the truth of its results, but rather judge the claims to truth of the results in terms of the merit of the method that produces them (assessing this merit by both internal [coherentist] and external [pragmatist] standards). We are not to evaluate an inquiry procedure by the truth of its results, but conversely, to assess the truthfulness of the results in terms of rational merits of the procedure (which merits are (1) internal, systematic, and coherentist, and (2) external, applicative, and pragmatist). With an *autonomous* inquiry procedure—where external "quality control" (check on output) is impossible—one has to rest content with checks on systematic functioning, including controls of pragmatic efficacy at the methodological level. The inversion at issue thus proceeds by *replacing* the direction of reasoning "demonstrably truer"→"worthier of acceptance" by a line of reasoning of an essentially *inverted* order: "better (i.e., more adequately) grounded"→"rationally more acceptance-worthy" →"presumptively truer." The direction of the reasoning thus does not proceed from "greater truth" to "more adequate warrant," but the very reverse. Precisely because the later stages of the application of our inquiry procedure are more fully developed and more fully warranted, we take the stance that it is *rational to view them as better qualified for endowment with the presumption of truth.*

On the standard, pre-Copernican, and seemingly most straight-forward view, an inquiry procedure is taken to acquire rational warrant on the basis of the truthfulness of its results. The reasoning is seen to proceed from "greater truthfulness" to "greater rational warrant," with truth as the independent variable and rational warrant for acceptance as the dependent variable in the linking equation between truth and warrant. But once we turn to our very mechanisms for determining where the truth may be taken to lie (which, in the factual area, is scientific inquiry), the matter can no longer be seen in this light. For one cannot avoid a vitiating circularity in seeking to validate the procedure in view through its capacity to lead to the truth, given that what is to count as true is to be determined by this very procedure itself. To be sure, the linking equation between truth and warrant need not be abandoned, but it must now be viewed in a very different light. For, at this stage, warrant must be seen as the independent variable and truthfulness as the dependent variable; and so, in consequence, it emerges that our inquiry procedures are not seen as warranted because truth-producing, but are presumed to be truth-producing because of their greater rational warrant. On this approach, it appears that to validate the propriety of an inquiry procedure in terms of its truthfulness is simply to pick up the wrong end of the stick: truthfulness should be seen as the output of warrant rather than its input—one does not approach warrant by way of truthfulness, but truthfulness by way of warrant.

Accordingly, there is no question here of denying the crucial fact that superior methodology is *correlative* with greater truthfulness. But the question is: which factor is the dog that wags and which the tail wagged? The inevitable implication of the Wheel Argument (*diallelus*) is that the proper view is *not* that one *possesses* a superior methodology thanks to the greater truthfulness of its results, *but rather* that their greater (presumptive) truthfulness derives from possession of a superior methodology (through the operation of a rational presumption connecting superior methodology with the rational warrant for truth-claims).

This line of approach calls for a shift of the center of gravity in regard to the issue of "self-correctiveness" away from *correction* as such to the enhanced methodological adequacy of our probative procedures. To characterize science as *self-corrective* in this sense is thus emphatically *not* to commit oneself to saying that science possesses methods that provide automatically effective cook-book procedures for finding alternative theories once the evidence in hand leads to a loss of trust in the existing ones. (And so the manner in which science is self-corrective does not help the scientist in his work—it does not afford him with any *devices* for replacing defective theories with more adequate ones.)

Our perspective postulates an effective reversal of the "natural" interpretation of the Hegelian dictum that the real is rational. This is now not so much a remark about the nature of the real, as one about the nature of cognitive rationality. The thesis is that we are warranted in our claims to truth (accuracy, correctness) in matters regarding reality insofar as these claims proceed from adequate methods of inquiry. The "real truth" is thus rational precisely in that it is determined through the output of a rationally warranted inquiry procedure.

6. COGNITIVE PROGRESS: ITS PRESUMPTIVE AND REGULATIVE ASPECT

Improvement in the warrant for claims to "scientific knowledge" is always possible, and it is in terms of such improvements that the idea of a "scientific progress" which leads "nearer to the truth" must be understood. Enhanced adequacy in the grounding of an inquiry procedure certainly does not *guarantee* a "closer approximation to the truth" for its deliverances. All one can say is that it is reasonable to *presume* the truth of the more adequately grounded alternative. This greater reasonableness of presumption neither guarantees nor requires actual correctness. The very fact of more adequate grounding is of itself enough for its establishment.

On the present view, scientific progress is not a process which (by its very nature) leads *directly* to a greater mastery of "the real truth." Rather the linkage moves *obliquely* along the following circuitous path:

(1) A more advanced and more fully developed application of an inquiry procedure leads (*ex hypothesi*) to more adequately based results.

(2) This provides a firmer rational basis for the step of *presuming* that the later results are true rather than the earlier ones.

Thus later applications do indeed—all our earlier counterargumentation notwithstanding—provide "truer" results than the earlier ones, but on the basis of *regulative* rather than *substantive* considerations (to use Kant's very useful distinction once more). That is, we adopt the stance that one does not here augment the stock of available truth through *assured possession*, but only through *reasonable presumption*.

The present theory thus interprets the issue of cognitive progress in the sciences by way of the route of rational presumption —rather than through any insistence upon the somehow enhanced correctness of later findings.[12] Given that we use science to determine where the truth lies in the domain of empirical fact, we cannot view the progress of science as a matter of successive approximation to an independently controllable fixed point, "the truth" located wholly outside the domain of scientific inquiry. When an inquiry procedure is autonomous and defeasible, then the linkage of the adequacy of the method to the truth of its products operates through the mediation of a rational presumption—a presumption whose rationality is underwritten ultimately by pragmatic considerations of increased success in the areas of predictive and manipulative control.

The present theory thus does not—and certainly need not—maintain that there is some sort of inevitable equivalence between

(1) the full set of implicit claims embraced within and consequent upon acceptance of a factual thesis that "*P* is true," and

(2) the (vastly lesser) set of data we must have in hand to claim with adequate rational warrant the factual thesis that "*P* is true."

There is a vast gulf fixed between the sum-total of the informational *content* of the thesis that "*P* is true" and the set of checks and balances within our reach of operative control in entering upon a *rationally warranted presumption* of *P*'s truth. An adequate basis of rational warrant stops well short of an unqualified guarantee.

William James—who recognized and emphasized this gap between the content of knowledge-claims and the evidence one has for them (this being the focus of his controversy with W. K. Clifford)—wrongly ascribed this difference solely to practical considerations, without recognizing that it holds at the *theoretical* (cognitive) level as well. Clifford (in "The Ethics of Belief"[13]) to all appearances flatly denies the difference between these levels in

---

[12] At just this point our evolutionary progressivism parts ways with the more traditional forms of the theory. Cf. for example, Herbert Spencer, *Principles of Sociology*, Vol. III, ch. VIII, "Intellectual Progress."

[13] In W. K. Clifford, *Lectures and Essays*, Vol. II (London, 1879).

his famous dictum that "It is wrong always, everywhere, and for everyone to believe anything upon insufficient evidence."[14] But Clifford's position is—as James rightly sees—ultimately indefensible, partly because of its tendency to stultify action, partly because his unrealistically rigoristic concept of the rationale of knowledge-claims leads to wholesale scepticism.[15] For in all contexts of factual inquiry, an "evidential gap" between the assertive content of our claims and the supporting data we have in hand for them is inevitable.

It is thus crucial for the workings of this ultimately regulative approach that in viewing science as *self-corrective* we do not maintain that later findings are somehow inherently "truer" than earlier ones by way of the actual-possession route to truth. However, our view of the nature of scientific progress emphatically does *not* call for *abandoning* the view that "science draws closer to the truth" in the course of its temporal development. It is a matter of just how this idea is to be construed. Clearly it must *not* be construed in some transcendent sense that places the locus of truth in an inaccessible realm to which all access is inherently precluded by the Wheel Argument (*diallelus*). Rather, the greater truthfulness of later claims is a matter of an increasingly more firmly rationally warranted presumption. It would be not necessarily *incorrect* but rather *rationally unconscionable* to give to the later results a lessened degree of credence.

Pierre Duhem, one of the founding fathers of present-day philosophy of science, recognized that no logically compelling grounds of general principle can be adduced on behalf of the contention that the development of science leads ever nearer to the "real relations among things" that define the objective order of nature. He wrote:

> Thus, physical theory never gives us the explanation of experimental laws . . . but the more complete it becomes, the more we apprehend that the logical order in which theory orders experimental laws is the reflection of an ontological order, the more

[14] *Ibid.*, p. 186. For the James-Clifford controversy and its wider background see Ralph B. Perry, *The Thought and Character of William James*, vol. 2 (Boston, 1935), pp. 245—8. For a contemporary treatment of the problem see Roderick Chisholm, "Lewis' Ethics of Belief," in *The Philosophy of C. I. Lewis* (La Salle, 1968).

[15] See pp. 42–7 above.

we suspect that the relations it establishes among the data of observation correspond to real relations among things. . . . The physicist cannot take account of this conviction. . . . But while the physicist is powerless to justify this conviction, he is nonetheless powerless to rid his reason of it. . . . Yielding to an intuition which Pascal would have recognized as one of those reasons of the heart "that reason does not know," he asserts his faith in a real order reflected in his theories more clearly and more faithfully as times goes on.[16]

However, Duhem's stance that the purported "advance towards truth" implicit in scientific development rests on some sort of metaphysical *faith* concedes too much to the demands of the sceptical rationalist opponent, who would surely regard this as hoisting the white flag of surrender. Fortunately, this resort to faith is unduly pessimistic. To be sure, the claims to progress in the sciences cannot be endowed with some *independent* demonstration at the strictly *theoretical* level of the greater truthfulness of later findings. But a pragmatically oriented line of rational legitimation can be deployed to provide the sort of extra-theoretical warrant that the circumstances of the case require.

7. SCIENTIFIC PROGRESS AND THE PROBLEM OF CONTINUITY

Some recent writers on the philosophy of science, influenced by the doctrines of Thomas Kuhn's influential book on scientific revolutions,[17] tend to stress the discontinuities produced by innovation in the history of science.[18] Scientific change, they rightly maintain, is not a matter of marginal revisions of opinion within a fixed and stable framework of concepts. The crucial develop-

[16] Pierre Duhem, *The Aim and Structure of Physical Theory*, tr. by P. P. Wiener (New York, 1962), pp. 26–7.

[17] *The Structure of Scientific Revolutions* (Chicago, 1962; 2nd ed., 1970). See also I. Lakatos and A. Musgrave (eds), *Criticism and the Growth of Knowledge* (Cambridge, 1970).

[18] The prime exponent here is Paul Feyerabend. See his essays: "Explanation, Reduction, and Empiricism" in Herbert Feigl and Grover Maxwell (eds), *Minnesota Studies in the Philosophy of Science*, Vol. III (Minneapolis, 1962); "Problems of Empiricism" in R. G. Colodny (ed.), *Beyond the Edge of Certainty* (Englewood Cliffs, 1965), pp. 144–260; and "On the 'Meaning' of Scientific Terms," *The Journal of Philosophy*, vol. 62 (1965), pp. 266–74.

ments involve a change in the conceptual apparatus itself. And when this happens there is a replacement of the very *content* of discussion, a shift in "what's being talked about" which renders successive positions "incommensurable." The change from the Newtonian to the Einsteinian concept of time, for example, represents a meaning-shift of just this sort. And such discontinuities of meaning make it impossible (so it is said) to say justifiedly that the latter stages represents a somehow "better treatment of the same subject-matter," since the very subject that is at issue at the later stage has become something different.

Such a theory of a radical discontinuity of meaning-shifts seems to throw the very concept of progress in science into question. For if the later stage of discussion is conceptually disjoint from the earlier how could one consider the later as constituting an improvement upon the earlier? The replacement of one thing by something else of a totally different sort can hardly qualify as ameliorative. (One can improve upon one's car by getting another, better car, but cannot improve upon it by getting a dishwashing machine.)

To draw this sort of implication from the meaning-shift thesis is, however, to take an unduly literary view of science. For at bottom the progress at issue does not proceed along theoretical but along practical lines. Once one sees the legitimation of science to lie ultimately in the sphere of its applications, the progress of science will be taken to center on its pragmatic aspect—the increasing success of applications in problem solving and control.

The traditional theories of scientific progress join in stressing the capacity of the "improved" theories to accommodate new facts. Agreeing with the emphasis on "new facts," it is, however, important to recognize two distinct routes to this destination:

1. *The Predictive Route*

$$\text{Research Program} \rightarrow \text{Theory} \xrightarrow{\text{prediction}} \text{New Facts}$$

2. *The Productive Route*

$$\text{Research Program} \rightarrow \text{Technology} \xrightarrow{\text{production}} \text{New Facts}$$

And it would appear proper to allow *both* of these routes, the predictive and the productive, to count as capable of building up the sort of credit at issue in evaluating the success of scientific research programs. To correct the overly literary bias of the purely *theoretical* stress of traditional philosophy of science requires a more ample recognition of the role of technology-cum-production. To say this is not, of course, to deny for one moment that the two (theory and technology) stand in a symbiotic and mutually supportive relationship in scientific inquiry. *Both* theoretical *and* applicative/experimental achievements must be allowed to count in assessing the success and viability of research programs.

Moreover, it is significant here that these applications are in large measure operative at the level of the ordinary, everyday concepts of natural-language discourse, concepts that remain relatively fixed throughout the ages, and that afford a stable element of intellectual continuity which lies deep behind the changing sophistication of scientific discussion. The ancient Greek physician and the modern medical practitioner might talk of the problems of their patients in very different and conceptually incommensurate ways (say an imbalance in humors to be treated by countervailing changes in diet or regiment vs. a bacterial infection to be treated by administering an antibiotic). But at the pragmatic level of control—i.e., a removal of those symptoms of their patients (pain, fever, dizziness, etc.) that are describable in much the same terms in antiquity as today—both are working on "the same problem."

We thus envisage a *complex* criterion of merit which stresses the technological/productive side of inquiry in natural science. And this introduction upon the stage of consideration of the technological sector as supplementary or complementary to the theoretical has far-reaching ramifications. The question of *technological* superiority (i.e., our ability at a given state-of-the-art level to obtain desired results—never mind for the moment if they are desirable or not) is something far less sophisticated, but also far more manageable, than the issue of *theoretical* superiority. The assessment of *technical* superiority is relatively easy *vis-à-vis* that of *theoretical* superiority, because the issues involved function at a grosser and more rough-and-ready level than those of theoretical meaning-content. At the level of praxis we can operate to a relatively large degree with the *lingua franca* of everyday affairs and make our comparisons on this basis—we need not worry about the problems of theory-comparison induced by the inaccessibility of a theory-neutral perspective for appraising "incommeasurable" theories. Just as the merest novice can detect a false note in the musical performance of a master player whose activities he could not begin to emulate, so malfunctioning of a missile or computer can be detected by the relative amateur. Dominance in technological power to produce intended results tends to operate across the board. (The superiority of modern over Galenic medicine requires few if any subtle distinctions of respect.) And technical progress tends to have a degree of continuity that the drastic trimmings of theoretical progress lack. The introduction of the technological aspect thus makes for a *practical* (i.e., *praxis*-oriented) standard of progressiveness that is vastly easier to implement than a standard which requires the comparative appraisal of the capacity of theories to accommodate—and so to receive support from—theory-laden "facts" whose capacity to serve in trans-theoretical comparisons is, to put it mildly, problematic.

On such a view, the technological and applicative aspect of science thus plays the pivotally determinative role in the assessment of "progress." The capacity of the theoretical science implicit in a certain technology of application to provide us with a more sophisticated means of "leaping the hurdles" of nature is the mark of its adequacy. Its claims to acceptability accordingly invoke no question-begging appeal to the superiority of the conceptual or theoretical framework of this body of science. The effectiveness of the technological instrumentalities of *praxis* can clearly be assessed in the absence of any invocation of the cognitive meaning-content of the body of theory brought to bear in their devising.

This pragmatic dimension endows science with the continuity it may well lack at the contextual level of the technical machinery of its ideas and concepts—a continuity that finds its expression in the persistence of problem-solving tasks in the sphere of *praxis*. Nor does such recourse to the continuity of our practical problems deny that these can themselves develop in point of complexity and sophistication in the wake of technological progress. But practical problems remain structurally invariant. The sending of messages is just that whether horse-carried letters or laser beams are used in transmitting the information. Often, the crude, molar aspects of the products of the *application* of scientific knowledge suffice for assessing the extent of its pragmatic efficacy.

Thus despite any *semantic* or *ideational incommensurability* between a scientific theory and its latter-day replacements, there remains the crucial *pragmatic commensurability* of a constellation of problem-solving tasks that can (by and large) be formulated in the ordinary everyday language that antedates scientific sophistication. The fundamentally pragmatic aspect of its applications in problem-solving and control at the level of everyday life manifests those continuities of the scientific enterprise with reference to which the idea of progress can be invoked.[19] And in this way, the applicative and technological dimension of scientific progress can be assessed comparatively—without any explicit reference to the semantical content of scientific theories or the conceptual framework used in their articulation. When the "external" element of *control over nature* is given its due prominence, the substantiation of imputations of scientific *progress* becomes a more manageable project than it could ever possibly be on an "internal," content-oriented basis.

[19] On this approach it is easy to account for the contrast between the growth of consensus in science and the cumulative progressivism of the enterprise on the one hand, and on the other the endless disagreements regarding questions of philosophy, ethics, or religion. The difference lies precisely in this, that the latter fields are less subject to the controls of pragmatic efficacy.

Chapter XI

THE LEGITIMACY OF DEFEASIBLE KNOWLEDGE

1. DEFEASIBILITY AND THE ROLE OF PRESUMPTION

The preceding chapter dwelt upon the self-correctiveness of the scientific method as a rational inquiry procedure in the factual domain. It maintained the defeasibility of our scientific knowledge—the fact that the corpus of science is everywhere open not merely to *addenda* but to *corrigenda* as well. A fallibilistic view of scientific inquiry is indicated.

An element of *putativity* or *presumption* will thus always be present with any inquiry procedure whose findings are inherently defeasible. As long as defeasibility is operative, there can be no absolute and inevitable rational *constraint* to acceptance. Since the procedure does not—*ex hypothesi*—yield certified and irrevocable truths, a suspension of judgment always remains a viable alternative in the face of defeasibility. The most such a defeasible rational inquiry procedure can accomplish is to determine what one *should* accept IF one is minded to accept anything at all in the circumstances of the case. Its incapacity to produce unconditionally and unqualifiedly certified truths means that its products are to be regarded in the light of *putative* or merely *presumptive* truths. (A claim to truth may, of course, be reasonably and warrantedly advanced in circumstances where an altogether definitive rational *guarantee* of truth may yet not be forthcoming.)

The epistemic situation in our factual context has the already familiar structure of an input-output process as pictured in Figure 1.

Figure 1

INQUIRY AS A PRODUCTIVE PROCESS

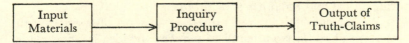

| Input Materials | → | Inquiry Procedure | → | Output of Truth-Claims |

The inputs are not validated truths but mere "data" of some degree of presumptive plausibility; the outputs are procedurally-validated truth-claims—i.e., putative truths. What is at issue is not a matter of *ex nihilo* production, but one of status-upgrading in the epistemic scheme of things. And this linear picture is itself misleading, because what is actually at issue is an iterative repetition of this sequence—a series of repetitions which endow the over-all process with an essentially cyclical structure, with the "last" compartment providing a feedback into the "first." The outputs thus serve as one among several controlling factors in the validation of the inputs as appropriate to the cognitive enterprise in hand. Accordingly, the overall process is a "cycle of revalidation" of the feedback-circuit type to which we have referred again and again in the previous discussion. Throughout this cycle we are never able to eliminate altogether the aspect of presumptiveness that still adheres to the inputs at every stage. And because the process never reaches any theoretically ultimate termination —but comes to an end only on the essentially practical ground that cost-benefit considerations indicate the futility of its continuation—we are never able to shake off an element of presumptiveness in a theoretically decisive way. Some degree of presumption (however small) attaches to our procedurally validated truths throughout this factual area where defeasibility is inherently operative. Our truth-claims must here remain defeasible in theory (if not in practice), and the theoretical line between "*our presumptive* truth" and what is, on some absolute plane, "*the real* truth" must be recognized.

There is, of course, no blinking at the fact that "*P* is *presumptively* true" does not *mean* "*P* is true." With presumption as with assertion there remains the "gap of commitment" between the thesis itself and the stance that some subscribing person or persons take towards it. With "It is *presumptively* the case that *P* is true," as with "It is *actually* the case that *P* is true," the relevant claim of *P*'s truth remains invariant: the content of the claim remains unaltered—it is its *status* that is alone affected. The *thesis* at issue that-*P*-is-true is the same, but is maintained in a somewhat different epistemic tone of voice: in the one case categorical and the other presumptive.

We are emphatically not proposing any sort of revision in the concept of *truth*. No attempt to *redefine* the idea is being made:

its meaning continues to stand where it always has—truth remains correspondence *ad rem*: "'*P*' is true" amounts to "It is actually the case that *P*." It is in this sense that truth-claims must be construed. A claim to truth—even one that is advanced hesitatingly and provisionally—is still just that, namely a claim to *truth. It is altogether wrong to equate a tentative claim to truth with a claim to tentative truth!* They are every bit as different as a hesitant confession of wrongdoing differs from a confession of hesitant wrongdoing. The fact that a claim to truth is provisional does not render it a claim to provisional truth.

There is thus no need whatever to take the view that a fallibilistic approach casts the idea of truth in a merely regulative role as governing only the ultimate aims of inquiry without any relevance to the here-and-now.[1] Defeasibility relates to the epistemic status of truth-claims, not to their nature as being perfectly authentic claims *to truth.* The concept of truth continues prominently operative: it is not abrogated by taking the view that truth-claims are put forward in a way recognized as ultimately tinged with some touch of provisionality.[2]

2. KNOWLEDGE CLAIMS AND THE ISSUE OF CERTAINTY

On such a fallibilistic epistemology of science, all claims to knowledge in the factual area are inherently defeasible. This poses difficulties that must be examined. We must face the question of whether defeasible knowledge, in which some element of presumption is inevitably present, can ever really deserve the proud title of *knowledge.* Since the time of Descartes absolute *certainty* has been hailed as the very hallmark of knowledge. Whatever is

---

[1] Peirce sometimes inclines in the direction of this view, and K. R. Popper accepts it outright. See his *Objective Knowledge* (Oxford, 1972), pp. 29–30.

[2] This section and the next one draw on the author's paper "The Illegitimacy of Cartesian Doubt," first published in *The Review of Metaphysics*, vol. 13 (1959), pp. 226–34 and reprinted with some revisions in *Essays in Philosophical Analysis* (Pittsburgh, 1969). For an interesting treatment of cognate issues see Robert Almeder, "Fallibilism and the Ultimate Irreversible Opinion" in N. Rescher (ed.), *Essays in the Theory of Knowledge* (Oxford, 1975; *American Philosophical Quarterly* Monograph, no. 9), pp. 33–54.

genuinely known must, so it is said, be certain. Indeed many philosophers would unhesitatingly maintain that the very idea of "fallible knowledge" is self-inconsistent—a contradiction in terms.

It is often pointed out "I know that P, but I may be mistaken" or "I know that P is the case, but it may possibly not be so" are self-contradicting statements whose first part gives something the second takes away. The complex thesis that X knows that P undeniably claims or concedes (*inter alia*) that the component thesis P is true, that what it asserts is the case. And so the further contention that this may well not be so cannot consistently be appended: it not simply qualifies but *negates* what has gone before. Accordingly, it is contended that the fallibilist who, following Peirce, is prepared to tolerate (or even insist upon) the claim that our knowledge is provisional—and so accepts the idea of potentially corrigible knowledge—is forced into occupying an untenable position. For he seemingly construes "knowledge" in such a way that the truth—nay the *certainty*—of P is not a necessary condition for knowing that P. This flies in the face of one of the very few points upon which *everyone* who has entered the lists of discussion in this area is agreed, namely that knowledge must be true and that one cannot be said to *know* something false.

The line of argumentation that is deployed here can be sketched roughly as follows:

The proposition "P is true" is to be regarded as a logical consequence of the proposition "I know (or X knows) that P". To say "I know that P" is to *claim* (*inter alia*) *that P*, and to say that "X knows that P" is to *concede* the correctness of this claim. And going beyond the implicit claim that P, the proposition "X knows that P" also claims (1) that X accepts P as certain, and (2) that X has adequate rational warrant for this acceptance. These observations establish the close link between knowledge and certainty. A claim to knowledge is a claim to certainty. It would make no sense to say (of oneself or another) that "X knows that P but he regards it as in some way doubtful whether or not P is the case." By their very nature knowledge-claims purport to be infallibly correct. The very idea of "defeasible knowledge" is not viable because it embodies an inner inconsistency.

Given these considerations, the objection is pressed that fallibilism opens the door to scepticism through the following form of argument:

(1) Fallibilism holds all our claims to factual knowledge to be defeasible.
(2) Now a defeasible claim is one that might have to be withdrawn, that is, one which is not altogether certain.
(3) But anything deserving of the name "knowledge" cannot fail to be certain: what is not really known for certain is not really known at all.

Therefore the attainment of factual knowledge is in principle impossible on the basis of a fallibilist position.

These considerations pose the fundamental problem with which any fallibilist theory of knowledge must grapple, that of reconciling claims to knowledge with a concession of even *possible* falsity. Any such theory of factual knowledge (be it inductivistic, probabilistic or coherentistic) faces the complaint that what it affords us is not "real" knowledge because what is known must be certain and it can provide no guarantee of certainty. Given the presently operative contention that what we take to be "our knowledge" results from a fallible methodological process, it becomes necessary to face up to the problem of calling something *knowledge* that is potentially defeasible.

But surely something's *being certain—or even true*—in fact just is not a necessary precondition for a rationally warranted claim to knowledge. Let us look more closely at the line of reasoning which delineates the difficulty. Consider the inference:

If—it is possible that P is false,
Then—no one can be justified in being certain of P.

This inference involves a fallacy. The *possible* falsehood of a proposition P constitutes grounds against one's being certain of P only for a person who has some information about this possible falsity, someone who is in actual possession of some evidence for it. The missing factor which underlies this inference, whose absence vitiates its correctness, is the element of evidence or information. Only for a person who possesses some indication of it can the merely possible falsehood of P serve as a ground for doubt.

This point can be brought out even more clearly by comparison with the analogous inference:

If—P is false,
Then—no one can be justified in holding that *P*.

Here again, and quite obviously, information as to the falsity of *P* (or at least awareness of some evidence for it) is a necessary presupposition for the correctness of the inference regarding justification. Only when evidence for the actual—or probable or prospective—falsity of *P* is *recognized* by a person, can this presumptive objective falsity serve as an operative factor which militates against *his* accepting, believing, or being certain of *P* (given that all the indications at his disposal conspire to point emphatically in that direction).

Consider the propositions:

P is justifiably held by *X* to be true.
P is true.

Does the first entail or require the second? Surely not. For the evidence-in-hand that suffices to justify someone in holding a thesis to be true need not provide a *deductive* guarantee of this thesis. And a strictly analogous situation obtains with the pair:

P is justifiably held by *X* to be certain.
P is certain.

Again, the first proposition does not entail or require the second. The standard gap between the epistemic issue of what someone justifiably holds to be and the ontological issue of what is again comes into the picture. One must be willing to admit in general the existence of a gap between *warranted assertability* and ultimate *correctness*, holding that on occasion even incorrect theses can be maintained with due warrant. And there is no decisive reason for blocking the application of this general rule to knowledge claims in particular.

Accordingly, we must distinguish between the two cases of:

(i)   warrant for a claim-to-be-certainly-true regarding *P*
(ii)   certainty-guaranteeing warrant for a claim-to-be-true regarding *P*

There is no room for degrees in the second case: once a warrant is conclusive that's simply that. But with warrant *per se* the case is different. The fallibilist thus does not want to drive certainty out of the arena of knowledge. He simply has his own views as to where it enters in.

The person who views a knowledge-claim as defeasible must be prepared to contemplate *in abstracto* the general prospect that a totally justified knowledge-claim may in the end actually be defeated (however much he may incline, in given cases, to exclude this prospect from the realm of "practical politics"). And of course, when a claim to knowledge is defeated, it must be withdrawn. But its *ultimate* failure does not show that the claim was not warranted in the first place.

Philosophers have often felt driven to a conception of knowledge so rigid that it results that there is little if anything left that one can ever be said to know. Thinkers of this inclination launch upon an explication of "the nature of knowledge" which sets the standards of its attainment so high that it becomes in principle impossible for anything to meet such hyperbolic demands.[3] Against this tendency it is proper to insist that while what is known must certainly be true, a doctrine that sees our claims to knowledge as *in principle* defeasible can nevertheless quite properly insist that there are circumstances in which claims to certainty are perfectly legitimate and justified.

Does such a concession that knowledge-claims are defeasible— that they are not certain and might (in conceivable circumstances) have to be withdrawn—not make it inadmissible or improper to invoke the sacred name of *Truth* in this connection? Is not the defeasibility doctrine tantamount to a confession that actual truth lies beyond our grasp and that one must speak instead of probabilities and conjectures? Not at all.

It is unquestionably correct to say that we cannot be said to *know* something to be that *is* not so. But we can assuredly have an adequate rational basis for a claim to knowledge even in cases when that claim proves insufficient in the final analysis because "we did not *really* know what we justifiably took ourselves to know." Here, as elsewhere, there is the familiar and inevitable gulf between one's *justifiedly taking* something to be so and its *actually being so.* A. J. Ayer has put this point in his characteristically trenchant way:

[3] For example, in Carnapian inductivism no factual theses of general content can ever be confirmed.

> But to allow that there are times when we may justifiably claim the right to be sure of the truth of . . . [a] statement is not to allow that . . . [we] are infallible. One is conceded the right to be sure when one is judged to have taken every reasonable step towards making sure: but this is still logically consistent with one's being in error. The discover of the error refutes the claim to knowledge; but it does not prove that the claim was not, in the circumstances, legitimately made. The claim to know . . . [a] statement is satisfied only if the statement is true; but it is legitimate if it has the appropriate backing. . . .[4]

The thesis that knowledge must be certain cries out for critical scrutiny and analysis in the light of these considerations. For "certainty" here must *not* be construed to mean "derived by infallible processes from theoretically unassailable premisses"; one is surely justified in "being certain" in circumstances that do not *logically* preclude any possibility of error. The operative mode of "certainty" here is not some absolutistic sense of logical infallibility. It is impossible to give too heavy emphasis to the crucial fact that to say of a thesis that it "is certain" is to say no more than *it is as certain as, in the nature of the case, a thesis of this sort reasonably could be.* It does not preclude *any* possibility of error, but any *real* or *genuine* possibility of error.

A closely analogous analysis must be made of the thesis that knowledge precludes any possibility of mistake. It is not any "logical" or "merely theoretical" prospect of mistake that is excluded, but any *real* possibility of being mistaken. This distinction between *absolute* and *real* possibilities of error is reflected in a parallel distinction between what might be termed *categorical* certainty on the one hand and *practical* or *effective* certainty on the other. The operative idea here is that of taking "every proper safeguard" or of doing "everything that can reasonably be asked" to assure the claim at issue. The evidential basis for effective certainty need not be "all the evidence there conceivably might be," but simply "all the evidence that might reasonably be asked for." On this approach, a stage could be reached when, even though further evidence might possibly be accumulated, there is *no reason* to think that further accumulation might be fruitful and *no reason* to believe that additional evidence might

[4] *The Problem of Knowledge* (London, 1956), pp. 43–4.

alter the situation. And by "reason" here we must understand not some synoptic, wholesale, across-the-board consideration of the sort favored by sceptics since antiquity, but case-specific considerations that bear in a definite and *ad hoc* way upon the particular case in hand.

A claim to knowledge extends an assurance that all due care and caution has been exercised to assure that any *real* possibility of error can be written off: it issues a guarantee that every proper safeguard has beeen exercised. Exactly this is the reason why the statement "I know *P*, but might be mistaken" is self-inconsistent. For the man who claims to know that *P* thereby issues a guarantee which the qualification "but I might be mistaken" effectively revokes. What is established by the self-defeating nature of locutions of the type of "I know that *P* but *might* well be wrong" is thus *not* that knowledge is inherently indefeasible, but simply that knowledge-claims offer guarantees and assurances so strong as to preempt any safeguarding qualifications: they preclude abridgment of the sort at issue in protective clauses like "I might well be wrong."

3. THE TENABILITY OF COGNITIVE FALLIBILISM

The thesis "*X* knows *P*" must be interpreted as claiming, among other things, that "*X* correctly accepts *P* as true, and does so on grounds that are in fact sufficient." An ambiguity is present here, as indicated by the question: Sufficient for what? Two alternatives are open, for "sufficient" might mean either:

(1) sufficient to establish *P* with absolute certainty (even beyond any merely theoretical prospect of error), or
(2) sufficient to provide rational warrant for the claim that *P* is certain.

The fallibilist approach must reject claims of type (1) in the domain of contingent fact, and there is no reason why it cannot do so. For it is in a position to trade upon the crucial difference between

(1) a *deductive* argument moving by unfailing processes of inference to the conclusion *P* from unassailable premisses,

with the result that one can claim that this conclusion, P, is absolutely certain

(2) a *nondeductive* argument moving to the conclusion "P is certain" from adequately secure premises, by an ampliative and evidential (and so not necessarily unfailing) process of inference.

In the former case, one demonstrates that-P with certainty; in the latter, one achieves *effective* or *practical* certainty by establishing with adequate (albeit not necessarily theoretically decisive) warrant that-P-is-certain. In cases of the second type, one obtains a *rational warrant* for claiming certainty short of requiring a theoretically failproof *demonstration*.

A fallibilist theory of knowledge accordingly stresses and exploits the crucial distinction between what is certain as such, and what is justifiably and warrantedly held to be so. It insists that a realization of fallibility-in-general—while indeed precluding *proofs or demonstrations* of certainty as such—does not preclude (in appropriate special cases) *the providing of rational warrant* for claims to certainty. Such an epistemology maintains that suitable considerations can provide a solid probative basis for a rationally tenable claim that something is certain.[5] But the fact that someone is so *warranted* in advancing claims to knowledge and certainty does not mean that he cannot possibly be mistaken—that a theoretically failproof guarantee against the possibility of error can be issued. It is ill-advised to fly in the face of the fact that there is here, in the case of certainty-claims (as elsewhere), a gap between the content of a duly warranted claim and the evidential base we have in hand for its support.

In cases where the evidential indications are strong enough, the burden of rationality shifts against the side of skeptical disbelief, precisely because the range of rational warrant inevitably outstrips that of demonstrative proof. To say "I know" or "He knows" is to claim or concede knowledge. Here, as with any other factual thesis that stakes a claim which—at least in principle— goes partially beyond the evidence, the claim that is staked may

---

[5] It should go without saying that what is at issue throughout this discussion of certainty is not psychologico/biographical, person-oriented claims of the type "I am certain of P" but epistemologico/ontological impersonally fact-oriented claims of the type "It is certain that P."

have to be withdrawn. To assert this claim in the strong language of "knowledge" is indeed to say that it is "inconceivable" that the claim would have to be withdrawn. But this inconceivability is not of a *theoretical* but of a *practical* nature. The fallibilist holds that a perfectly justified knowledge-claim may prove wrong, but yet that—recognizing and conceding this—one may be entirely justified in insisting that *in this case* such a theoretical prospect can reasonably be put aside.

Theoretical fallibilism at the level of an epistemological theory of defeasibility thus does not create a basis for doubt at the concrete level of particular situations. In suitable circumstances, case-specific considerations may well indicate that it would be quixotic to hold that there is still "room for doubt." Once everything that realistically *need* be done *has* been done in a particular case of claim-substantiation, it becomes not only unrealistic but *unreasonable* to ask for further assurances. Thus a fallibilism at the theoretical, abstract, and generic level of epistemological theory is perfectly compatible with an unabashedly cognitivistic stance at the practical, concrete, and particularized level of specific claims.[6]

4. SUMMARY

The three key points to emerge from this discussion are:

(1) A knowledge-claim of the type "I know that *P*" is just that: a claim. As with other claims, its *substance* may well go beyond the warranting *evidence-in-hand* for making it, and may do so without transcending the bounds of the reasonable.

(2) The *certainty* at issue in knowledge-claims is not absolute: it is simply that the evidence in hand is good enough to render the need for further substantiation dispensable, because it suffices to give every reasonable assurance that the thing at issue is as certain as anything of its sort possibly can be.

[6] This was also the position of Peirce. See David Savan, "Peirce's Fallibilism," *Studies in the Philosophy of Charles Sanders Peirce*, ed. by E. C. Moore and R. S. Robin (Amherst, 1964), pp. 190–211 (see especially p. 205).

(3) The sort of "possibility of mistake" that a knowledge claim proposes to exclude is not a possibility in the absolutistic sense of what is hypothetically possible from the merely conjectural point of view. It is not the *remote* possibility of purely theoretical considerations of the "merely logical" sort, but a *real* or *genuine* possibility relative to the practicalities operative in the circumstances.

The last of these points is crucial. To be sure, certainty is correlative with the "impossibility" of being mistaken, construed in some suitable sense. But this impossibility is not, in our present context, a matter of the lack of any hypothetical room for error. Rather, it relates to the absence of any and all substantively specific reasons to think that whatever formally generic prospect of error there may indeed be is presently realized. It is denied that the merely generic possibility poses a prospect which need genuinely concern us under the circumstances of the case in hand. A fallibilist epistemology maintains an ever-present possibility of error at the *theoretical* level of abstract conceivability—it need not deny that a *real* possibility of error can in many cases be excluded from the sphere of what might be called the "practical politics" of the matter.

The issues of defeasibility, fallibilism, and certainty have been dealt with in the present chapter in such a way as to block the objection that fallibilism inexorably brings scepticism in its wake. But the methodologically pragmatic approach to the validation of knowledge opens the way to a still more far-reaching critique of scepticism. Its development calls for a new chapter.

Chapter XII

A REBUTTAL OF SCEPTICISM

Time and again throughout these pages, the idea of the provisional "acceptance" of claims on a merely presumptive basis has been invoked as a central element of argumentation. The moment has come to take a closer look at this idea, its originative setting, and its theoretical ramifications. This exploration is particularly apposite now, because the concept of presumption is a crucial device in enabling us to cope with the sceptical tendencies of thought that surfaced in the preceding chapter.

I. Burden of Proof

1. THE LEGAL ASPECT

The idea of "burden of proof" (*onus probandi*) is at root a legal concept. It relates to an adversary proceeding where one party is endeavoring to establish and another to rebut some charge (involving guilt, responsibility, default, etc.) before a neutral adjudicative tribunal. The very phrase (*onus probandi*) derives from classical Roman law. The idea deals with the ground-rules of probative procedure, specifically the division of the labor of argumentation between plaintiff and defendant, providing a specification of tasks in terms of who is supposed to do what with respect to the marshalling of evidence. Under the Roman system, nothing was conceded in legal actions as admitted: the plaintiff, as the initiating agent in laying a charge, had his case to make out first (*agenti incumbit probatio*) and if this did not fail, the defendant's counter-case was argued on his *exceptio,* then again the plaintiff's on his *replicatio*, and so on. The burden rested with the plaintiff in civil cases and with the state (as surrogate plaintiff) in criminal cases. Throughout, the "burden of proof" lay with the side active in making the allegations—conformably to the fundamental rule: *necessitas probandi incumbit ei qui dicit non ei qui negat.*[1]

Various aspects of Anglo-American legal procedure derive from this conception. The principle that the accused is "innocent until proven guilty" is, in effect, a straightforward device for allocating the burden of proof. And the "Scots verdict" of *not proven* affords a way of saying that the burden has been discharged in part—sufficiently for the correlative presumption (of innocence) to come to an end, without, however, an actual proof of guilt having been formally established.

The idea of burden of proof is interlocked with that of evidence. The concept articulates a basic rule of the evidential game. To say that the burden of proof rests with a certain side is to say that it is up to it to bring in the evidence to make out its case. Thus in the face of the presumption of innocence the prosecution is, in criminal law, obliged to present to the court at least a *prima facie* case for maintaining the guilt of the accused. This is to be accomplished by presenting evidence which is sufficient to show the guilt of the accused in the absence of appropriate counter-evidence. Thus in California, a level of blood alcohol in excess of 1/10th percent (as indicated by a blood or breath test administered to a driver at the scene of an arrest) is considered *prima facie* evidence of driving while intoxicated. But, of course, the development of such a *prima facie* case is capable of rebuttal by the deployment of further evidence (e.g., its being shown that the inebriated person was merely a passenger of the vehicle, not its operator).[2]

This sketch points towards a fact which careful students of the matter have long realized, viz., that there are really two distinct albeit related conceptions of "burden of proof":

(1) The *burden of an initiating assertion* (I-burden of proof). The basic rule is: "Whichever side initiates the assertion of a thesis within the dialectical situation has the burden of supporting it in argument." The champion of a thesis

---

[1] Sir Courtenay Peregrine Ilbert, art. "Evidence," *Encyclopaedia Britannica* (11th ed.), vol. 10, pp. 11–21 (see p. 15).

[2] For a clear and comprehensive exposition of the legal issues see Richard A. Epstein, "Pleadings and Presumptions," *The University of Chicago Law Review*, vol. 40 (1974), pp. 556–82.

—like the champion of a medieval joust—must be prepared to maintain his side in the face of the opposing challenges. This burden of *agenti incumbit probatio* remains constant throughout.

(2) The *burden of further reply in the face of contrary evidence* (E-burden of proof). Whenever a counter-argument of suitably weighty evidential bearing has been given, this argument may be taken as standing provisionally until some sufficient reply has been made against it in turn. Thus the opponent of any contention—be it an assertion or a denial—always has the "burden of further reply." This "burden of going forward with evidence," as it is sometimes called may shift from side to side as the dialectic of controversy proceeds.

One authority has put the matter as follows:

> In modern law the phrase "burden of proof" may mean one of two things, which are often confused—the burden of establishing the proposition or issue on which the case depends, and the burden of producing evidence on any particular point either at the beginning or at a later stage of the case. The burden in the former sense ordinarily rests on the plaintiff or prosecutor. The burden in the latter sense, that of going forward with evidence on a particular point, may shift from side to side as the case proceeds. The general rule is that he who alleges a fact must prove it, whether the allegation is couched in affirmative or negative terms.[3]

This formulation neatly summarizes the two basic modes of burden of proof. The former mode (I-burden) is static and rests with the inaugurating side constantly and throughout; the latter (E-burden) is subject to the idea that a suitably weighty amount of evidence can, as it were, succeed in *shifting* the burden from one side to the other as the course of argumentation proceeds. The role of *presumptions* also emerges more clearly in this context. They indicate at just which points counter-evidence is called for—the exact positions at which the E-burden ceases to bear upon a contending party.

[3] Sir Courtenay Ilbert, *op. cit.*

2. THE DISPUTATIONAL ASPECT

A major development in the history of the conception of burden of proof occurred with its shift from a legal to a scholastic setting. The formal disputation was one of the major training and examining devices in academic instruction in the middle ages in all four faculties, arts, medicine, and theology, as well as law. The procedure of disputation, of course, has substantial analogy with the confrontation process of a law-court: a formal disputation was closely akin to a trial both in setting (the *aula* was set up much as a courtroom) and in structure. It was presided over by a "determiner," the supervising *magister* who also "determined" it—that is, summarized its results and ruled on the issue under dispute (*quaestio disputata*), exactly as with the verdict of the judge in a law-court.[4] The disputant was faced by a specifically appointed respondent (*respondens*), who, like a prosecuting attorney, attempted to reply to his points (*respondere de quaestione*).[5]

Here again there must be general rules to fix the burden of proof between proponent (*proponens*) and opposing respondent (*respondens, opponens,* or *quaerens,*). And these were taken over bodily from the procedure of the Roman law-courts. Throughout the dialectical process of contention and response, the burden of proof lay with the assertor (*ei qui dicit non ei qui negat*). This, of course, supposes the simple thesis/denial case. In the case of a thesis/counterthesis, on the other hand, where the respondent advances a positive statement as evidence to the contrary of a position maintained by the proponent, the burden of proof will shift to the respondent's side. Consequently, as the dialectic of the

[4] A rather romanticized view of the basic set-up can be seen in the famous fresco "The Dispute of St. Thomas Aquinas with the Heretics" in the Church of Santa Maria sopra Minerva in Rome. It is particularly interesting that the foreground is littered with the books used by the disputants as sources for their proof-texts.

[5] On medieval academic disputations see A. G. Little and F. Pelster, *Oxford Theology and Theologians* (Oxford, 1934), pp. 29–56. A vivid account of the conduct of scholastic disputations is given in Thomas Gilby, O. P., *Barbara Celarent: A Description of Scholastic Dialectic* (London, 1949); see especially Chapter XXXII, "Formal Debate," pp. 282–93.

debate proceeds, the burden of proof may shift from one side to the other (though, of course, a different thesis bears the burden at each stage).

The dialectical structure of a disputation can be most simply represented by means of the flow-chart given in the diagram of Figure 1:

Figure 1

THE STRUCTURE OF A DISPUTATION

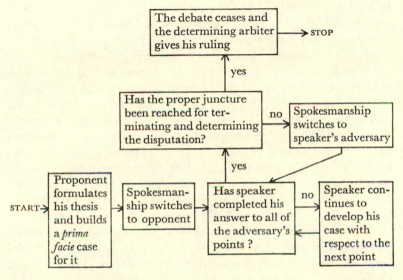

It is, accordingly, useful to distinguish a special mode of burden of proof that might be characterized as a *burden of refutation* (or rebuttal), along the lines of the "burden of further reply" considered above. For insofar as the opposition is able to bring in substantial arguments against a thesis, it is incumbent upon the initiating side to adduce considerations that blunt or deflect the impetus of these counter-arguments.

Disputation was, as we have seen, modeled rather straight-forwardly on the precedent of legal practice.[6] The explicit shift

---

[6] See, for example, Cicero, *De inventione*, I: 10–16. Cicero's analysis of four types of disputable questions and his description of the successive stages through which a dispute passes is drawn up with a view to the legal situation.

of the relevant legal conceptions to the context of the theory of debate in rhetoric was clear already to the ancients (e.g., in Aristotle's *Rhetoric* and Cicero's *De inventione*). But what is, for our purposes, a crucial step was taken by Richard Whately, in his *Elements of Rhetoric* (London, 1828). Though part of the law of evidence since antiquity, the ideas of *burden of proof* and of *presumptions* were first introduced explicitly into the theoretical analysis of *extra-legal* argumentation in Whately's treatment of rhetoric. And from that time onwards to the present day they have figured prominently in the theoretical discussions of textbooks of college debating.[7] This continuity of debating with medieval disputation has itself a solid historical basis. A good case can be made out for holding that the extracurricular disputations of the 15th–17th centuries—especially those between rival universities —were the direct precursors of modern intercollegiate debates.[8]

It also warrants note that disputation long continued as a testing method in universities, providing a format for *viva voce* examinations, in particular those for doctoral candidates in German universities (*Doktoranden*). Not only in humanistic fields but even in the natural sciences, the candidate had to undertake a formal public defense of specified theses against designated opponents, his professors presiding over the exercise. In latter days all this became very much a formality, the candidate having arrived at a friendly understanding with his "opponents" in advance.[9] In the American context, such disputation continues in a vestigial form in the final oral examination for graduate degrees, when the candidate defends his thesis or dissertation before a group

---

[7] See, for example, A. J. Freeley, *Argumentation and Debate* (2nd ed., Belmont, California, 1966), chap. III, sect. III, "Presumption and Burden of Proof," pp. 30–4.

[8] See Bromley Smith, "Extracurricular Disputations: 1400—1650," *Quarterly Journal of Speech*, vol. 34 (1948), pp. 473–6.

[9] See the report given by Max Planck of his own experiences at the University of Munich in 1879:

The *viva voce* examination was followed by the ceremonial *Promotion* in which—according to the regulations of the day—the doctoral candidate had to defend [in disputation] certain theses which he put forward. My "opponents," with whom—as was customary—I had already reached friendly accomodation in advance, were the physicist Carl Runge and the mathematician Adolf Hurwitz. (Max Planck, *Vorträge und Erinnerungen*, 5th ed. [Stuttgart, 1949], p. 4.)

of his principal professors, who play a dual role: first in the public part of the examination playing out the role of opponents, and thereafter deliberating *in camera* as evaluative judges, with the dissertation-director acting as counterpart to the determiner of a medieval debate.[10]

3. THE EXPOSITORY ASPECT

Written exposition of persuasive intent is closely comparable to disputation. The author is cast in the role of a proponent, and his reader is cast in a dual role: both as the sceptical opponent and as the determiner (both as the attorney for the other side and as the judge, so to speak). Reasoning in written exposition can and should be regarded as *argumentation* aimed at winning over an opponent (in both of the senses of "winning over"—i.e., *defeating* his objections qua opponent, and *persuading or convincing* him in the role of an adjudicative determiner). It warrants incidental remark that this probative character of written exposition is particularly striking in the case of philosophy, where books very commonly have a heavily dialectical aspect. The examples of this phenomenon include the dialogues of Plato, the explicitly disputational aspect of medieval treatises (which tended to take on the overt structure of a disputation, with the full panoply of thesis, counterthesis, objection and reply, etc.), Spinoza's procedure of *more geometrico* demonstration with its interjection of argumentative *scholia*, or the quasi-judicial manner of argumentation encountered in philosophical authors like Berkeley and Hume.

The author, as the proponent, is thus subject to the dialectical disabilities that go with this role. The burden of proof rests on his

---

[10] The present treatment leaves wholly out of account the vast body of philosophical discussion—inaugurated by Zeno, enlarged by Plato revivified by Kant, and launched upon seemingly endless seas by Hegel— dedicated to the theme of *dialectic*. I have done so not because I am under the (blatantly wrong) impression that this theme is without inherent interest and value—quite the reverse!—but rather simply because it does not lie sufficiently close to the direction of the present concerns. The reader interested in a brief account of this range of issues is referred to the long article "Dialektik" in J. Ritter (ed.), *Historisches Wörterbuch der Philosophie*, vol. 2 (Basel and Stuttgart, 1972), pp. 163–226.

side: it is incumbent on him to make out a case for any positive thesis he advances as a contention.

While the burden of proof always inclines against the person who, as it were, tables a thesis for acceptance, one must, of course, make it *possible* for him to build a substantiating case. The adducing of supporting considerations must be something that is not made in principle impossible under the circumstances: not *everything* can be disqualified as failing to count in this regard. All rational discussion presupposes an exchange of contentions, and it will not do in such a context simply to silence one of the parties by an extraneous act of *force majeure* that precludes him from the very outset from developing a case.

Accordingly, the situation must be such that there are always *some* considerations that are "allowed to count." Thus there must always be established ground-rules that specify certain categories of contentions to carry evidential weight. It makes sense to speak of a "burden of proof" only in the context of established rules regarding the discharge of such a burden. In rational controversy, there must be some impartially fixed common ground as to what is to count as evidence. This leads straightaway into the topic of *presumption*.

4. PRESUMPTIONS AND THE STRUCTURE OF BURDEN OF PROOF

Presumption represents a way of filling in—at least *pro tem*—the gaps that may confront us at any stage of information. The French *Code civil* defines "presumptions" as: *des conséquences qui la loi ou le magistrat tire d'un fait connu à un fait inconnu.*" (Bk. III, pt. iii, sect, iii, art. 1349). The conception of burden of proof is correlative with that of a presumption, with "presumptions of innocence" capable of serving as a paradigm example here. Such a *praesumptio juris* is an inference from a fact which, by legal prescription, stands until refuted. Ilbert has elucidated the conception of presumption in the following terms:

A presumption in the ordinary sense is an inference. . . . The subject of presumptions, so far as they are mere inferences or arguments, belongs, not to the law of evidence, or to law at all, but to rules of reasoning. But a legal presumption, or, as it is sometimes called, a presumption of law, as distinguished from a presumption of fact, is something more. It may be described, in [Sir James] Stephen's language, as "a rule of law that courts and judges shall draw a particular inference from a particular fact, or from particular evidence, unless and until the truth" (perhaps it would be better to say "soundness") "of the inference is disproved."[11]

The specifically defeasible presumptions are closely interconnected with the conception of burden of proof:

> The effect of a presumption is to impute to certain facts or groups of facts a *prima facie* significance or operation, and thus, in legal proceedings, to throw upon the party against whom it works the duty of bringing forward evidence to meet it. Accordingly, the subject of presumption is intimately connected with the subject of burden of proof, and the same legal rule may be expressed in different forms, either as throwing the advantage of a presumption on one side, or as throwing the burden of proof on the other.[12]

In effect, a defeasible presumption is coordinate with—or to be more exact, is simply the reverse of—a burden of proof (of the "burden of further reply" variety). Such a presumption indicates that in the absence of specific counterindications we are to accept how things stand "as a rule"—and such a general presumption retain its force in general even if subject to exceptions in particular cases.

Whenever there is a "burden of proof" for establishing that X is so, the correlative defeasible presumption that not-X stands until the burden has been discharged definitively. Archbishop Whately has formulated the relationship at issue in the following terms:

> According to the most correct use of the term, a "presumption" in favour of any supposition means, not (as has been sometimes erroneously imagined) a preponderance of proba-

[11] Sir Courtenay Ilbert, *op. cit.*, p. 15.
[12] *Ibid.*

H

bility in its favour, but such a *preoccupation* of the ground as implies that it must stand good till some sufficient reason is adduced against it; in short, that the *burden of proof* lies on the side of him who would dispute it.[13]

It is in just this sense, for example, that the "presumption of innocence" in favor of the accused is correlative with the burden of proof carried by the state in establishing his guilt.

In line with this idea, the circumstance that the burden of proof always rests with the party that introduces a thesis by way of initial assertion leads to the view that there is automatically a *presumption against* any initiated thesis. But, of course, if the adducing of evidence in the dialectic of rational argumentation is to be possible at all, this circumstance must have its limits. Clearly, if the burden of proof inclined against *every* contention —if there were an automatic presumption of falsity against every proposition—it would become in principle impossible ever to provide a persuasive case. The rule that each contention needs evidential support through the adducing of further substantiating contentions cannot reasonably be made operative *ad indefinitum.*

This, of course, does not mean that we need to invoke the idea of *unquestionable* theses, theses that are inherently uncontestable, certain and irrefutable. To take this view would involve a misreading of the probative situation, by succumbing to the tempting epistemological theory of *foundationalism.* This doctrine insists on the need for ultimate primacy of absolutely certain, indefeasible, crystalline truths, totally beyond any possibility of invalidation. The search for such self-evident or protocol theses, inherently inviolate and yet informatively committal about the nature of the world represents one of the great quixotic quests of modern philosophy.

There is no need to enter on any such hunt in the context of present purposes. The probative requirements of disputational dialectic do not involve any category of irrefutable claims. All that we need is that some theses, or rather, some *types* of theses— are such that the presumption of truth inclines in their favor— that the burden of proof is to be carried by someone who wishes to reject a contention of this sort. Once a thesis of this sort is introduced—and established to be such—there is, as it were, a

[13] Richard Whately, *Elements of Rhetoric (op. cit.),* Pt. I, ch. III, sect. 2.

pro tem presumption of truth in its favor, one that persists until it is overthrown in its turn. The crucial thing, then, is the availability of certain families of contentions that inherently merit the "benefit of doubt," that are able to stand provisionally—i.e., until somehow undermined—in short, that, however vulnerable to refutation, have at any rate a *presumption* of acceptability in their favor. There is, in this domain, a crucial contrast between "decisive" (or "conclusive") evidence and "prima facie" evidence—the former resulting from the latter only if it is not defeated or overridden by further countervailing considerations.[14]

Such presumptions, though possessed of significant probative weight, will in general be defeasible—i.e., subject to defeat in being overthrown by sufficiently weighty countervailing considerations. In its legal aspect, the matter is expounded by one writer as follows:

> [Such] a presumption of validity . . . retains its force in general even if subject to exceptions in particular cases. It may not by itself state all of the relevant considerations, but it says enough that the party charged should be made to explain or deny the allegation to avoid responsibility; the plaintiff has given a reason why the defendant should be held liable, and thereby invites the defendant to provide a reason why, in this case, the presumption should not be made absolute. The presumption lends structure to the argument, but it does not foreclose its further development.[15]

The concept of presumption plays a crucial epistemological role in the structure of rational argumentation. Clearly there must be some class of claims that are allowed at least *pro tem* to enter uncontested into the framework of argumentation, because if everything were contested then the process of inquiry could not progress at all. Such a class may, but need not, constitute a stable

---

[14] Although *probability* can in certain circumstances serve as a guide to presumptions, complications do arise in this connection. We cannot pursue the issue here, but refer the reader to the discussion in the author's *Plausible Reasoning* (Assen, 1976). On the legal aspects of the presumptive role of probabilities, see R. A. Epstein, "Pleadings and Presumptions," *The University of Chicago Law Review*, vol. 40 (1973), pp. 556–82 (see pp. 580–82).

[15] R. A. Epstein, *op. cit.*, see p. 558–9.

category. It could be determined on a contextual basis, by strictly *local* (rather than *global*) ground-rules—so that theses which figure as presumptions in some situations need not do so in others. Above all, presumptions are not uncontestable. In "accepting" a thesis as such one concedes it a probative status that is strictly provisional and *pro tem*; one does *not* say to it: "Others abide our question, thou art free."

In accordance with this line of thought, we may introduce the idea of an "evidentially sufficient" contention (ES-contention), namely a contention that succeeds in effecting a shift in the burden of proof with respect to the thesis on whose behalf it is brought forward. Unlike *decisively* established contentions (self-evident protocols or the like), such ES-contentions will in general be defeasible. They do not stand unshakeable for good and all, but only provisionally and "until further notice"—or rather until considerations have been adduced that succeed in setting them aside. Such ES-contentions must be of a sort that (1) there is a substantial presumption of truth in their favor, and (2) the evidential force they are able to lend to the thesis in whose behalf they are adduced is sufficiently weighty that the burden of proof is shifted in its favor.

The idea of evidential sufficiency is closely connected with that of the *weight* of the burden of proof or of the *strength* of presumption (to look at the other side of the coin). British law, for example, adopts different standards of proof in criminal and civil cases. In criminal cases guilt must be established "beyond reasonable doubt," in civil cases it is sufficient to show that the defendant is guilty "on the balance of probabilities." And both standards are flexible: In criminal cases, "What is reasonable doubt ... [should vary] in practice according to ... the punishment which may be awarded."[16] Moreover "The standard [of proof for cases of fraud] is the civil one of preponderance of probabilities, but what is 'probable' depends upon the heinousness of what is alleged ... 'in proportion as the offense is grave, so ought the proof to be clear'...."[17] In general (and in disputation particularly) what is evidentially sufficient in shifting a burden of proof will hinge on the inherent seriousness of the contention at

[16] *Phipson on Evidence* ed. J. H. Buzzard *et. al.*, 11th edition (London 1970), p. 230.

[17] *Ibid.*, p. 232.

issue. The more *outré* a contention the weaker the force of what-ever presumptions may operate in its favor.

For a proposition to count as a presumption is altogether different from its counting as a truth, just as a man's being a presidential candidate is something far different from his being a president. Presidential candidates are not presidents; data are not truths. Truth-candidacy does not require or presuppose truth: quite different issues are involved. A potential truth is a truth no more than an egg-enclosed embryo is a hen. The "acceptance" of a proposition as a presumptive truth is not *acceptance* at all, but a highly provisional and conditional epistemic inclination towards it, an inclination that falls far short of outright commitment.

Such a presumption is—in the traditional sense—a "given." But a proposition may be given in two ways:

(1) as a *truth* or as *actually* true; to be classed as true *sans phrase.*

(2) as a *truth-candidate* or as *potentially* or *presumptively* true; to be classed as true provided that doing so creates no anomalies.

A presumption is a proposition that is "given" not in the first, but only in this second mode: it is a *pretender* to truth whose credentials may well prove insufficient, a runner in a race it may not win.

Our stance towards presumptions is unashamedly that of fair-weather friends: we adhere to them when this involves no problems whatsoever, but may abandon them at the onset of diffi-culties. But it is quite clear that such *loose* attachment to a pre-sumption is by no means tantamount to no attachment at all.[18]

The following objection might be made: How can you speak of asserting a proposition merely as a presumption but not as a

[18] As I. Scheffler puts a similar point in the temporal context of a change of mind in the light of new information: "That a sentence may be given up at a later time does not mean that its present claim upon us may be blithely disregarded. The idea that once a statement is acknowledged as theoretically revisable, it can carry no cognitive weight at all, is no more plausible than the suggestion that a man loses his vote as soon as it is seen that the rules make it possible for him to be outvoted" (*Science and Subjectivity* [New York, 1967], p. 118).

truth? If one is to assert (accept, maintain) the proposition in any way at all, does one not thereby assert (accept, maintain) it *to be true*? The answer here is simply a head-on denial, for there are different modes of acceptance. To maintain *P* as a presumption, as *potentially* or *presumptively* factual, is akin to maintaining *P* as *possible* or as *probable:* in no case are these contentions tantamount to maintaining the proposition as true. Putting a proposition forward as "possible" or "probable" commits one to claiming no more than that it is "*possibly* true" or "*probably* true." Similarly, to assert *P as a presumption* is to say no more than that *P* is *potentially* or *presumptively* true—that it is a truth-candidate—but does not say that *P* is *actually* true, that it is a truth. As with assertions of possibility or probability, a claim at issue with presumptive truth definitely stops short—far short—of being an unqualified claim to truth. Adequate warrant of presumptive truth does not render a thesis true as such.

We do not intend the conception of a presumption to "open the floodgates" in an indiscriminate way. Not *everything* is a presumption: the concept is to have *some* logico-epistemic bite. A presumption is not merely something that is "possibly true" or that is "true for all I know about the matter." To class a proposition as a presumption is to take a definite and committal position with respect to it, so as to say "I propose to accept it as true insofar as this is permitted by analogous and possibly conflicting commitments elsewhere."

There is a crucial difference between an *alleged* truth and a *presumptive* truth. For allegation is a merely *dialectical* category: every contention that is advanced in discussion is "allegedly true" —that is, alleged-to-be-true. But presumption—that is, *warranted* presumption—is an *epistemic* category: only certain special sorts of contentions are of such a sort that they merit to be accepted as true provisionally, "until further notice," until the path to acceptance is clear, in that the crucial issue that "remains to be seen" has been clarified, viz., whether the presumptive truth will in fact stand up once "everything is said and done."[19]

[19] For an interesting analysis of presumptive and plausibilistic reasoning in mathematics and (to a lesser extent) the natural sciences, see G. Polya's books *Introduction and Analogy in Mathematics* (Princeton, 1954) and *Patterns of Plausible Inference* (Princeton, 1954). Polya regards the

To be sure, if presumption is to have any probative bite, it stands in need of some justification: there will have to be some rationale for counting presumptions as presumptions in the first place. Here our standard methodological line comes into play. A presumption is justified in the first instance—but in the first instance only—in terms of certain presumption-establishing *criteria* (e.g., the blanket rules of presumption in favor of "uniformity," regularity, simplicity, and all the other key parameters of orthodox inductivism). These criteria themselves are then justified on a metaphysical basis—i.e., the world-picture we build up by their means resubstantiates them. This entire informational complex is then in turn legitimated by the methodologico-pragmatic cycle—when we put its purportedly reality-characterizing products to work in actual implementation, things by and large work out to satisfaction. The "double helix" approach of p. 122 above comes into play here. The presumption-establishing criteria are retrospectively revalidated through the adequacy of the whole system in both its theoretical and its pragmatic dimensions.

5. PRESUMPTIONS AND THE CONCEPTION OF A "PRIMA FACIE" CASE

The conception of a *prima facie* case is intimately connected with that of burden of proof in the evidential, E-burden of proof version. A *prima facie* case is, in effect, one that succeeds in *shifting* the burden of proof—it "demands an answer" and, until one is forthcoming, inclines the balance of favorable judgment to its side. To make out a *prima facie* case for one's contention is to adduce considerations whose evidential weight is such that—in the absence of countervailing considerations—the "reasonable presumption" is now in its favor and the burden of proof (in the sense of an adequate reply that "goes forward with [counter-] evidence") becomes incumbent on the opposing party.

In the dialectic of controversy the burden of proof in this

---

patterns of plausible argumentation as defining the "rules of admissibility in scientific discussion" on strict analogy with the legal case, regarding such rules as needed because it is plain that not *anything* qualifies for introduction as probatively relevant.

evidential sense (E-burden of proof) shifts back and forth between the parties in accordance with the evidential merit of their
case at each stage. The key idea here is that of adducing probative considerations whose weight is "sufficient" to fix or to shift
the burden of proof.

A controversy will be "won," in ideal circumstances, when
one side manages to embed all of its relevant contentions in evidentially adequate considerations (ES-contentions) which are
presumptively correct, and to which no adequate reply is forthcoming within the framework of discussion. When such an
argument has been constructed the case is no longer of *prima
facie* status but indeed has been made out, having proved itself to
be, under the circumstances at issue, an effectively "unanswerable" one.

A winning position of the dialectical game is reached when
every initiating burden of proof has been discharged. That is, all
the pertinent contentions have been carried back in the process of
evidentially supportive argumentation to theses that are left in
the status of presumptive truths because no adequately weighty
counterargument against them is forthcoming within the dialectical context of the dispute. (When presumptive truths are at issue,
an unanswered contention is presumed unanswerable.)

Presumptions are thus the (only provisionally fixed) points to
which the spider's web of dialectical case-building must be an-
chored. For the structure of the over-all argument can be set as
a tree-like configuration of the sort given in the following
diagram:

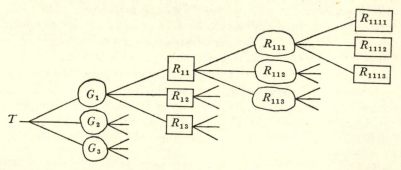

Here T is the basic thesis to be maintained by the proponent. The
G_i are the proponent's supporting considerations adduced as

grounds in constructing a *prima facie* case for maintaining *T*. The R_{ij} are the counter-considerations adduced in rebuttal or refutation of these grounds as adduced by the opponent (whose contributions are schematized in boxes, to distinguish them from the propenent's emplaced in ellipses). The R_{ijk} are the proponent's rebuttals of the opponent's R_{ij}. And so on. Now the proponent is in a "winning position" as long as *all* the opponent's rebuttals are covered by counterarguments whose component premises are *all* presumptive truths. The opponent is in a "winning position" whenever any one of the proponent's contentions is left unprotected in terms of their support through presumptive truths. Each party to the debate strives to be in a winning position when the time arrives to terminate the debate. The disparity in probative status of proponent and opponent is manifested by the fact that to realize a "winning position," the initiating proponent must be "protected" everywhere—and that a single "unprotected" proposition in his case leaves the victory in his opponent's hands. Just this disparity manifests the operation of the concept of a *burden of proof*.

6. THE LOCUS OF PRESUMPTION

To render this idea of *presumption* clearer and more vivid, it may be useful to survey its workings in a range of relevant cases.

(1) *Law*

Legal presumption (*praesumptio juris*) specifies an inference that is to be drawn from certain facts (or their absence): It indicates a conclusion which, by legal prescription, is to stand until duly set aside.

Such legal presumptions are sometimes irrefutable (as with the presumption that a child of less than seven years cannot commit a crime, or that the testimony of an incompetent [disqualified] witness is worthless). Such are the so-called "conclusive presumptions of law." More generally, however, the presumption is refutable, as with the "presumption of innocence" itself, the presumption that a person seven years lost is dead, the presumption that a child born or conceived in wedlock is legitimate, and the presumption that a document at least thirty years old is genuine. In all these cases the presumption can be defeated by appropriate evidence to the contrary.

(2) *Disputation*

In disputation (unlike law) all presumptions are, of course, of the defeasible sort. This is true not only of the fundamental presumption of falsity regarding freshly introduced theses, but also of the presumptions in favor of certain species of evidence, such as matters of "common knowledge" or the attest of suitable "authorities." Such refutable presumptions in effect serve to demarcate the rules of the evidential game in the dialectic of disputation.

(3) *Debate*

Most debating textbooks seem agree that in debate a presumption of truth must be accorded to what might be characterized as the cognitive *status quo:* the domain of what is "generally accepted" and/or qualifies as "common knowledge."[20] A related case is that of the testimony of "experts" which is also generally conceded as entitled to a presumption of truth. In both these cases one is dealing with presumptions of the evidential type.

(4) *Theory of Knowledge*

The concept of presumption also has important uses in philosophy. A tradition in the theory of knowledge that reaches from the later Stoics and Academic Sceptics of antiquity to the British Idealists of the turn of the present century insists (not always *expressis verbis*, but in effect) on a presumption of truth in favor

---

[20] One of the best modern books on the rhetoric of rational debate is Ch. Perelman and L. Olbrechts-Tyteca, *The New Rhetoric: A Treatise on Argumentation* (Notre Dame, 1969; original French version, Paris, 1958). On presumptions see pp. 70–4.

of the deliverances of memory and of the senses. Theses based on observation or recollection are to have the benefit of doubt; a presumption of truth operates in their favor—they are to stand unless significant counterindications are forthcoming.

It deserves stress that an epistemic quest for categories of data that are *prima facie* acceptable (innocent until proven guilty, as it were) is altogether different from the quest for absolutely certain or totally self-evidencing theses that has characterized the mainstream of epistemological tradition from Descartes via Bretano to present-day writers such as Roderick Chisholm.

Against the claims of the senses automatically to afford us the truth pure and simple, one can deploy all of the traditional arguments of the sceptics, and take for one's precept the dictum of Descartes: "All that up to the present time I have accepted as most true and certain I have learned either from the senses or through the senses; but it is sometimes proved to me that these senses are deceptive, and it is wiser not to trust entirely to any thing by which we have once been deceived."[21] But, of course, such arguments in support of the potential untruthfulness of sensory data serve only to reemphasize their role as *data*—i.e., truth-*candidates*—in our presumptive sense, rather than outright *truths* as such. In our technical sense of these terms we must thus speak not of "the *evidence* of our senses" but rather of "the *presumptive data* of our senses." (That potential fallibility proves actual falsehood and that these truth-candidates are in principle to be excluded from the realm of truth—in short that what is not known to be true is thereby known to be false—is something no sceptic has claimed to establish in even his most extravagant moments. And this being so, the door to truth-candidacy will remain open.) While in the face of potential inconsistencies among sensory (or other) reports one must yield up any insistence on truth, the factor of truth-*candidacy* yet passes by unscathed, and is not damaged by the fact that some candidates occasionally fail. This illustrates the general line of the *modus operandi* of the concept of presumption in epistemology.

The conception of presumptive truth must play a pivotal role throughout all such various contexts in which the notion of a "burden of proof" is operative. In any essentially dialectical

21 René Descartes, *Meditations on First Philosophy*, No. I, tr. R. M. Eaton.

situation in which the idea of burden of proof can figure, the very "rules of the game" remain inadequately defined until a suitable determination has been made regarding the nature, extent, and weight of the range of presumptions that are to be operative. Burden of proof and presumption represent correlative conceptions, inevitably coordinate with one another throughout the context of rational dialectic.

7. THE EPISTEMOLOGICAL ASPECT: RATIONALITY

Our present concern is with *cognitive* rather than *behavioral* rationality, rationality in regard to what a person believes in contrast to rationality in regard to his actions. (Admittedly the two are interrelated.) Now cognitive rationality has two significantly distinguishable aspects:

(i) *Substantive or probative rationality* in relation to the utilization of evidence. This has to do with the initial introduction of accepted theses into a person's belief-system (and hence is a *material* issue of the substantive content of that system). Here the key question is: does the person abide by the established evidential ground-rules in coordinating his credence with the nature of the evidence in hand?

(ii) *Logical or inferential rationality* in relation to the interconnections among beliefs in point of their consistency and their mutual implications. This has to do with the internal structure of the collection of theses that consitute a person's belief-system (and hence is a *formal* issue of the internal components of that system). Here the key question is: does the person abide by the established inferential ground-rules? This is primarily a matter of maintaining consistency among beliefs, of identifying and recognizing the consequences of accepted beliefs, and of acknowledging the acceptability of the recognized consequences of accepted theses.

Cognitive rationality embraces both of these aspects of thesis-introduction and thesis-attunement within a coherently articulated belief-system. Both *thesis-introduction-moves* and *thesis-derivation-moves* are indispensable to the dialectical enterprise of rational argumentation in discourse or discussion.

This distinction deserves stress because it underpins the crucial point that the idea of burden of proof relates *solely to the first* of these components of cognitive rationality. Rational argumentation demands reason-introduction moves, and the way in which probative theses are introduced and treated in rational argumentation reflects the ground-rules revolving about the concept of burden-of-proof. The crucial connection between presumption and rationality may be seen in this light as articulated via the correlative precepts that a warranted presumption is one which should carry weight with the rational man, and that the rational man is prepared to accord to presumptions the weight that is their just due.

It cannot be emphasized too emphatically that the idea of burden of proof is not a *logical* concept. Putting aside for the moment the special category of "purely logical truths," logic has no dealings with the issue of probative obligations or even with the (categorical) truth-status or presumptive truth-status of propositions. Its concern with truth is wholly in hypothetical mode ("if certain theses are [assumed to be] true, then certain others must also be [assumed to be] true"). Logic concerns itself with thesis-derivation moves, not with thesis-introduction moves.

Rather than being a *logical* concept, burden of proof is a *methodological* one. It has to do not with valid or invalid reasoning, but with probative argumentation in dialectical or crypto-dialectical situations. The workings of the conception of burden of proof represent a procedural or a *regulative principle of rationality* in the conduct of argumentation, a ground-rule, as it were, of the game of rational debate.

II. Scepticism

8. SCEPTICISM AND RATIONALITY

A useful way of viewing the historic doctrine of cognitive scepticism is to regard it from the perspective of the ideas of presumption and burden of proof. From this angle it appears that the sceptic simply *rejects* the common-sense and virtually universal practice of granting a presumption of veracity to our senses, our memory, our practices of inductive reasoning etc., thus denying the serviceability of the very materials from which alone our knowledge of the world is—or can be—constructed. Accordingly, the sceptic moves towards such positions as agnosticism in point of factual knowledge about the world, solipsism in abstaining from belief in the existence of other people, cognitive solipsism in the rejection of the vicarious evidence of others, etc. Such positions are the immediate consequence of rejecting the presumptive veracity of the senses, memory, inductive inference, analogy, etc.

Now on their own ground of purely theoretical argumentation, these positions are secure and irrefutable. They win an easy victory, but an ultimately empty one—*because they systematically deny evidential weight to those considerations which alone could be brought to bear in making out a case to the contrary.* This very fact marks the profound irrationality of the sceptic's position. For cognitive rationality turns—as we have seen—not upon derivation-moves alone but introduction-moves as well. This is not just a *hypothetical* issue of making proper inferences from given premises; it involves also the *categorical* issue of giving a proper probative weight or epistemic status to the premises themselves.

In refusing to give to evidential considerations the presumptive and *prima facie* weight that is their established value on the market of rational interchange, the sceptic, rather than being the defender of rigid reason, is in fact profoundly irrational. The probative rules must be allowed to do their proper work of showing where presumptions lie and how the burden of argumentation can be shifted—one cannot be allowed to redesign them so as to cut one's opposition off from all further prospect of argumentation. The victory of the man who systematically refuses to grant the evidential weight of considerations contrary to his position is at once inevitable and Pyrrhic. For scepticism profoundly misreads the dialectic situation: it insists on taking the *initial* situation (viz., a burden of proof against the thesis maintained at the outset) as *ultimate* (viz., a burden of proof against *every* contention, even those introduced evidentially at later stages.)

The ordinary and standard probative practice of empirical

inquiry stipulates a presumption in favor of the senses, of memory, etc. We take the data deriving from these sources as veridical until proven otherwise. When the sceptic refuses to grant this presumption, he blocks any prospect of reasoning with him *within* the standard framework of discussion about the empirical facts of the world. The sceptic is in effect unwilling to play the rationality-game, because he refuses to abide by the evidential ground-rules that govern its management. The sceptic is not a defender of reason, but a fugitive from the enterprise of rational discussion.

A totally committed sceptic could, of course, attempt to argue as follows:

> When I denied the common presumption in favor of the data of memory, sense, etc., you shifted to a methodological ground. Looking on memory, sense, etc., as cognitive methods for the validation of beliefs, you invoke the presumption in favor of generally successful methods. But since granting this presumption leads to results I do not accept, I shall deny it as well.

But this tactic represents a desperate and ultimately unavailing move. To be sure, it is clear that within the framework of *any* controversy one can deny an inferred conclusion by denying the premises from which it derives. But when these premises themselves relate to the ground-rules of procedure for the conduct of rational discussion itself, this generic tactic is no longer a genuine option. For to make *this* move is—in effect—to withdraw from the lists of rational controversy: and to confess that the position one has undertaken to defend in reasoned argumentation is not in fact supportable in this way.[22]

---

[22] C. S. Peirce put the case for presumptions on a somewhat different basis, viewing them as needed to maintain the line between sense and foolishness:

> There are minds to whom every predjudice, every presumption, seems unfair. It is easy to say what minds these are. They are those who never have known what it is to draw a well-grounded induction, and who imagine that other people's knowledge is as nebulous as their own. That all science rolls upon presumption (not of a formal but of a real kind) is no argument with them, because they cannot imagine that there is anything solid in human knowledge. These are the people who waste their time and money upon perpetual motions and other such rubbish. (*Collected Papers*, Vol. VI: 6.424.)   [Continued]

When it comes to the validation of our empirical beliefs about the contingent arrangements of what goes on in the world, the sceptic in effect refuses to play the usual evidential game. When we adduce the data of the senses, of memory, etc., in support of such beliefs, the sceptic simply denies their probative weight. "You admit," he says in a Cartesian tone of voice, "that these data-sources occasionally deceive you; so how can you be confident that they do not go amiss in the case in hand?" Given that the only sort of evidence we could possibly adduce in the specific circumstances will itself have to be of the very type whose probative weight the sceptic calls into question, we have no way of meeting his argument head-on. But surely, whatever victory the Pyrrhonian sceptic is able to gain by this sort of strategy will have to be altogether Pyrrhic.

Philosophical sceptics generally set up some abstract standard of absolutistic certainty and then try to show that no knowledge-claims in a certain area (sense, memory, scientific theory, etc.) can possibly meet the conditions of this standard. From this fact, the impossibility of such a category of "knowledge" is accordingly inferred. But this inference is totally misguided. For what follows is simply the inappropriateness or incorrectness of the standard at issue. If the vaunted standard is such that knowledge-claims cannot possibly meet it, the moral is not "too bad for knowledge-claims," but rather "too bad for the standard." The sceptic's argument is double-edged and inflicts the more serious damage upon itself. It is senseless to impose on something conditions which it cannot in the very nature of things meet: an analogue of the old Roman legal precept is operative here, one is never obliged beyond the limits of the possible (*ultra posse nemo obligatur*). The cognitivist who claims in the sceptic's despite to know that P need not insist that he has intrinsically irrefutable and logically conclusive evidence that P. And it is not necessary for him to make good a claim of this sort. It is sufficient that his

---

Peirce is very emphatic regarding the role of presumptions in scientific argumentation, and adduces various examples, e.g., that the unknown parts of space and time are occupied as are the known, or that the universe is inherently indifferent to human values and does not in its own workings manifest any inclination towards being benevolent, just, wise, etc.

evidence for *P* is as good as that for anything of *P*'s type possibly could be. The "certainty" that must attach to knowledge-claims need not be absolute—it suffices to construe it in the sense of *effective* certainty. A claim to knowledge does not commit the sceptically reproached transgression of issuing in principle infeasible guarantees; it simply embodies the assurance that everything that can reasonably be done under the circumstances to ascertain the fact at issue has indeed been done.

9. SCEPTICISM AND THE DEMANDS OF RATIONALITY

Why not simply let discretion be the better part of epistemic valor and systematically avoid accepting anything? If our knowledge of factual issues is defeasible—if it is always *potentially* flawed—caution might well be the best policy, and we would be well advised to resort to a Carnapian stance and avoid accepting anything whatsoever. Why not, then, adopt the sceptic's traditional policy of a systematic suspension of judgment?

To take this stance is to involve oneself in a serious misreading of the very *raison d'être* of the cognitive enterprise. For its aim is not just to avoid error but to engross truth. Throughout the book we have taken the position that the aim of inquiry is to provide information about the world (and this, at any rate, is what it *purports* to do). And here, as elsewhere, "Nothing ventured, nothing gained" is the operative principle. To be sure, a systematic abstention from cognitive involvement is a sure-fire safeguard against error. But it affords this security at too steep a price, for it requires one simply to opt out of the cognitive enterprise.

Note that this line of thought does not involve any immediate resort to pragmatic considerations. Since the days of the Academic Sceptics of Greek antiquity, philosophers have often answered our present question "Why accept anything at all?" by taking the following line: Man is a rational animal. *Qua* animal he must act, since his very survival depends upon action. But *qua* rational being he cannot act availingly save insofar as his actions are guided by what he accepts. The practical circumstances of the human condition preclude the systematic suspension of belief as a viable policy.

But this pragmatic appeal has *not* been operative in the present line of argumentation. Instead, this has addressed itself wholly to the issue of *cognitive* rationality. The line we take runs *not* "If you want to act effectively then you must accept something" but rather "If you want to enter into 'the cognitive enterprise'—that is, if you wish to be in the position to obtain information about the world—then you must accept something." Both approaches take a line that is not categorical and unconditional, but rather hypothetical and conditional. But in the pragmatic case, the condition relates to the requisites for effective action, and in the cognitive case to the requisites for rational inquiry. (The tactic of probing for the justificatory presuppositions for securing "information" about the world has governed our proceeding throughout the book.)

The traditional pragmatic argument against scepticism goes roughly as follows:

> On the plane of abstract, theoretical reasoning the sceptical position is, to be sure, secure and irrefutable. But scepticism founders on the structure of the human condition—that man finds himself emplaced *in medias res* in a world where his very survival demands action. And the action of a rational being requires the guidance of belief. Not the inferences of theory and cognition but the demand of practice and action make manifest the untenability of the sceptic's position.

Essentially this argument is advanced by such diverse thinkers as David Hume and William James.[23] Conceding that scepticism cannot be defeated on its own ground, that of theory, it is held to be invalidated by an incapacity to support the requisites of human action.

Unfortunately, however, this position leaves it open for the sceptic to take to the high ground of a partisan of rigorous rationality. For the sceptic may well take the following line:

> This charge of stultifying practice is really beneath my notice. Theoretical reason and abstract rationality are what concerns

---

[23] The argument derives from the Academic Sceptic Carneades (c. 213–c. 128 B.C.) who headed the Platonic Academy, but its essentials are due to Pyrrho (c. 360–c. 270 B.C.), founder of the Sceptical school.

the true philosopher. The issue of what is *merely practical* does not concern me. As far as "mere practice" goes, I am perfectly prepared to conform my actions to the pattern that men in general see fit to follow. In matters of *practice* let us by all means go along at the common level. But one should recognize that the clarity of the theoretical intellect points in another—and altogether sceptical—direction.

The present line of argumentation does not afford the sceptic this comfortable option. Its fulcrum is not the issue of *practice* as such, but the issue of *rationality*. It revolves around the question of the sorts of considerations (viz., teleological success) that establish the rationality of a practice. And then it applies these generic considerations to the specific case of cognitive practices to reach a scepticism-contradicting conclusion.

In affecting to disdain *this* line of approach, it is not simply the practice of ordinary life, but rationality itself on which the sceptic must now turn his back. And at this juncture he is no longer left in possession of the high ground.

In the final analysis the sceptic runs afoul of the demands of that very rationality in whose name he so high-mindedly claims to speak. Rationality, after all, is not a matter of *logic* alone—of commitment to the logical principles of consistency (i.e., not to accept what contradicts accepted premisses) and completeness (i.e., to accept what is entailed by accepted premisses), which are, after all, purely hypothetical in nature ("If you accept. . . , then—"). Thesis-derivation principles do not exhaust the issue; thesis-introduction principles also enter in. Rationality indispensably possesses a categorical and substantive dimension inherent in the conception of evidence—that of abiding by the established evidential ground-rules of various domains of discussion in terms of the locus of presumption and the allocation of benefit of doubt. To be sure, there will always be a rationale of justification for such ground-rules. And if it were simply this rationalization that the sceptic asking for, his demands would *not* be unreasonable, and could always in principle be met. But in transmuting the need to justify the principles for allocating benefit of doubt into a ground for shifting the nature of this allocation (turning it, so to speak, against the theses it initially favored), the sceptic takes an ultimately unwarranted step. After all, if it were a *request for justification* that were at issue, then this should be understood as itself subject to the usual ground-rules of evidence in the building up of a justificatory case. And in undertaking a blanket rejection of the usual principles of presumption and benefit of doubt, the sceptic would render it in principle impossible to provide the sort of case which is, from this present perspective on the issue, exactly what he is in fact demanding. Accordingly, the sceptic's stance is, in effect, *question-begging* by laying down conditions which block at the very outset the development of the case he challenges his opponent to produce. Whatever victory he can gain in this way is ultimately meaningless.

One could—to be sure—press the issue one step further. One could say "Very well, so acceptance is necessary to the project of rational inquiry or what you have called 'cognitive enterprise.' But why should you seek to play this game at all?" At this stage, of course, considerations of theoretical rationality can no longer be deployed appropriately and one must take the pragmatic turn. One clearly cannot marshal an ultimately adequate defense of rational cognition by an appeal that proceeds wholly on its own ground. Now one must look for a cognition-external rationale of justification, and at a later stage the aforementioned pragmatic appeal to the conditions of effective action properly comes into operation.

10. SCEPTICISM AND THE METHODOLOGICAL TURN

We have arrived at the upshot that the sceptic is being unreasonable because he simply withdraws from the rationality game, since the basic rationale of reasonableness in the factual area at issue is fixed by certain ground-rules that the sceptic refuses to heed. In striving against this conclusion it is open to the sceptic to argue thus: "If I'm departing from what by your rights is 'rationality,' that doesn't show anything I'm prepared to regard as a genuine flaw. Indeed my very thesis is that your 'rationality' is, in a certain regard, deficient." To meet this desperate but profound sceptical objection we must shift the ground. It now becomes advantageous to stop talking about *beliefs* directly (the acceptance of *theses*), and to approach the issue from a different point of departure, namely that of practices, procedures, and methods.

In one of its classical forms, the sceptic's argument goes as follows:

The rational man must, of course, have a basis for his beliefs and opinions. When asked *why* he accepts some accepted belief or opinion, he will cite one (or more) others that support it. But we can now ask him why he accepts these in turn, and this process can be continued as long as one likes. As a result, we will either move in a circle—and so ultimately provide no justification at all—or become involved in an infinite regress, supporting the elephant on the back of a turtle on the back of an alligator, etc. The only way to terminate the regress is by a dogmatic acceptance, somewhere along the line, of an *ultimate* belief that is used to justify others but is not itself justified. But any such unjustified acceptance is by its very nature arbitrary and irrational.

So reasons the philosophic sceptic.[24] His position, though strong, is not altogether unanswerable. The answer lies in recognizing that the things one rationally accepts are not of a piece. Specifically, it is necessary to heed the essentially Kantian distinction between those substantive *theses* that constitute our knowledge, on the one hand, and our cognitively regulative *methods* on the other.

It is indeed ultimately unsatisfactory to adopt the purely discursive course of justifying theses in terms of further theses and so on. But reflection on the structure of rational legitimation shows that this is not our only option. Rather, we justify our acceptance of certain theses because (ultimately) they are validated by the employment of a certain method, the scientific method, thus breaking outside the cycle of justifying thesis by thesis through the fact that a thesis can be justified by application

[24] Considerations along these lines have led various recent epistemologists of the *foundationalist* tradition (as it might be called) to give up all prospects of "knowledge" in the sense of rationally-validated-acceptance-as-true. Exactly this is the position of Rudolf Carnap with respect to empirical generalizations (see his *Foundations of Probability*, Appendix H). Cf. also the more radical position of Keith Lehrer, "Why Not Scepticism?", *The Philosophical Forum*, vol. 2 (1971), pp. 283–98, as well as Peter Unger, "A Defense of Skepticism," *The Philosophical Review*, vol. 80 (1971), pp. 198–219, where further references to the recent literature of the subject are given.

of a cognitive method. And in turn we justify the adoption of this method in terms of certain *practical* criteria: success in prediction and efficacy in control. (With respect to *methodology*, at any rate, the pragmatists were surely on firm ground— there is certainly no better way of justifying a *method* than by establishing that it "works" with respect to the specific tasks held in view.)

This dialectic of justification thus breaks out of the restrictive confines of the sceptic's circle, and does so without relapse into a dogmatism of unjustified ultimates. We justify the acceptance of theses by reference to the method by which they are validated, justifying this method itself in terms of the classical pragmatic criterion of methodological validation. The line of approach adopted here thus blocks the route towards philosophical scepticism by a complex, two-stage maneuver, combining the methodological justification of the *theses* that present our claims to knowledge with the pragmatic justification of the cognitive *method* by whose means they are validated.[25]

11. THE CRUCIAL SHIFT OF PRESUMPTION AT THE LEVEL OF PRACTICE

The systematic bearing of the methodological turn taken in the preceding section must be considered more closely. It is necessary, first of all, to pay heed once more to the ancient recognition of the essentially amphibious nature of man as a creature of intellect and will, of thought and action; a creature capable both of beliefs and deeds, of sayings and doings.

In this regard, it is important to recognize the distinction between (1) the essentially *intellectual/theoretical* issue of having certain *beliefs* (viz., accepting that P is the case); (2) the essentially *practical* issue of espousing certain *actions* (viz., accepting that A is to be done), and (3) the complexedly Janus-faced issue of methodology (tools, procedures, policies, and rules for action, etc.) which looks both in theoretical and in practical directions.

As a *rational* being, man must certainly have some sort of

---

[25] Cf. the author's book, *The Coherence Theory of Truth* (Oxford, 1973), pp. 323-4, for a further development of this line of reasoning in another context.

adequate *rationale* for proceeding in all three of these cases: the beliefs he deems worthy of acceptance, the actions he deems worthy of performance, and the procedures he deems it proper to follow. And, of course, in all such cases the burden of proof goes against the proposer—in each instance there is an initiating burden (I-burden of proof) that rests against the item at issue. But when we consider the evidential aspect of the issue (E-burden of proof) the matter stands rather differently in the different cases.

Established *theses* and established *methods* stand on a quite different footing. The fact that *a certain belief has generally been held* with respect to some issue at best consitutes an item of very weak evidence in its favor. Unless further special aspects of the case are involved, the factor of general adoption will provide a rather feeble evidential basis, which can go only a relatively short distance in shifting the impeding presumption and re-allocating the burden of proof.[26] When it has been shown that a certain belief is generally accepted, it may still be plausibly maintained that—in view of the gullibility of men—the burden of proof yet pretty much remains against it. But when it has been shown that a certain *method* has come to be generally adopted, the situation changes. The very fact that a given *modus operandi* has come to be generally adopted (in a community of rational agents) as means for realizing the relevant teleology of given objectives thus constitutes a significant evidential factor in its favor. General acceptance of a method within a community of rational agents implies success in reaching the objectives in view with respect to the method, and success is a valid—indeed *the* valid—criterion of methodological appropriateness. It is clearly debatable whether or not an established *belief* deserves to have a presumption of truth conceded in its favor (the probative situation is unquestionably murky here). But there can be no real question that an established *method*—one which has, as it were "proven itself" in various applications lying within the range of its correlative objectives—has solid claims to a presumption in its

[26] Some may think this position too cautious. For a spirited defense of the evidential significance of general acceptance see D. Goldstick, "Methodological Conservatism," *American Philosophical Quarterly*, vol. 8 (1971), pp. 186–91. Goldstick argues the position that "*a priori* and in principle, it is possible (at least sometimes) to make out a good *prima facie* case for a proposition by citing the fact that it is believed by us" (*op. cit.*, p. 186).

favor. There is no reason why even a perfectly rational inquirer acting cautiously on the best evidence at his disposal might not exchange true theses for false ones whenever "the evidence at his disposal" simply points in the wrong direction. And this can even happen when a "superior" method of inquiry is being used. But it is vastly less likely that an inquiry-method of inherently superior performance-capabilities would ever be replaced by an inherently inferior one, given that the rational man adopts methods on the basis of their *manifest* superiority, and that, where a method of the range and many-sidedness of an inquiry procedure is concerned, manifest superiority in performance is well-nigh decisive for *inherent* adequacy. (At this level, *gratuitous* success through *systematic* malfunction is effectively excluded by the range of metaphysical suppositions that lie at the background of the discussion.)

But why should even relatively few instances of success be accepted as rationally justifying continued use of a method when this would clearly not suffice to justify acceptance of any corresponding thesis? Why, in short, is the probative rationality of the *practical* realm more lenient than that of the *theoretical*?

The answer lies in the crucial difference between the domain of theory and that of practice. Pure theory is never under any constraint to arrive at any resolution—by its very nature it operates in the absence of such pressures. Whenever the evidence seems somehow imperfect or insufficient, theory is free to suspend judgment and await further information. But in the sphere of action, the case is very different. For even inaction is a mode of action in this domain. And because we must act on the best available evidence—however imperfect it may be from some ideal point of view—the ground-rules for rationally warranted action are bound to differ substantially from those which govern rational belief in the purely theoretical side. Thesis-acceptance requires strong or conclusive evidence if the demands of strict rationality are to be met. But the circumstances of the practical sphere are such that relatively weak considerations on the side of attained success can serve to reverse the presumption against a method of proceeding.

The crucial factor of this pragmatically methodological approach to the critique of scepticism in relation to matters of fact lies in the consideration that different facets of rationality come into play in different settings. In particular, the rationality of practice has (and *must* have) different ground-rules from the rationality of theory, and the principles of presumption and burden of proof are bound to differ in the two contexts.

This difference expresses itself in the context of the Principle of Sufficient Reason. We know full well that it is imprudent (i.e., impropriety-risking) to operate in the theoretico-cognitive setting on the principle: "If no differences between two cases are *known* to us, it *is reasonably safe to believe* that no differences exist." But its *pragmatic* counterpart is perfectly rational (prudent, proper): "If no differences between two cases in *which we must act* are known to us, then it is proper to proceed uniformly in both of them—there is no rational basis for different action and *it is reasonable to act on the supposition* that no differences exist."[27]

The critical point is that in the context of justificatory argumentation with respect to methods and procedures one is *not* dealing with the establishment of a factual thesis at all—be it demonstrative or presumptive—but rather with the rational validation of a practical course of action. And the practical warrant that rationalizes the use of a method need not call for a guarantee of success (which is, in the circumstances of the case in view, altogether impossible), but merely for having as good reasons as, under the circumstances, we can reasonably expect to lay our hands upon. In the realm of action—unlike that of theory —the concept of rationality operates in a variant manner. For here the presumption in favor of established methods (but not theses!) tilts the burden of proof in this context against a sceptical opponent. And this difference between theses and methods is crucial for our present purposes. It provides the rationale for taking the fact that a method has worked in certain other cases as basis for its application in the present case (in the absence of any explicit counter-indications).[28]

---

[27] We deliberately ignore here those cases in which we wish to "hedge our bets" across a plurality of cases for reasons of statistical fluctuation.

[28] Here lies the cash-value of our thesis that while a methodological pragmatism requires some appeal to the principle of the uniformity of nature, it need not (in the first instance) treat this principle as a constitutively substantive factual thesis, but rather as a regulative principle of practical rationality: Do what has worked out in similar cases until there's a jolly good reason for proceeding differently!

Thus at the deeper, methodological level, the flaws of the sceptic's procedure become manifest in a clear and decisively damaging light. Considerations of *onus probandi* here provide the saw which cuts off the doctrinal limb onto which the sceptic has chosen to climb.

Chapter XIII

THE PROBLEM OF ALTERNATIVE
LOGICS

1. PLURALISM IN LOGIC

The proceeding chapters have dealt with the pragmatic legitimation of *factual* knowledge. Let us now shift our focus from the factual to the formal area—in particular to the domain of logic (as well as to that sector of mathematics which, being *pure*, deals with strictly hypothetical truth whose basis of veracity is altogether logico-conceptual). The problem-area of present concern is thus the *formal* counterpart of our previous concern with the legitimation of truth-claims in the *factual* domain.

There can be little doubt that one of the most significant and striking features of logic in the twentieth century is the development of a large proliferation of logical systems. Even in the sphere of propositional logic alone, a plethora of systems confronts us— the various many-valued logics, intuitionistic logic, the multiplicity of modal systems, the systems of material and strict implication, and other modes of entailment. In a persuasively argued article entitled "Are There Alternative Logics?" Friederich Waismann has put the matter trenchantly in supporting an affirmative answer to this question:

> . . . we do already possess distinct logics—if this term is used to denote precisely elaborated formalized systems; e.g., logics including or excluding a Theory of Types, systems admitting or barring the law of excluded middle, etc. Perhaps one might add that the rise of a conventionalistic mode of thinking— emanating from mathematics—today favours attempts to construct novel logics.[1]

This proliferation of logical systems has had a stimulating effect

---

[1] Friederich Waismann, "Are There Alternative Logics?", *Proceedings of the Aristotelian Society*, vol. 46 (1946), pp. 77–104 (see p. 77).

upon philosophical theorizing. The philosophical problems posed by the multiplicity of systems of logic have a fundamental interest transcending that of the technical issues of logical theory involved. Looking backward toward the first impact of Lukasiewicz's work in many-valued logic, Z. Jordan writes:

> But it is difficult to fully realize now all the consequences of Lukasiewicz's discovery. Investigations in this direction have gone little beyond the first shocking conclusion that logical truth has got a multi-form character and that there is a variety of ways in which it may be considered. In some respects the discovery and the foundation of many-valued logic makes us think of the shattering blow dealt by the discovery of the Non-Euclidean geometries to the deeply-rooted conviction that there is one and only one way of constructing the spatial reference-frame of our experiences. Similarly it was supposed that a consistent deductive system must follow the Aristotelian pattern, in accordance with his most general "law of thought." In particular it was believed that a statement must be either true or false. In some circles there arose doubts concerning this principle when Brouwer constructed definite examples of mathematical theorems—dealing with "the infinite" as it occurs in analysis—which are neither true nor false. The construction by Lukasiewicz of a self-consistent deductive system in which the proposition "a statement is either true or false" no longer holds turned the balance definitely against the Aristotelian assumption.[2]

The prospect of basically different alternatives to the traditional logic built up over the centuries upon the groundwork of Aristotle excited the minds of many thinkers, and has exerted a powerfully stimulative impetus in freeing the logical imagination from the narrow-guage tracks of the prior tradition.

But here, as elsewhere, innovation has despite its interest and fruitfulness brought serious problems and difficulties in its wake.

---

[2] "The Development of Mathematical Logic in Poland Between the Two Wars" in S. McCall (ed.), *Polish Logic* (Oxford, 1967), pp. 346–97 (see pp. 394–5).

2. THE PROBLEM OF CHOICE

The undeniable fact of a proliferation of logical systems leads straightaway to the question of how a choice between them can be made. How is one to decide which alternative represents *the correct* system of logic?

Three alternative postures are available with respect to this question, all of which have been espoused by some writers on the subject.

(1) the question is misguided because there is no real choice: there is in fact only one system of logic—the putative "alternatives" are spurious. (Platonic Absolutism)

(2) the question is inappropriate because cast in the wrong terms; the search for the correct logic is pointless: all (duly suitable) systems are on the same level, and the choice between them is a matter of essentially arbitrary convention. (Conventionalism or Indifferentist Relativism)

(3) the question is legitimate: a genuine choice between genuine alternatives is at hand, a choice which can and must be resolved on some rational but context-dependent and purpose-oriented basis (Instrumentalistic Relativism).

The first position (Platonic Absolutism) holds that logical pluralism is an illusion: there simply is no plurality of genuine alternatives as regards logic. Thus the eminent late Polish logician Stanislaw Lesniewski held (according to an oral communication by J. M. Bochenski) that all the variant nontraditional systems are merely idle games. There is but one single authentic system of logic: the orthodox and standard one. In the same spirit Paul F. Linke relegates all the nonclassical pluri-valued logics to the position of "logic-like formalisms" (*logoide Formalismen*).[3] This points towards a conception of logic which is inherently absolutistic. Since there is one correct system of logic, logical principles are in the final analysis either correct or not—and so certain logical principles will stand on a secure, uncontested footing.

The *instrumental* conception of logic is, on the other hand, inherently relativistic. If there is a plurality of viable systems of

[3] "Die mehrwertigen Logiken und das Wahrheitsproblem," *Zeitschrift für philosophische Forschung*, vol. 3 (1948–9), pp. 376–98 and 530–46.

logic, then—even if some of them have, for certain purposes, an advantage over others in serviceability—logical principles are at the mercy of competing systematizations; principles standardly operative in some systems will fail to hold in others.

In putting forward the case for relativism in logic, let us (for the sake of having a concrete example) consider a particular logical principle, say the Law of the Excluded Middle in the form of the Principle of Bivalence asserting that every proposition either takes on the truth-value T (*true*) or the truth-value F (false), in short, that every proposition is either true or false. Now consider the two questions:

(1) Does the Principle of Bivalence hold for system X?
(2) Does the Principle of Bivalence hold (*simpliciter*)?

These questions are strikingly different. The question of type (1) is obviously warranted and proper, for there is a variety of many-valued systems of logic, and in some (e.g., the classical propositional calculus) the Principle of Bivalence obtains, whereas in others (e.g., the 3-valued system of Lukasiewicz) it does not. Everyone can agree with respect to considerations of *this* sort, regardless of any doctrinal position on the issue of the nature of "logic itself."

The case is altogether different with regard to the question of type (2), where logical principles appear to function without any aspect of system-relativity. Here the instrumentalist could plausibly argue that this type of question is inappropriate and improper. Logical principles like that of Bivalence hold for some systems and not others (a universally admitted fact). And there is little alternative to granting that the choice between logical systems is not dictated by any inevitable necessity, but is in the final analysis a matter that must be *decided* on some basis. The decision may well be regarded as not arbitrary but guided by purposive and contextual considerations; yet all the same, it is a decision admitting of a resolution whose suitability is a moot point. And on this perspective the status of the "laws of logic" is held to be system-relative and thus subject to a genuine choice between logical systems.[4]

Such a relativism can take two forms, depending upon its

---

[4] It should be stressed that such an instrumentalism by no means destroys or even undermines the standardly vaunted apodeictic necessity of logical

view of the nature of the choice between alternative systematizations. On the one hand we have *conventionalism*, which views such systems as basically abstract formalisms, the choice between which is unconstrained by objective considerations, but is a matter of essentially arbitrary preference, whose sole basis is subjective: matters of personal convenience, subjective taste, or aesthetic "style" (or else simply a matter of historical tradition). On the other hand we have an *instrumentalism* which views the choice between alternative systematization as teleologically guided (rather than being essentially arbitrary) subject to the constraint of purpose-relative considerations of effectiveness, efficiency, economy, and the like.

3. THE GEOMETRIC ANALOGY: A FALSE START

In the historical development of the debate on logical pluralism and relativism, the central role has been played by the analogy of geometry and the plurality of geometric systems. This analogy provides a good starting-point for our own analysis.

Charles Sanders Peirce aside, the founding fathers of many-valued logic—V. A. Vasil'ev, Jan Lukasiewicz, Emil Post, and C. I. Lewis—all assimilated the diversity of logical systems to the existence of non-Euclidean geometries.[5] All these logicians were motivated by a conception of non-Aristotelian logic along lines of

---

principles. That a given thesis holds with ironclad necessity in a certain system of logic is nowise questioned. But *this* sort of necessitarian "logical truth" is clearly a system-internal issue: it assumes we are dealing with a *given* logic and are asking whether certain principles obtain *within it*. The necessity of logical truth is accordingly seen as operative at this *internal* level. But when one cuts loose from any commitment to this or that specific system and approaches the issue from a system-external perspective, then logical principles become negotiable and the question of their obtaining can no longer be settled on a basis of necessity. Yet nothing in this system-external relativism conflicts with a system-internal absolutism: an instrumentalistic approach need not abrogate the necessitarian cast that is the hallmark of logical truth.

[5] E. L. Post placed emphasis on one interesting feature of the analogy: From the standpoint of intuitive naturalness, a three-dimensional space wins out on the geometric side of the analogy even as a two-dimensional truth-space wins out on the logical side. But neither fact is to preclude the development of other systems of higher dimensionability. "Introduction to a General Theory of Elementary Propositions," *American Journal of Mathematics*, vol. 43 (1921), pp. 163–85 (see p. 182).

an analogy with the situation in geometry, where one finds a great proliferation of systems—not merely that of Euclid alone, but the variant geometries of Bolyai, Lobachevski, and Riemann, among others. On neither the geometric nor the logical side can a choice between alternative systems be validated on the basis of purely formal considerations. This comparison, upon which virtually all discussions alike have (largely independently) placed heavy stress, represents a striking, almost astonishing convergence of perspective.

The distinction between a *pure* (i.e., wholly abstract and purely formal) and a *physical* (i.e., physically interpreted) geometry must play an important role in this analogy. It is quite plain that, on the side of pure mathematical theory, no rational preferential choice can be made among alternative possibilities: no one among the variant systems can possibly be validated *vis-à-vis* its competitors by purely formal considerations. The issue of relative correctness simply cannot arise here. But when one makes the transition from *abstract* to *applied* geometry—that is to *physical* geometry, bringing upon the scene such physical realizations of mathematical *abstracta* as meter sticks or light rays—then only one particular system will presumably prove itself to be apposite and "correct." However, (and this point is crucial) with logic we have to do solely with the *applied* side of the fence. Only the applied, *physical* sector of the geometric case is relevant to the analogy with logic. For there can be no "pure"—i.e., wholly uninterpreted—logic. A system of "logic" must deal with specifically predefined notions. Its materials—propositions and their assertion and denial, propositional operators like conjunction, propositional classifiers like falsity—are all predetermined. An abstract calculus which is not suitably connected with these pre-systematic ideas cannot qualify as a *logic*. It would be pointless to offer an uninterpreted formalism that leaves meaning-specification to its axioms themselves. The geometric analogy, then, must be construed as being drawn between logic, on the one hand, and, on the other, *physical* (i.e., intepreted) geometry.

So drawn, the analogy *suggests* that empirical considerations become predominant in a choice between alternative logics. Just as one physical geometry will presumably turn out to be the right one—the only one that correctly applies (under the specified conditions) to the actual world—so only one logical system is acceptable as the actual logic (once all the relevant facts are known). This suggestion is in actuality very much mistaken. (It will be criticized in detail below.) The consideration that analogy has such misleading consequences indicates that something is amiss with it.

The contention that the proliferation of logical systems is to be traced to sources similar to the multiplicity of non-Euclidean geometries is misguided because there is a crucial disanalogy between the two cases. The key point which—though it is generally neglected—cannot be given sufficient stress is this: *We cannot formulate (give exact articulation to) a system of logic without ourselves using logical principles* (even if only tacitly). The semantical factors of meaningfulness, truth, consequence, inconsistency, and their congeners must inevitably play an overt and prominent role in the development of a system *of logic*. In the course of formulating as a system the materials of "a logic" one must inevitably make an at least implicit use of logical principles. To articulate a *systematic* logic we necessarily employ some *presystematic* logical machinery. The principles of the presystematic logic need not, of course, themselves be *formulated*— otherwise one would be caught up in an infinite regress. But they will surely be *formulable*. For one can reason logically without explicit resort to an articulated logic, even as one can speak grammatically without awareness of grammatical principles. Presumably (and in normal circumstances) the system of logic at issue seeks to capture the presystematic logic used in its development—the formal system being so articulated that we can see intuitively that it largely or wholly succeeds in systematizing the logical principles employed in its own articulation.[6]

Now this feature that a systematic logic is bound up with a presystematic logic as its *sine qua non* is a point of crucial disanalogy with geometry. There just is no need for any *pre-*

[6] The historic controversy—which raged both in antiquity and medieval times—as to whether logic is a *special branch* of knowledge or *general instrument* for the realization of knowledge throughout all its branches is to be resolved along just these lines. Systematized logic is a special branch of knowledge; but the presystematic logic used generically in the formulation of all branches of knowledge (systematized logic included) is a general instrument. (And, of course, a systematized logic can *also* be applied —say in mathematics—as an instrument in developing other branches of knowledge.)

I

systematic geometry to be in hand before one can proceed to give exact articulation to a "system of geometry."

This disanalogy is highly significant from the standpoint of the present considerations of alternativeness and relativism. For the situation it puts before us is this: that the development of a geometric system is unfettered and free of involvement with presystematic geometric principles, while that of a logical system requires the use of presystematic logical machinery. This critical disanalogy between the situation in logic and that in geometry shows that different sorts of alternativeness are at issue in the two cases, so that the nature of the choice between alternative systems in the two cases will have to differ decisively.

These shortcomings of the geometric analogy indicate the desirability of exploring yet another, very different line of approach.

4. THE GRAMMATICAL ANALOGY

In traditional discussions of the matter, deriving from Aristotle and continuing within the Aristotelian tradition of antiquity and the Middle Ages, logic was held to be analogous not with geometry, but with *grammar*. The analogy of grammar may thus be regarded as the historically standard approach to the question of the nature of logic as a branch of knowledge. This analogy goes as follows:

> Both with grammar and with logic we begin with a pretheoretical corpus of practice: *speech* in the one case and *reasoning* in the other. In either case, a *theoretical systematization* of the (best and most correct) practice in this area can be made, codifying the procedural principles governing this practice in actual operation. With *speech* the framework of rules that present the theoretical systematization of the pretheoretical practice is *grammar*, and with *reasoning* it is *logic*. Logic is thus the systematic articulation of the principles of (correct) reasoning, even as grammar is that of the principles of (correct) speech.

This classical analogy is not only in large measure appropriate, but also illuminating. Its main, but perhaps its only, major shortcoming arises in connection with the normative qualifiers that occur in the characterization just given. For the modern grammarian has abandoned the traditional normative appraisals of right and wrong, whereas the logician (modern or otherwise) is neither willing nor able to do so. Traditional or classical grammar, conceiving its role in the normative terms of a search for *correct* rules of usage, thus comes nearer to satisfying the conditions of a correct analogy.

With the latter-day non-normative version of grammar, the nature of the observed presystematic practice is decisive: the systematization must, on pains of inadequacy, conform to it. The empirical aspects of the presystematic practice are taken as altogether determinative for the systematization. But in logic the situation is otherwise. Early in the game, one abstracts certain of the key *regulative* features of the logical enterprise from an informal examination of the presystematic practice of reasoning. Thereupon one injects the requirement of conformity to these regulative features into the consideration of systematizations (as well as introducing "pragmatic" considerations relating to the specific area of application at issue).

Thus the principles of logic—unlike those of grammar on the currently fashionable view—have a *normative* force: logic must maintain the ideas of correctness and incorrectness in operation. To be sure, logic begins with merely descriptive considerations as to how persuasively effective argumentation in fact proceeds. But while it begins with the descriptive, logic ends with the normative. Logic must root in a teleological analysis of the purposes of the presystematic practice of reasoning that is its object. Then, early on, it transmutes *de facto* persuasive efficacy into the concept of *de jure* probative force. Thus the normative "right" and "wrong" of the logician's account of how reasoning is to be conducted are of simply *instrumental* weight, relating to how one "ought" to reason to achieve efficacy in conviction and security against objections and possible counter-moves. Given the teleology of efficiency and effectiveness in probative argumentation, the normative aspect enters in through this *purposive* door.

Let us consider logic along grammatical lines, looking at grammar in the way of the traditional normative grammarians. We have to do, then, with a presystematic practice of reasoning in a wide variety of relatively demanding contexts—mathematics, science, political disputation, legal argumentation, etc. In this connection the situation of logic becomes crucially disanalogous with that of the purely descriptive grammar of the contemporary grammarians.

In taking such a stance, the logician (unlike the modern grammarian) veers away from primary emphasis upon the empirical features of the presystematic practice with which he deals: his insistence upon certain regulative principles limits the extent to which he can rest satisfied with any merely empirical survey of inferential practice. Regulative and functional (and so teleologically oriented and normative) considerations come to bear a relatively greater weight. In this respect, the logical situation is disanalogous with that of modern grammar, and our guiding analogy of the nature of logic must thus be construed with reference to the traditional normative approach to the grammatical enterprise.

The initial "practice of reasoning" with whose systematization logic commences is very diversified, variegated, and largely inconsistent (perhaps even less uniform than linguistic practice). This being the case, significant scope is left for divergent systematizations. For when a corpus of practice is inherently non-uniform and incoherent, different (mutually inconsistent) rule systematizations can at best organize parts of it. Not only may such divergences arise as between different groups of reasoners and different subject-matter fields of inquiry—they can arise in the practice of one group within one area.

The resulting systems will be linked by a network of family resemblances based on the sharing of various principles by any two systems—although no particular group of principles will hold "all across the board." The lack of such an essentialistic "hard core" of logical principles—principles that will inevitably have to be features of *any* logical system—has significant consequences for the study of alternative logics. It means that we cannot here proceed essentialistically through the increasingly sufficient specifications of necessary conditions for what it is to be "a logic." We cannot say: "A logical system *must* embody the specific principles $P_1, P_2, \ldots P_n$, and can then vary in other respects."

To take this view is to abandon the conception of a core of principles that *must inevitably* be present in all logical systems. But it does not commit us to denying that there may be a *statisti-*

cal core of principles that will *generally* be present in logical systems. For example, the rules of inference by substitution and *modus ponens* are almost universally present as inferential principles in propositional logic. To say this is not, however, to make the essentialistic contention that a system that wholly lacked these two principles could not conceivably count as a "logic."[7] The whole idea of *inevitable* logical principles is given up.

5. ABSOLUTISM AND RELATIVISM IN LOGIC

Let us review the various alternative positions regarding the justificatory rationale of logic. Some major approaches to the issue of resolving the choice between alternative systems of logic are summarized in Table 1.

The *Platonist* conceives of logic as descriptive, but as describing not human practices of reasoning but the geography of an abstract realm of concepts. The leading idea of Platonism is that there is a real but abstract realm of logical entities (say abstract propositions) and the aim of logical theory is to study the real but abstract interrelationships among the entities comprising this realm. The principles of logic are thus universal truths about one fundamental—though admittedly abstract—sector of reality.[8]

From the point of view of *psychologism*, logic is regarded as a fundamentally *descriptive* enterprise. Its task is seen as the devising of a "theory of reasoning"—a formalized and systematized account of the way in which men actually proceed when reasoning successfully (i.e., when managing to avoid confusion and error). Logic is now construed as a discipline whose ultimate roots are factual: the logician studies the actually observed process of reasoning (perhaps only on the part of a very selective group of highly intelligent people—say mathematicians) much as

[7] In various contexts one speaks of "the principles of logic," and this mode of thought is not incompatible with the present analysis. For it is clear that one then has in mind inference processes such as those of substitution and *modus ponens* and conjunct-separation (etc.) which obtain with respect to virtually all of the commonly encountered systematizations of logic. But one need not then espouse the essentialistic hard-core view of principles that must inevitably characterize any "genuine" logic.

[8] See, for example, Morris R. Cohen's *Reason and Nature* (New York, 1931).

Table 1

APPROACHES TO ALTERNATIVE LOGICS

Genus	Species	Difference: The choice between various systems of logic is:
1. Absolutism	Platonism	*constrained*, being dictated by the abstract conceptual objects of logic
2. Absolutism	Psychologism	*constrained*, being dictated by the empirical realities of human reasoning processes
3. Relativism	Conventionalism (formalism)	*wholly free*, being unconstrained by any objective considerations; purely a matter of arbitrary preference, subjective taste, and personal "style"
4. Relativism	Instrumentalism (functionalism)	*teleologically guided*, being circumscribed by purpose-relative considerations of effectiveness, efficiency, economy, and the like

the social sciences make a descriptive study of political or economic behaviour.[9] Construed in this way, the question of the content of the appropriate system of logic is a strictly empirical issue. Alternative systems of logic stand in an outright doctrinal conflict. Logical principles are (for a given target group of reasoners to be studied) either correct or not—they do or do not describe satis-

---

[9] I do not actually know of any serious writer who has explicitly espoused this position in this extreme form, although perhaps certain Oxford philosophers in the entourage of J. L. Austin tended to move in this direction.

factorily the way they actually go about conducting their inferential business.[10]

This conception of logic as the empirical science descriptive of actual (but correct or at any rate successful) reasoning stands in contrast with the position of *relativism*. This position embraces two distinct poles.

At the conventionalist pole of relativism, the construction of logical systems is regarded as a free exercise in creative ingenuity. We have to do with the unfettered construction of abstract procedures systematizing possible inferential practices. According to such a view, the task of logic lies in the construction of systems codifying *possible* instrumentalities for deductive (i.e., truth-preserving) inference. These would be *available* (should someone want to make use of them) for possible adoption as an organon of reasoning, but no empirical claims are made that anyone has (or will) avail himself of this opportunity. The logician devises a tool or instrument for correct reasoning, but does not concern himself about the uses of such formal mechanisms. That is the essence of the conventionalist position.

However, at the *instrumentalist* pole of relativism there is a strong injection of normative considerations, and great emphasis is placed on the convenient and efficient usability of some of these instruments as opposed to others. The case for such an instrumentalism was clearly argued by C. I. Lewis.[11] Lewis maintains:

Sufficiency for the guidance and testing of our usual deductions, systematic simplicity and convenience, accord with our psychological limitations and mental habits, and so on, operate as criteria in our conscious or unconscious choice of "good logic." Any current or accepted canon of inference must be pragmatically determined. That one such system should be thus accepted does not imply that the alternative systems are false: it does imply that they are—or would be thought to be—relatively poorer instruments for the conduct and testing of our ordinary inferences.[12]

10 The issue may, of course, become a ramified one: the "logic" of one group may go one way; that of another, another.
11 "Alternative Systems of Logic," *The Monist*, vol. 41 (1931), pp. 481–507.
12 *Op. cit.*, p. 484.

On an instrumentalistic approach of this sort, there is no danger of irrationalism. One postulates, at the metalogical level, a clear, nonrelative criterion for the *validity* of inference principles in an acceptable logic—viz., truth preservation, i.e., leading from true premisses to true conclusions. Apart from this consideration, the choice between alternative systems is—for the instrumentalist— heavily hedged about by considerations of a functionalist and purposive sort.

Psychologism and Platonism are both absolutistic and inherently monistic doctrines: they support the view that there is— actually or most probably—one single "correct" logic. Formalistic conventionalism remains inherently pluralistic: it envisages a virtually endless procession of logics, the choice between which is purely arbitrary and conventional and is guided by considerations of stylistic preference (if by anything at all). Instrumentalism takes a more restrictive view. Admitting a plurality of logics, it regards the choice between them as not as arbitrary and wide open, but as narrowly delimited by a whole host of *functional* or purpose-relative considerations of effectiveness, economy, and efficiency given the inferential tasks and purposes upon which the logical apparatus at issue is to be deployed.

Neither a version of absolutism nor an indifferentist relativism (conventionalism) is inherently very appealing. Absolutism founders on the fact that alternative logics are not merely formal games: they are serious instruments capable of accomplishing serious work. Conventionalism, on the other hand, carries the burden of its indifferentism. Once considerations of correctness or appropriateness are ruled out, and the matter is seen as one of an arbitrary choice between conflicting but essentially indifferent systems, doubt comes to be cast on the preeminent status of logic as such. For the question of the credentials that establish logic as superior to illogic now becomes ominously pressing. The way from indifferentism to a kind of anti-logic or even illogic and irrationalism is dangerously smooth and tempting.

The discussion could (and perhaps should) be prolonged, but its upshot remains the same. Our own commitments point towards a constellation of three principles: (1) that the pluralism of logical systems confronts us with the situation of a real choice among genuine alternatives, (2) that this choice that must be resolved on some appropriate rational basis, and (3) that functional considerations of purposive efficacy provide the pivot-point here, so that an essentially purpose-oriented justification is called for. This, then, is the core of the instrumentalist position.

The fact of alternative systems of logic thus confronts us with a situation of a real choice. However, this choice is—on the view propounded here—heavily laden with teleological considerations. This functional perspective opens up the prospect of an instrumental approach as a convenient middle course between the Scylla of a rigid absolutism and the Charybdis of an indifferentist conventionalism. The closer appraisal of this prospect is the task of the next chapter.[13]

---

[13] The present chapter has drawn upon Chapter 3 "The Question of Relativism in Logic" of the author's *Many-valued Logic* (New York, 1969).

Chapter XIV

THE INSTRUMENTAL JUSTIFICATION OF LOGIC

1. THE INSTRUMENTAL TURN: LOGIC AS DOCTRINE VS. LOGIC AS INSTRUMENT

A "conflict" can arise between rival systems of logic in two significantly distinct ways, according as alternative *doctrines* or alternative *procedures* are understood to be at issue. For logic clearly has a dual aspect in this regard. On the doctrinal side, logic is construed as a body of *theses*: it is systematic codification of a special class of propositions, the "logical truths." On the other, methodological side, logic represents an *operational code*, a *modus operandi* for conducting the business of reasoning. It is important to recognize this dual aspect of logic as a *doctrine*, a collection of theses, on the one hand, and as a *method*, a procedural organon for the conduct of inference, on the other. The distinction at issue carries back to the old dispute—carried on throughout late antiquity and the Middle Ages—as to whether logic is to be considered as a part of knowledge or as an *instrument* for its development. The best minds of the day rightly refused to resolve this issue on an either/or basis: they insisted that the proper answer is simply that logic is *both* of these—at once a *theory* with a body of theses of its own and a *tool* for testing arguments to determine whether they are good or bad.

This duality is not, however, a partnership of equals in a situation of strict parity. The *instrumental* character of logic as codifying "the principles of right reasoning" (as the traditional formula puts it) must be accepted as primary. For the very aim is to systematize, formalize, and rationalize the practice of reasoning in all of the many contexts—practical and theoretical alike— where inferences are drawn or brought to bear. Accordingly, logical rules must be attuned to the practice of reasoning in these domains. And logical theses must consequently be grounded in this practice, for such *theses* effectively formulate the import of the inferential *rules* that characterize the practice of reasoning. The instrumental aspect of logic as a tool of argumentation is thus fundamental.

A conflict between codified systems considered as alternative *doctrines* involves a conflict in truth-claims: some theses that are true according to one system are false according to the other. Various systems of geometry represent a doctrinal conflict of just this sort—Euclidean and Riemannian geometry, for example. For there will be theses (e.g., the Euclidean parallel postulate) which are true according to the one, but false according to the other system. Again, two discordant theories in physics—classical and relativistic dynamics, for example, or Maxwellian and quantum electro-dynamics—will also disagree in such a way that conflicting assertions are involved.

On the other hand, diverse systematizations involve alternative *instrumentalities* when they provide different instruments or specify different procedures for the accomplishment of a task. This clash is of a weaker sort. The sets of instructions "Take first a pound of *A*, stir it up well, and then add an ounce of *B*" and "Take first an ounce of *B*, then add to it a pound of *A* and stir well" do not represent a logical conflict among contradictory *theses*, but rather a practical conflict among *procedures*. Such procedural complexes are "inconsistent" only because both cannot possibly be carried out in one and the same case. The conflict here is analogous to that encountered among different rule books or different codes of etiquette. It is a clash of conflicting things *to be done*, and not of conflicting things *asserted*.

Systematic diversity accordingly has two very different modes: the one involving a *doctrinal* conflict between *purportedly* available alternative sets of logical theses, and the other involving an *instrumental* conflict between *actually* available alternative sets of inferential *procedures*. In the context of our inquiry the pivotal question is: Which of these two modes of conflict is at issue with respect to alternative logics? Our present answer lies squarely on the instrumental/methodological side. In the case of a doctrinal conflict one can appropriately ask: *Which is in fact correct?* But one cannot do so in the case of an instrumental conflict. The question that can appropriately be raised with respect to alternative methods or procedures is that quintessentially *instrumentalistic* question: *Which is optimally effective for specified purposes?*

This instrumental approach accepts the aspect of logic as inferential practice as basic, and views the theses of logic as attempts to capture the workings of this practice in articulated propositions. From such a perspective, the factor of *procedural* diversity is the fundamental issue as regards logic, and the doctrinal conflict of logical systems is secondary and *supervenient* —a merely derivative consequence of the instrumental conflict of inferential procedures.

Accordingly, we maintain that the weaker type of instrumentalistic alternativeness is fundamental with respect to different systems of logic. Given, say, the desideratum of avoiding the semantical paradoxes, one may well consider the question whether this is more efficiently accomplished by adopting a many-valued logic (and accepting the added complications so introduced), or by keeping to a two-valued logic as our inferential apparatus and adopting a more complex theory of meaningfulness to rule out the paradox-generating statements.

On taking this view of logic as primarily an instrument for the management of reasoning (in both its practical and theoretical settings), one can routinely apply the standard strategy of instrumental justification as set out in the first chapter. For *any* practice—inferential practice included—is correlative with its characteristic objectives, and we can use the standard approach of assessing the merits of the instruments in terms of their efficiency in the realization of these goals. When logic is construed as an instrument for the conduct of reasoning in the various contexts of exact argumentation, the machinery of instrumental justification can be brought into operation, and logic examined in the functional and teleological terms that make the instrumentalist approach routinely applicable. This teleological view of logic places it squarely within the framework of our general strategy of instrumentalistic analysis.

2. THE PRAGMATIC LIMITS OF PLURALISM

Let us return to our point of departure in the recognition of a plurality of viable systems of "logic," alternative to one another with respect to their common capacity to satisfy the fundamental objectives of any system of "logic": the systematic codification of procedures of reasoning in those multiple practical and theoretical contexts that require resort to rigorous inferential mechanisms. This plurality of systems provides alternative instrumentalities; for certain purposes some of these instrumentalities may be better (e.g., two-valued logic for classical mathematics), for other purposes, other systems may be superior (as 3-valued logic may turn out to be a better instrument for systematizing quantum theory, or infinite-valued logic may be the best medium for developing set theory). Since the goals themselves are varied—due to the fact that reasoning in a great many diverse areas is at issue (physics, mathematics, law, etc.)—there can be no theoretical *guarantee* of a uniformity of result. We must be prepared for the possibility of finding that our "logic" is a complex structure of many branches, and that there may not necessarily be one single all-purpose tool, but a variety of special-purpose tools: various specialized "logics" that represent distinct sectors of *logic* in the broader sense.

An instrumentalist approach can no more count upon validating a universally and generically "correct" logic than one could expect to find a universally and generically "correct" woodworking tool. (To say this is not to deny that a pencil will not be a woodworking tool at all, nor will an axiomatized theory of classical mechanics be a logic.[1]) On the instrumentalist approach there will be room for maneuver among the plurality of logical systems. But this room is limited. The operative limits are primarily of two kinds. those relating to *regulative feasibility*, and those relating to *teleological suitability*. Both demand somewhat closer attention.

(i) *Regulative Feasibility*

Let us begin with limits imposed by considerations of *regulative feasibility,* for these must weigh heavily in the present context.

[1] This indicates a line of reply to the proposal: "If there are different systematizations that seem on first sight qualified to serve as 'logics,' why not regard as a part of genuine logic only what belongs to their common core—i.e., those principles on which all 'logics' across the entire spectrum are in agreement?" The answer is simply that too little would remain; that we would obtain a "system" so impoverished as no longer to qualify as a "system of logic" at all.

After all, proposed logical systems will not qualify for serious considerations if they do not satisfy minimal standards of precision (e.g., in avoiding ambiguity and equivocation). These feasibility-aspects appear in clearest focus not so much by looking at the assertive content of the logical system from its own internal perspective, as by taking an essentially external perspective upon the metalogical aspects of the matter. Certain important features now stand out. The first and most important of these is the necessity of meeting at least minimal regulative standards of coherence in the articulation and development of a logical system. For example, such a system must be *consistent*. (Regardless of whether or not the system contains something deserving of the name of a "Principle of Noncontradiction," it must itself avoid self-contradiction.) Moreover, all the characterizing features of such systems must be explicitly and unambiguously specified. Thus the system must be objective, in that its composition must be fixed intersubjectively, obtaining *with respect to that system* for any person, regardless of his own preferred logical perspective. If this requirement were not satisfied, we would not have succeeded in putting a well-defined system forward at all. We may designate this second requirement—additional to that of coherence—as the requisite of precision.

(ii) *Functional Suitability*

Considerations of *teleological suitability* specify the *functional desiderata* of a systematization of logic (in contrast with its inevitably necessary requisites). Such factors enter in through the crucial question: What kind of thing do we expect a logical system to do? A "logic" is, after all, a very general, but yet definite *sort* of thing. Certain qualifying conditions of a purposive sort should be fulfilled by the axioms (if any) and inference rules of a system *of logic*. (An uninterpreted axiomatization of mathematical group theory or of classical mechanics would not qualify.) One—admittedly imprecise—requirement is that a semantical interpretation *along something like the usual lines* must be possible. (The italicized phrase here indicates a problem to which we shall return—that of the priority-claims of classical logic.) Above all, any logically acceptable (i.e., *valid*) process of inference must be such that it can under no circumstances lead us from true premises to a false conclusion.

On this view, there is range of legitimate choice among logical systems, but this range is not without limits. In the first instance this choice is restricted by regulatively grounded principles, delimiting an area within which various alternatives are viable. The residual choice among these remaining alternatives is defined not in terms of the distinction of "correct" vs. "incorrect" but that of "effective" vs. "ineffective." Within this range, then, a choice between systems cannot be made in a once-and-for-all fashion on the basis of abstract *theoretical* considerations, but must be made on the basis of *purposive* considerations concerning the specific, lower-level objective at issue.[2] The choice among systems now hinges on questions of their instrumental role in the intended applications. Logic is accordingly viewed as a many-roomed mansion rather than a single vast hall—a much-inclusive *discipline* of internally variegated theories rather than one monolithic all-embracing *theory*.

Above all, any proposed logical system must conform to regulative principles at the metasystematic level—certain minimal but universal regulative standards of coherence and precision (*inter alia*). Moreover, there is the crucial factor of *conformity with our presystematic understanding of what logic is all about.* The devising of systems is constrained by functionalistic considerations of their serviceability for the purposes for which the systematization of logic is undertaken. And this has important consequences for the issue of relativism. For it places definite limits on any defensible form of logical relativism.[3]

These considerations point back to our initial recognition of the existence of alternative logics and the resultant concessions to

[2] Thus it is only with respect to this limited range that we can endorse the position of J. B. Rosser and A. R. Turquette in their book *Many-Valued Logics* (Amsterdam, 1952); see p. 1.

[3] We cannot spell out in any detail here the implications of this position for the concept of *logical truth* (and of *analytic propositions*). This will now *to some extent* become context-relatively dependent upon the logical framework operative in a given range of discussion. Generally speaking, the area of application of the concept will now be fuzzy-edged: there will be a definite interior and a definite exterior separated from one another by a wide penumbral border.

system pluralism. But there is good reason to think that this pluralism is hedged by regulative principles in such a way that it does not issue in a relativism or conventionalism of any unfortunate sort—to say nothing of illogic or irrationalism. For despite its intrinsic pluralism, the instrumentalistic view of logic does not underwrite the arbitrariness of indifferentism. The delimitative force of purposiveness is crucial here.

3. A CLOSER LOOK AT THE FUNCTIONAL/REGULATIVE ASPECT

An instrumental line of approach thus cannot avoid facing the difficult question: What is the *function* of a "system of logic"? Logic, after all, has an inherent teleology: it is inherently purpose-oriented and application-directed,[4] and this teleological dimension of the issue must not only be acknowledged, it must be clarified.

Certainly a system of logic must bear upon the formal structure of inference and reasoning. It must systematize our informal intuitions in this sphere in a way akin to that in which systems of arithmetical calculation formalize the informal computations we can "do in our head." Confronted with an austerely formal system, a purely abstract calculus, we are not even entitled—and would not in the slightest be tempted—to speak of it as a "logic" until a semantical interpretation has been provided (involving such concepts as those of the *meaning* and *truth* of propositions, and relationships of *consequence* and *inconsistency* among groups thereof).[5] Only a system that achieves this objective of systematizing the formal, generic features of inference and reasoning—as we conduct it in the context of precise inquiries like those of mathematics and science—can qualify for characterization as a

---

[4] No writer has stressed this point more emphatically than C. S. Peirce: "Logic has to define its aim, and in doing so is even more dependent upon ethics, or the philosophy of aims, by far, than it is. . .upon mathematics." (*Collected Papers*, vol. IV: 4.240.)

[5] Some formal systems, such as the many-valued systems of quantification theory developed by Rosser and Turquette, do not have any semantic interpretation, but base whatever claims they have to being a "logic" on purely syntactical analysis. On our view, such systems can be called "logics" only provisionally in the hope that the syntactic analogy gives grounds for expecting the future discovery of a workable semantics.

"system of logic." The theses which constitute such a systematization must be given a justificatory warrant because they represent simply one alternative among others. There certainly are no logical principles which must indispensably figure as overt theses within any and every systematization deserving the name of a "logical system." Thus, at the *constitutive* level of the issue, much can be said for the doctrine of relativism.

But this is not the end of the matter. What we might call the doctrine of the *Constitutive Relativism of Logical Theses* must be tempered by the no less correct doctrine of the *Regulative Absolutism of Metalogical Principles*. To see what is at issue here, let us begin by distinguishing between two distinct versions of such logical principles as the "Principle of Contradiction" and the "Principle of Excluded Middle": (1) On the one hand, as explicit formulas of a system—the analogues of "$\neg(P \,\&\, \neg P)$" and "$P \lor \neg P$".[6] (2) On the other hand, such logical principles may be viewed as metasystematic principles ("Do not affirm a proposition and its negative," "If you do not class a proposition as true, you must class it as false, and conversely"). In this latter, essentially regulative role, these principles have a very different sort of status, and they cannot be written off as easily as in the first. Here logical principles function as regulative rules that operate *outside* any specifically formulated system, rather than as explicit members of an overt systematization.

The key point emerges that while the *internal*, constitutive principles are relativistic and negotiable—some may be traded off against others—the *external*, regulative, metalogical principles are absolute. These latter, being definitive of the very "nature of the enterprise," must be maintained come what may. However, notwithstanding their seeming solidity, even these principles may, from one angle, be said to have feet of clay. For such regulative metaprinciples are of essentially negative import. Consider for example, this key principle:

[6] It may be said that, strictly speaking, there is no such principle as (e.g.) that of the Excluded Middle, since there are many different logical systems in each of which there is (or may be) something akin to the principle. (One might even argue for a family-resemblance approach along lines made familiar by the later writings of Ludwig Wittgenstein.) But in fact, there is a certain core idea operative throughout. Cf. M. Farber, "Logical Systems and the Principles of Logic," *Philosophy of Science*, vol. 9 (1942), pp. 40–54; see especially p. 52.

A logically valid principle of inference must be truth-preserving: it must not, under any circumstances, lead from true premisses to a false conclusion.

Note that this—like all other metaprinciples—is purely restrictive in its bearing. It *eliminates* certain inferential principles and narrows the range of what is admissible. But it is not determinative of any particular result (any more than the negative morality of the "thou shalt not" commandments can determine any positive course of action). Neither alone nor in conjunction with other similar metaprinciples can such rules delimit a specific system of logic (for just as total *inaction* is compatible with any number of instructions to refrain on the order of the Decalogue commandments, so a simply agnostic refusal to draw any inferences at all will be compatible with the honoring of any and all negativistic metaprinciples).

The important feature of such metaprinciples of regulative feasibility is that—together with the suitability requirements of convenience, economy, efficiency, effectiveness, and the rest—they represent constraints that *underdetermine* the structure of any specific systematization of a "logic." The metaprinciples impose limiting conditions, without fixing a single solution—analogously with such problems as constructing an equilateral triangle with two of three given points as vertices, or solving n (independent) linear equations with $m > n$ unknowns. This analogy illustrates our own pragmatic approach. It leaves the choice between various "alternative" logics *genuinely open*—so much we must concede to relativism. But nevertheless it sees the resolution of this choice as constrained within an (absolutistically) delimited range of viable alternatives, and even within this range as *guided* by instrumentalistic and purpose-oriented considerations.

A "logical law," as we are now considering it, is not a thesis which holds within each and every system of logic. Rather it will be a regulative metasystematic principle: It holds not *in*, but *of* the various systems. It is *regulative* in its bearing upon what should be done; and it is normatively restrictive, having for its basis the contention that if such-and-such is not done, then certain untoward consequences ensue.

At the regulative level, every candidate that can be put forward as a logical system must conform to certain general canons of rationality. These regulative canons ensure a substantial degree of metatheoretical uniformity across the whole range of diverse logical systems. They impose absolutistic constraints on any "system of logic"—constraints which, being underdeterminative, may still leave open a relativistic area of genuine choice. Yet even this choice is not totally free and unfettered, but limited by pragmatic considerations.

4. THE SYSTEMATIZATION OF LOGIC AND ITS INSTRUMENTAL JUSTIFICATION

The analysis in Chapter XIII of the Geometric Analogy showed that, unlike the case of pure mathematics, the systematization of logic does not proceed *in vacuo*, free from implicit restraints inherent in the teleology of the subject. For in the case of the formalization or codification of logic, one must satisfy the demands imposed by the prior existence of a relatively well-defined presystematic practice with rules and requirements of its own. The present approach to logic sees this teleological and purposive nature of the enterprise as central. To be what a logic *is* is to do as a logic *does*. And if a logic is to accomplish its function it must at least succeed in systematizing and justifying the multitude of our specific intuitions regarding the validity and invalidity of arguments. The systematization or codification of an explicitly formulated logic always proceeds with reference to data—viz., the presystematic practice. These data are not sacrosanct. Our new-found sophistication can lead us to criticize and even reject some of them. Yet while not *individually* decisive, these data are yet controlling *in the aggregate*. The existence of a basic practice is crucial, for its nature exercises a significant determinative influence throughout the entire process of systematization.

A cyclic process of reciprocal interaction is thus at issue in the systematization of logic, a feedback-process whose rough structure is set out in Figure 1.

Such a cyclic process of alternation between a (relatively) presystematic and a consciously resystematized codification reflects the distinction (borrowed from the scholastics) between a *logica utens* and a *logica docens* which played a central part in Peirce's theory of logic.[7]

[7] *Collected Papers*, vol. II: 2.186–89.

Figure 1

THE PROCESS OF LOGICAL SYSTEMATIZATION

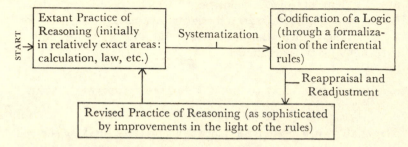

One facet of this process deserves particular stress. The construction of a logic to systematize inferential practice is *not* a purely descriptive project. Logic makes emphatically normative claims of *right* and *wrong* in the context of inference and argumentation, and does so on essentially purpose-oriented grounds. The very foundation of logic involves an insight into the teleological nature of the entire enterprise of exact reasoning, which makes it clear (for example) that arguments which lead from true premisses to false conclusions are "bad." The reasoner who accepts such arguments is thereby *defeating his own purposes*; he is "inconsistent" with himself in that his actions violate the very reason for being of the practice in which is he avowedly engaged. *This* sort of consistency is the logician's touchstone. It affords him an instrument for the normative appraisal of arguments which his calling demands of him. Accordingly, logic does not slavishly summarize the presystematic practice which provides its basis. At every stage of its development it criticizes this practice, rejecting some of it as unworthy of serious attention (exactly as grammarians of the old school reject some sectors of actual linguistic practice as improper). Thus logic does not simply *reflect* our inferential intuitions, it also *re-educates* them.

In giving a central place to the idea of logic as the *normatively construed* systematization of a presystematic practice of reasoning, we must note the role which *regulative principles* play in the construction of such a "systematization." What is at issue here revolves about such conceptions as those of *precision* and *exactness*, of *economy* and *simplicity*, of *generality* and *extensiveness*, and of *coherence* and *consistency*. Above all, we must emphasize again the regulative ideal of by-and-large *conformity* to the key features of the presystematic practice—of "saving the phenomena" involved in the presystematic practice.

Thus while the systematization at issue may refine the presystematic practice of inference in matters of occasional detail, it cannot readjust this to the point of abandonment. A significant element of purposive continuity must be maintained. Thus the systematization must be what has been called *autodescriptive:* it must afford logical mechanisms adequate for its own development.[8] In the evolutionary long run, the matter must work itself out so that at successive stages of sophistication our "presystematic" practice and the rules of our formalized logic must be brought into a workable coordination. Autodescriptivity represents one facet of the systematic coherence that must obtain between the systematized theory of inference and the presystematic data of inferential practice.

It appears from this standpoint that an oversimplification was at work in our earlier talk of "choosing" or "adopting" a logic. One is never called on to synthesize a logic *ex nihilo*, to extract it from a vacuum in which there are no influential ground-rules to yield guidance. At each and every stage there is at hand an (absolutely or relatively) presystematic logic—one which is simply *given* and not "chosen" at all, and without which (or some functional equivalent thereof) no reasoned choice whatever is possible. But, of course, one *can* explicitly choose to modify this pre-existing logic, abandoning it in favour of some duly systematized or resystematized variant (this being done on the basis of instrumental considerations of purposive efficacy). And by an evolutionary process along these lines one may ultimately arrive at a systematized logic that is substantially different from the initial presystematic logic—even as intuitionistic or many-valued systems differ radically from the so-called "classical" logic.

The working of cyclic processes of this sort is familiar from analogous points in the earlier discussion. As John Myhill has aptly put it, "our formalizations correct our intuitions while our

---

[8] See the discussion of this point in the author's *Many-valued Logic* (New York, 1969).

intuitions shape our formalizations."[9] A repeating process of continuing reciprocal adjustment is in question. As always, the important issue is that of a "closing of the circles." But the mutual attunement need not be perfect at any stage—our presystematic practice may need some marginal correction and adjustment at every level. The crucial factors are those of meshing, coordination, conformation, mutual accommodation, and considerations of best-fit. And no *vicious* circularity is involved in this circular process. What is fundamentally at issue is a cyclic feedback process of evolutionary development through successive stages—a process of just exactly the sort at work at various points in the preceding discussion. It is not maintained that we need a logical practice to develop a logical system, and a logical system to have a logical practice. For this would be overly simplistic. By distinguishing between pre- and post-systematic levels of inferential practice we are freed from any enmeshment in paradox.

These considerations make it clear why an argument along the lines of the Wheel Argument (*diallelus*) cannot block the prospects of legitimation in the logical sphere. The cyclic process does not call for justifying our logic with reference to some fixed, independent, external standard (a kind of super-logic whose legitimation would itself be moot). For justification becomes a matter of the stepwise resystematization of a pre-existing practice (for which a logical machinery is never lacking at any stage). What assures the truthfulness of a "conceptual truth" is in the final analysis its implicit containment in the ground-rules of our logico-conceptual practice. Consequently, there is no ampliative gap between the claim-content of a logical thesis and its "evidential" basis, as there is in the factual case, where the *diallelus* accordingly poses a more formidable challenge to the viability of justificatory reasoning.

The general structure of this process has been clearly perceived by Nelson Goodman. He writes:

How do we justify a *de*duction? Plainly, by showing that it conforms to the general rules of deductive inference. . . . Yet, of course, the rules themselves must eventually be justified. . . .

[9] John Myhill, "Remarks on Continuity and the Thinking Subject" in I. Lakatos (ed.), *Problems in the Philosophy of Mathematics* (Amsterdam, 1967), p. 175

Principles of deductive inference are justified by their conformity with accepted deductive practice. Their validity depends upon accordance with the particular deductive inferences we actually make and sanction. If a rule yields inacceptable inferences, we drop it as invalid.... This looks flagrantly circular. I have said that deductive inferences are justified by their conformity to valid general rules, and that general rules are justified by their conformity to valid inferences. But this circle is a virtuous one. The point is that rules and particular inferences alike are justified by being brought into agreement with each other. *A rule is amended if it yields an inference we are unwilling to accept; an inference is rejected if it violates a rule we are unwilling to amend.* The process of justification is the delicate one of making mutual adjustments between rules and accepted inferences; and in the agreement achieved lies the only justification needed for either.[10]

It is clear that a feedback-loop of the sort we envisage will qualify as what Goodman charmingly calls a *virtuous circle*.

This "circular" aspect of alignment with a pre-existent practice endows the over-all procedure of systematization with the cyclical structure of an iterative feedback process, along the lines shown in Figure 2.

Figure 2

THE EVOLUTIONARY DIALECTIC OF LOGICAL
SYSTEMATIZATION

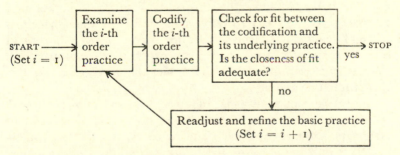

10 *Fact, Fiction, and Forecast* (Cambridge, Mass., 1955), pp. 66–7.

As one advances through the iterations of this process one increasingly moves further from the initial, descriptively given, *de facto* practice of reasoning (as determined through empirical investigation into the inferential procedures in fields like mathematics, law, etc.) to the increasingly refined and "rationalized" codifications that fit an ever more sophisticated and normatively restructured practice.

As this process of continual refinement moves on—both on the side of the actual practice of reasoning and on that of its systematic codification—there is ultimately a "closing of the circle." A point is reached where there is, if not a total coincidence, then at least a sufficiently close fit between the operative rules of the practice at issue and its normatively articulated codification.

Such a "closing of the circle" occurs when a condition of diminishing returns sets in with respect to revision and recodification—that is, when the results of the n-th and the $(n + 1)$st and the $(n + 2)$nd (etc.) steps in the iteration simply yield successive codifications that differ only trivially if at all. Such a state is reached when the improvements generated by successive iterations have become so miniscule that it is simply not worthwhile to carry the process on through still further iterations. Accordingly, the characteristic indicator of the crucial "closing of the circle" is simply the stability and equilibrium of the process itself. The systematic coherence being sought for is manifested at the temporal (or quasi-temporal) level by the stability of this process of successive refinement and mutual attunement of presystematic practice and postsystematic codification. At this stage there comes to be a due conformity between one's *protological practice* and one's *formulated logic*—the theory or formalized organon of reasoning adopted as normative codification of the "principles of right reason." The medieval question "Is logic a *branch* of science or an *instrument* of scientific exposition?" is answered in the medieval way: it is *both*—but under the proviso that the two conform to one another.

But in the context of logic, the normative aspect of good/bad, appropriate/inappropriate does not revolve about the factor of systematic coherence alone. Coherence when narrowly interpreted is only a matter of the *internal* conditions of adequacy, whereas the normative aspect must also include *external* considerations of functional adequacy and purposive efficacy. These external considerations reflect the purposes for which a logic is instituted as a problem-solving (and so an end-serving) methodology—the range of particular inferential tasks for whose sake a mechanism of this sort is deployed. Coherence becomes coherence *with something*—namely practice. At this stage our instrumentalism takes a pragmatic coloration, and an explicitly logical purposive aspect is introduced here, exactly as in the factual case.

5. THE EVOLUTIONARY ASPECT

As already observed in Chapter I, *any* instrumental justification can—given suitable assumptions about the rationality of the agents in its operative environment—yield an essentially evolutionary pattern of development in its dynamical application over the course of time. This general fact applies specifically to the present case—that of logic. Consider the basic feedback cycle set out in Figure 3:

Figure 3

THE FEEDBACK CYCLE OF SYSTEMATIZATION

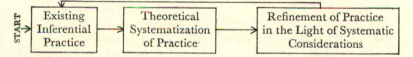

What is, on the systematic side of rational validation, a *process of probative justification* in the order of reasons becomes, in its historical dimension, *an evolutionary process of development.* This historical perspective provides for a variational modification and improvement by natural selection of the mechanisms of logical inference. Thus historical survival once again serves as an index of suitability—given the usual assumptions of pragmatic rationality, etc., survival has justificatory value because it serves to manifest functional adequacy. Subject to metaphysical assumptions of the sort by now familiar, evolutionary development replicates a line of substantive validation. Our previous deliberations concerning evolutionary epistemology carry over bodily to the present context.

As a concrete instance of an argument which has been "abandoned" in the actual course of logical evolution, consider the case of *subalternation*, exemplified by such inference as:

All S are P	All men are mortal
Some S are P	Some men are mortal

Throughout most of the history of logic, such a process of immediate inference from a universal affirmative premiss to a particular affirmative conclusion was regarded as valid. But as the doctrine of "existential import" began to be explored more fully, logicians tended to change their mind about this. G. J. Massey (from whom I borrow this apt illustration) has put the issue as follows:

> Change in logical theory has effected a re-education of intuition, so that . . . [subalternation] is no longer recognized as valid by those who have been indoctrinated in the revised logical theory. . . . There are precedents, then, for amending intuitive judgements of validity no less than for revising theories of valid argument forms.[11]

This evolutionary aspect of justification has crucial implications for our position. At an earlier stage (p. 246) we contrasted:

(i) An *absolutistic psychologism* which holds that the choice between alternative systems of logic is *actually constrained*, being dictated by the empirical realities of human reasoning processes

and

(ii) A *relativistic instrumentalism* which holds that the choice between alternative systems of logic is *merely guided*, being circumscribed by purpose-relative considerations of effectiveness, efficiency, economy and the like.

But it is clear that in the light of the sort of evolutionary process envisaged here, these two approaches—however much they may

[11] "Are There Any Good Arguments That Bad Arguments Are Bad," (see p. 71). *Philosophy in Context*, vol. 4 (Cleveland, 1975; published by the Department of Philosophy of Cleveland State University), pp. 61–77.

differ from a purely theoretical point of view—are driven into close contiguity and agreement. The approach of the mechanism of rational selection is bound to force these two seemingly divergent doctrines into increasing convergence.

6. CAN ONE EXPECT UNIQUENESS?

Given the structure of our instrumental/evolutionary approach to the validation of logic, the question arises: Can we reasonably expect to validate a unique result? Is it plausible to suppose that one single logic will win out over all the rest?

One's initial inclination may well be towards a simply negative response. No limpid reason of general principle is available in the *logical* sphere (in contradistinction with the *factual* case considered above) to assure that the justification-process must issue in a unique result. In the comparative appraisal of logical systems, no considerations of abstract theory can block the prospect of diversification—with different logical systems legitimated as apposite with respect to different problem-areas of application.

But this statement of the position—taken by itself and without context and commentary—distorts the actual situation. For the range of relativistic choice is sharply reduced by instrumentalistic considerations of purposive efficacy. And one among these deserves particular stress because its restrictive role is especially significant. One of the prime "criteria of adequacy" for a *logic* concerns its inherent generality: its claims to be capable of organizing the principles of inference "across the board" of a vast multiplicity and wide variety of uses. (Traditionally this is said to inhere in the *formal* nature of logic, in that logic is devoid of any material contents restricting its applicability to this or that range of discourse.) The claims a system can lay to being "a logic" require an open-ended and virtually universal effectiveness for its inferential rules throughout the entire range of exact reasoning. The claims of Logic are grandiose: one does not even have a "logic" unless the system at issue is of virtually universal efficacy. Clearly this requisite of comprehensively universal adequacy and open-endedness of operation itself affords a powerful constraint on the theoretically possible plurality of solutions that inhere in the aforementioned underdetermination. The situation is thus far more uniform and determinate than an orthodoxly instrumentalistic perspective suggests.

One related issue deserves exploration. Present-day grammatical theorists (of both the *generative* and the *transformationalist* schools) tend to conceive of the grammatical enterprise along the following lines:

> The grammar of a natural language has a *surface structure*, a structure which is characterized relatively adequately by traditional grammar. But behind this surface structure there lies implicit another, more fundamental structure—the deep structure. The surface structure of a sentence is linked to its deep structure by a sequence of levels related to one another by a series of transformations (i.e., paraphrases). The deep structure of a sentence is its primal ancestor in this transformational regress.

Now recently a sizable group of linguists have come to adopt the daring theory that the grammarian's and the logician's pictures of language must ultimately coincide.[12] On their view, the logician's analysis of a statement into logically basic form and the grammarian's analysis of it into its deep-structure composition will yield *precisely the same result* because "the rules of grammar are just those rules that relate logical forms and surface forms."[13] This theory that an in-depth analysis of logical and grammatical forms will yield conformal results is generally known as *generative semantics*. It poses the prospect of determining what Lakoff calls *natural logic*; i.e., the "logic" inherent in the grammatical mechanisms of deep structures and transformations via the principle that *grammatical form is isomorphic with logical form*.[14] If there is a natural logic of this sort—i.e., if the unification of logic and grammar as proposed by generative semantics can actually

---

[12] For an account of the theory and references to the literature see Gilbert Harman, "Deep Structure as Logical Form" in D. Davidson and G. Harman (eds), *Semantics of Natural Languages* (Dordrecht, 1972), pp. 25–47. See also the articles in this collection by J. D. McCawley and George Lakoff.

[13] George Lakoff, "Linguistics of Natural Logic," *Synthese*, vol. 22 (1970), pp. 151–271. Reprinted in D. Davidson and G. Harman (eds), *op. cit.*, pp. 544–655; see p. 590.

[14] See Lakoff, *op. cit.*

be carried out—this moves a great way towards logical absolutism. For it would mean that one specific logical system is built into the very structure of human thinking as in its language-utilizing resource. It would lead to the conclusion that man—as "rational animal"—is *programmed* to reason in a certain way in the context of natural-language use.[15]

This position would carry us far towards absolutism, but not all the way. Man is not constrained to use natural language: its replacement by other artificial devices is possible and indeed—insofar as mathematics is the "language" of science—even necessary. Our drive to understand the world may (here or elsewhere) lead us to forego "doing what comes natural." As Lakoff puts it:

> If natural logic requires that space and time be independent dimensions, then it is claimed that people conceive of space and time as independent dimensions, not that space and time *are* independent dimensions (which we know they are not). If one wants a logic capable of dealing with the physical facts of an Einsteinian universe, then it seems pretty sure that one doesn't want a natural logic.[16]

This indicates the nonabsolutist and underdeterministic upshot of even this absolutist approach. We remain exactly where we began: with a plurality of logical systems, differently attuned to different settings. The result is once more a situation in which a purpose-oriented instrumentalistic approach seems pretty well inevitable.

But is such a conclusion really warranted? Is such an upshot of a restricted pluralism circumscribed by instrumentalistic considerations indeed inevitable? Does not even an instrumentalistic approach indicate a superior status of near-absolutistic primacy for the "classical" systematization of logic—considering all its tremendous successes in the context of mathematics and science?

7. THE "PRIORITY" OF CLASSICAL LOGIC

It is necessary and unavoidable that one should have *some*

---

[15] Cf. the author's essay "A New Look at the Problem of Innate Ideas," in *Essays in Philosophical Analysis* (Pittsburgh, 1969), pp. 255–80.

[16] *Op. cit.*, p. 650.

criterion—or at least some cluster of *partial* criteria—for deciding when a body of formal apparatus deserves to be considered as a "logic." In the final analysis, this can only be done in terms of functional similarity—in certain fundamental respects—to orthodox "classical" logic. It makes sense to ask whether a system constitutes a "logic" on in the context of *some pre-existing idea* of what *logic* is. And this pre-existing idea must be drawn from the actual condition of the subject—in whatever state the historical vagaries of its development have produced. It must, in short, be derived from the ongoing traditions of the discipline. Such a stance patently endows orthodox, classical two-valued logic with a place of special prominence.

But this "priority" of classical logic does not authorize it to lay claims to being more than a *point of departure*. Its claims in this regard will be a matter of historical accident—the result of contingent historical developments which are irrelevant, at the *theoretical* level, to the claims of this system *vis-à-vis* any proposed "improvements" upon it.

In this respect the situation regarding *logic* is analogous to that of *arithmetic*, the theory of "calculation" with "numbers." No doubt the arithmetic of natural numbers came first historically. And so the mechanisms for calculation with fractions, real numbers, integers modulo *n*, complex numbers, and the like, which came historically later, also came to the subsumed under the rubric of "arithmetic." What entitled them to be called so? Clearly only the patterns of their agreements and analogies with the previously known cases, especially the classical arithmetic of natural numbers. But few mathematicians (Kronecker apart) take this to mean that the arithmetic of the natural numbers is the one and only proper or true or correct arithmetic

Moreover, it must not be forgotten that the historical claims of the orthodox, two-valued system to be the paradigm systematization of logic by which alone all others must be judged are by no means irreproachable. Syllogistic and modal logic both antedate the Stoics' invention of a propositional calculus akin to the orthodox, two-valued system. Variant theories of (non-truth-functional) implication have deep historical roots. And the idea of denying certain propositions a definite truth status as *T* or *F*—a conception which tends towards some sort of many-valued logic—has deep roots in classical antiquity and a notable place in medieval logic. Thus the "classical" two-valued logic can hardly with propriety be counted as the sole or prime arbiter by reference to which alone the issue of what is and what is not to qualify as a system of "logic" is to be resolved. The classical, two-valued propositional calculus can appropriately lay claim to a place of special *prominence*, but it is certainly not the sole or even necessarily the *predominant* standard for judging what is a system of logic.

8. CONCLUSION

The result of these deliberations can be summarized in brief compass. From a *system-internal* perspective, the theses of a system of logic no doubt qualify as "necessary truths." But the fact that different systematizations of logic are possible undermines the absoluteness of this necessity by raising the issue of justification—at the systematic level and from a *system-external* perspective—for the choice of one alternative in place of others. The *methodological* aspect of logic as a systematization of our inferential practice means that this issue of choice-validation can be tackled in the standard instrumentalistic manner. While such an instrumentalism does issue in a relativistic position regarding the justificatory rationale of logic, there is nevertheless good reason to expect a relatively definite resolution of the under-determinism of the theoretical situation by an instrumentalistic and functionally teleological narrowing of the range of alternative choices. Moreover, because of its heavy reliance upon considerations of purposive efficiency and effectiveness, such an instrumentalistic approach, does *not* lead to an arbitrary conventionalism or indifferentism. When all is said and done, the acknowledgement of pluralism does not issue in an indifferentist arbitrariness, but yields a rationale of strongly preferential justificatory considerations articulated along instrumentalist—i.e., function-oriented—lines. With logic too, the strategy of instrumental justification plays a pivotally important role.[17]

[17] Parts of the present discussion have been drawn from the author's *Many-valued Logic* (New York, 1969). Some of the work on this chapter and the following was supported by an NSF research grant (GS–43160) awarded for 1974–5 for an investigation of the role of pragmatic considerations in the justification of logic.

Chapter XV

THE DIALECTICAL INTERRELATION OF FORMAL AND FACTUAL KNOWLEDGE

I. THE ORIENTATION OF THE INSTRUMENTAL JUSTIFICATION OF LOGIC

The preceding chapter has argued that logic can also be brought into the general instrumentalist framework of a methodological pragmatism. It maintained that the correct position in the controversy between the absolutistic and the relativistic conceptions of logic lies somewhere in the middle—with the functionalistic or instrumentalistic version of the relativistic approach. Thus the legitimation of logical machinery must—as we see it—be taken to hinge, in the final analysis, on its instrumental superiority with respect to the governing context of relevant purposes. But it merits stress that this approach to the rational credentials of logic takes a line that is *in the first instance* generically *instrumental* rather than specifically *pragmatic* in its immediate bearing. For a pragmatic justification revolves about a teleology specifically oriented towards issues of *welfare*, proceeding with a view to our affective well-being if not actual physical survival. Now the present approach to the rationalization of logic is certainly *not* predicated on the view that the justification of a logical system hinges upon considerations of this welfare-oriented sort. Rather, it takes a teleological tack quite different from the specifically pragmatic: the relevant range of purpose has been construed in terms of the efficient and effective systematization of our presystematic processes of inferential reasoning. The teleological focus of this instrumentalist analysis was consequently not located in the area of practical life at all, but rather in that of man's theoretical concerns. The prime work of logic, thus regarded, is to smooth the transaction of our *intellectual*, not our *practical* business. But this is not quite the end of the matter: the analysis can—and must—be pressed further.

There can be little question that the "presystematic practice of reasoning"—which is thus accorded a pivotal place—is itself *ultimately* the evolutionary product of a prior process of initially natural and eventually rational selection. Such a presystematic *modus operandi* in intellectual affairs clearly represents an instrumentality in whose development factors of survival-conduciveness and affective adequacy unquestionably played a formative role. When the matter is viewed in this light, it becomes clear that pragmatic considerations do actually figure even in our "merely instrumental" approach to the justification of logic: the issue of *praxis* is thus not utterly irrelevant, though it enters in only obliquely and at a significant remove.

In effect, what is at issue is a *two-phase approach*:

(1) Logic is justified not along specifically pragmatic lines, but in terms that are generically instrumental, and revolve about the *telos* of effectively systematizing a presystematic practice of reasoning.

(2) However, this presystematic practice is seen as itself possessed of a presumably strongly pragmatic rationale in terms of promoting the furtherance of human purposes in general, and pre-eminently those of furthering welfare and the prospects of survival.

Accordingly, the presystematic practice of reasoning is seen as a mediating link between the justificatory rationale of logic and the operation of specifically pragmatic considerations. But this link bridges a genuine gap; a considerable distance separates the present instrumental legitimation of logic from the operative range of specifically pragmatic considerations.

Such considerations indicate the substantial difference between our instrumental and only *obliquely pragmatic* line of justification as regards *logic* (i.e., the methodology of "pure reasoning") and our specifically and *directly pragmatic* approach to legitimating *the criteriology of factual truth* (i.e., the methodology of empirical inquiry). This recognition of a diversity of approach leads to another issue, the problem of the mutual relationships and interconnections that obtain on the present instrumentalistic approach between the domain of logic and that of factual knowledge.

K

2. THE STUCTURE OF THE INTERRELATIONSHIP

On this view, rather different modes of justification are at issue in the formal and factual areas, with our criteriology of factual knowledge receiving a *specifically pragmatic* justification (in terms of the welfare-conduciveness of action guided by its deliverances), while our body of formal knowledge receives a *generically instrumental* justification (with reference to its effectiveness in systematizing our inferential practices). The operation of two teleologies of decidedly different orientation means that the over-all rationalization of our total body of knowledge will involve two quite different phases (or Hegelian "moments"), in that the legitimation of *formal* knowledge will have to proceed with reference to a set of purposive considerations quite different from that envisaged in the legitimation of *factual* knowledge.

From this methodological perspective, it appears that knowledge, though one whole, is certainly not a seamless one. Distinct legitimative procedures are operative in its two major divisions. Yet the wholeness of knowledge does mean that they must, in the end, be interrelated and interconnected. We must examine somewhat more closely the nature of this relationship.

In considering the relation between the logico-conceptual and the empirico-factual sectors of knowledge, one must begin with the crucial consideration that *inferential mechanisms are needed to operate any viable inquiry instrumentality for the validation or substantiation of factual claims.* The fundamental issue of the determination of *formal* truth can thus be viewed as a separable matter—one that is conceptually prior to the deployment of a viable criterion of *factual* truth, because it affords part of the very machinery needed to make any such a criterion work. We thus arrive at the pattern of dependency-interrelatedness shown in Figure 1.

But this as yet unidirectional picture of a two-stage process with a logical phase preceding a factual phase is not the end of the matter. It involves a drastic oversimplification. For the division into two sequential stages has proceeded in the timeless present characteristic of all too much methodological discussion, and has left out of account the crucial aspect of historical process. Actually, at any given historical juncture there is *both* a logic for the conduct of our abstract reasoning *and* a scientific organon for the securing of empirical facts. And the process of rational validation and assessment has a strong element of reciprocity across these two different sectors. We may well test the capacity of our logic-in-hand to systematize efficiently and effectively our total

Figure 1

INQUIRY PROCEDURES PRESUPPOSE LOGICAL MECHANISMS

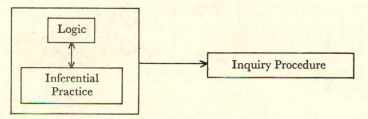

body of knowledge (in the formal and factual areas alike), with the result that this logic itself may be sharpened and revised, this being done in part with a view to our knowledge—or purported knowledge—of "the empirical facts." (Note that this process itself will call for the use of logical machinery—be it the old, previous one or, perhaps hypothetically, the new one to which we are conjecturally inclined.) And we will then presumably deploy this "improved" logic in appraising our methodological resources for empirical cognition. The result leads to a new stage, parallel to the initial situation, with both a logic and a substantiation-procedure for the provision of factual knowledge once more available as a "given" basis. And now a further iteration of the whole process can get under way. The over-all structure of this iterative process is not merely sequential, but essentially cyclic, along the lines of the diagram of Figure 2.

As this diagram makes clear, a process of reciprocal feedback of the type met with several times before is at issue. Since logic formalizes our inferential apparatus in the systematization of knowledge —*all* knowledge, the factual sector specifically included—it eventuates that changing practices in the structuring of our empirical knowledge will exert modificatory pressures upon our logic itself. Thus *if*, for example, it were to turn out (as has been suggested) that the systematization of quantum physics could be accomplished with substantially greater ease and effectiveness by a non-standard logic—such as a system of many-valued logic— then there would arise a pressure towards the modification of our "prior" logic so great as to prove ultimately decisive.

Figure 2

THE FEEDBACK INTERACTION BETWEEN LOGIC
AND INQUIRY

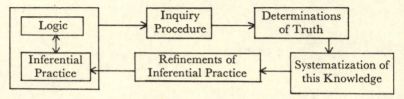

This brings to view the essentially cyclic aspect of the interrelationship between the formal and the factual mechanisms of truth-criteriology. Such an iterative process must include a series of mutual accommodations and readjustments until there is an eventual "closing of the circles" when the various components dovetail with one another in smooth coordination.

Of course, the critical disparity remains that a logic of some sort is indispensably requisite at each stage of the process, whereas the validation of a logic itself need not inevitably involve a reference to factual issues—since its basis of reference could in principle be limited to the domain of the formal sciences alone. Thus while the over-all structure of epistemic validation may well be cyclic, *at each stage* it remains sequential, with the issues of the logical machinery of inference and contradiction always enjoying the rather weak priority of a merely relative fundamentality.

On this approach, one obtains the same sort of self-sustainingness for *deductive* logic that was considered above (in Chapter VII) with respect to "inductive" logic (i.e., the evidential-argumentation sector of our procedures of factual inquiry). The structure of the situation that is obtained in the two cases is depicted in Figure 3.

As these diagrams show, the justificatory situation is essentially isomorphic in these cases, a circumstance which brings two

Figure 3

THE ISOMORPHISM OF SUBSTANTIATION IN DEDUCTIVE AND INDUCTIVE LOGIC

A. *The Case of Deductive Logic*

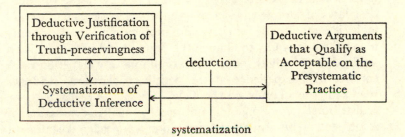

B. *The Case of Inductive Logic*

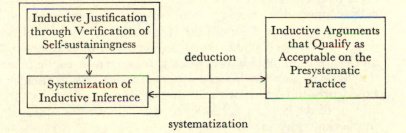

crucial aspects of "inductive reasoning" (empirical inquiry procedures) to the fore: (1) the fact of the justificatory dependence of "inductive" logic on an in-hand mechanism of deduction (as mentioned above), and (2) the fact that—interestingly enough—while the over-all legitimation of inductive inference is not itself inductive, it is nevertheless a crucial element of this legitimation that an inductive justification of induction should be forthcoming.

3. QUINE'S PRAGMATIC VALIDATION OF LOGIC

It may serve the interests of clarity to set out explicitly the contrast between the present pragmatic theory and the pragmatism of W. V. Quine's influential essay on "Two Dogmas of Empiricism." Quine vividly formulates his position in the following terms:

> The totality of our so-called knowledge or beliefs, from the most casual matters of geography and history to the profoundest laws of atomic physics or even of pure mathematics and logic, is a man-made fabric which impinges on experience only along the edges. Or, to change the figure, total science is like a field of force whose boundary conditions are experience. A conflict with experience at the periphery occasions readjustments in the interior of the field. Truth values have to be redistributed over some of our statements. Re-evaluation of some statements entails re-evaluation of others, because of their logical interconnections—the logical laws being in turn simply certain further statements of the system, certain further elements of the field. Having re-evaluated one statement we must re-evaluate some others, which may be statements logically connected with the first or may be the statements of logical connections themselves. But the total field is so underdetermined by its boundary conditions, experience, that there is much latitude of choice as to what statements to re-evaluate in the light of any single contrary experience. No particular experiences are linked with any particular statements in the interior of the field, except indirectly through considerations of equilibrium affecting the field as a whole.[1]

On Quine's approach, this ongoing reappraisal of "the totality of our so-called knowledge or beliefs" is to be all-encompassing without any prior differentiation between logical and factual truths, and is to be carried out in terms of pragmatic criteria of adequacy and effectiveness. Quine sees "total science" as one vast and seamless whole. It involves an all-embracing allocation of truth-values to the propositions of the formal and the empirical disciplines alike, and proposes to judge the adequacy of this allocation by the pragmatic standard of practical satisfactions:

---

[1] "Two Dogmas of Empiricism" reprinted in *From a Logical Point of View* (Cambridge, Mass., 1961), pp. 42–6 (see pp. 42–3).

Carnap, Lewis, and others take a pragmatic stand on the question of choosing between language forms, scientific frameworks; but their pragmatism leaves off at the imagined boundary between the analytic and the synthetic. In repudiating such a boundary I espouse a more thorough pragmatism. Each man is given a scientific heritage plus a continuing barrage of sensory stimulation; and the considerations which guide him in warping his scientific heritage to fit his continuing sensory promptings are, where rational, pragmatic.[2]

Accordingly, Quine has it that (1) *all* statements comprising the total body of knowledge—logical and factual alike—lie, so to speak, on the same plane, and come up for critical pragmatic evaluation *at one and the same time*. Moreover, (2) this evaluative test is to be carried out in terms of "considerations of equilibrium affecting the field *as a whole*." Nothing could be more synoptic and totalistically all-embracing than Quinean approch.

The instrumentalism of the present theory differs from Quine's at both of these crucial points. It refuses to combine logical with factual considerations so as to throw everything holus bolus into the melting-pot of simultaneous re-evaluation. We are prepared to retain the traditional distinction between logical and factual theses, and regard the issue of logical and factual truth as one to be resolved in a *separate* and *sequential* way. The validation of logical machinery—itself, to be sure, an instrumental choice, as we see it[3]—is to be resolved first with primary reference to the non-empirical domain of mathematical, semantical, and logical considerations. Only *after* the mechanisms of logic are at least provisionally secured can we press on—guided in large measure by their means—to deploy some criterion of truth in the factual domain. Here too, the process of legitimation is also seen as ultimately instrumental, but in a manner that invokes quite different objectives in another setting.

This approach differs from Quine's not so much as regards his pragmatico-instrumentalist methodology, but as regards his deployment of it in a once-for-all evaluation. Instead, we have envisaged a two-phase, *sequential* process that makes logic available as a *given* instrument for analysis in the factual sphere.

[2] *Ibid.*, p. 46.
[3] See also the author's *Many-valued Logic* (New York, 1970), pp. 213–35.

There are very general and fundamental reasons for adopting the present approach of a sequential procedure, providing the normative standards of logic prior to the validation of factual standards. Think of the very structure of Quine's conception of a network of propositions structured in "a loose association reflecting the relative likelihood, in practice, of our choosing one statement rather than another for revision in the event of recalcitrant experience." Difficulties arise at this very fundamental point.

How in the absence of *given* logical standards, can one possibly even begin to determine what sorts of experiences are to count as "recalcitrant"? What—other than logic—is to tell us that a *conflict* has come about with the result that "revision" among various believed statements is in order?[4] What of the "relative likelihood in practice" of a choice between conflicting statements? Is this to be a purely *descriptive* matter—a matter of the sociology of knowledge in various human communities of thinkers? Are we concerned merely descriptively with what people *will in fact* be disposed to choose? Are we not rather concerned normatively with what—under the epistemic circumstances—they *ought* to be disposed to choose? For epistemological purposes, it is clearly the issue of normative appraisal that is crucial, and this imperatively requires the utilization of logical machinery. Without logic to guide us we might conceivably be in a position to describe how people do reason, but we are muzzled on the topic of how they ought to reason so as to resolve belief-conflicts.

The key point is that a pragmatic analysis regarding the internal adequacy of what Quine calls "the totality of our so-called knowledge or beliefs" is in principle not feasible unless logical mechanisms already lie to hand for our guidance. And this is why an intrinsic advantage accrues—quite as a matter of general principle—to any multi-stage procedure of validation such as that envisaged here. By validating our logical mechanisms at the outset of the epistemological journey we assume their

---

4 To be sure, it might be suggested that this logic is provided as an *internal* constituent of that great seamless web that constitutes Quine's "total knowledge." But this will not do. When this forms an inconsistent set (because it includes recalcitrant elements) we need an "external logic" even to *recognize* this fact, let alone to work out ways of overcoming it.

subsequent availability to provide the required guidance at later junctures.

We thus join Quine in adopting an approach of the pragmatic *genre*. But our pragmatism is decisively different from his. For we deploy pragmatic considerations at the *methodological* level rather than at the level of statements or classes of statements. And we resolve the problem of method in two phases, the first of which addresses itself to the validation of the mechanisms of logic, and the second to the (subsequent) validation of the methodological standards of factual knowledge. However, we envisage a cyclic process of dialectic where these two phases are repeated time and again (as per Figure 2 above).

This iterative aspect means that the upshot of our position in the final analysis draws close to that of Quine's. He rejects any absolute distinction between truths of reason (logical truths) and truths of fact (empirical truths). The present theory maintains this distinction, albeit in a way that is ever provisional and tentative, regarding these categories as interlocked in a complex feedback process where each category can exert pressures upon the other. It envisages a distinctness of categories, but not their total separation as regards all prospects of reciprocal interaction.

As his talk of a pragmatic assessment of distributions of truth-values over statements makes patently plain, Quine's approach takes the form of what we have characterized as a thesis-pragmatism. In this orientation to theses, Quine is a thesis pragmatist of the traditional, Jamesian variety. Here, then, is a pivotal difference between the Quinean theory and our present approach. Quine's instrumentalism addresses itself to *theses;* ours addresses itself to *methods.* On this methodological approach, theses enter in only in a very oblique way—when it is specifically thesis-establishing methods that are at issue—and accordingly pragmatic considerations are never brought to bear directly upon theses, but mediately through their operation upon the inquiry procedures by which theses are validated.

A direct orientation on theses would make it natural (though, to be sure, not inevitable) to take an undifferentiating approach across the whole range of theses, without troubling to draw any lines of division between theses of various sorts. A thesis-pragmatism that addresses itself to the allocation of truth-values to statements might just as well take a synoptic totalitarian line and lump all statements together in one single, all-embracing whole.

By contrast, it would seem natural and only to be expected that a *methodological* pragmatism would take a more highly differentiated line. The definitive orientation of the present approach lies in its addressing itself to methods (not theses!), and it seems plausible enough—indeed almost inevitable—that distinctly different modes of inquiry should be operative in the formal and factual spheres. Nothing could be more *plausible*, nay more *invitable* than that different approaches should be used to settle a question like on the one hand (e.g.) that of the number of rabbits in a cage, and on the other that of the number arrived at when 4 is multiplied by 13, considering that calculation and reasoning alone will suffice to settle the latter issue, whereas no amount of calculation or reasoning can of itself serve to settle the former, for whose resolution one has no alternative but to "consult nature."

Some questions of truth one settles by calculation, some by inquiry into language-use, some by experimentation or observation of nature. These *procedural* differences are pivotal for the present methodological approach. The common fact that all of them have to do with establishing parts of our "total knowledge" is regarded as overly abstract to be of much epistemological utility. When one approaches the theory of knowledge from the direction of the methodologies of inquiry appropriate for resolving certain sorts of questions (or for establishing certain sorts of theses), the issue clearly takes on a more highly differentiated (but *naturally* differentiated) aspect than that which it bears when everything is run together in the guise of "assigning truth values to statements." The key issue now is not *that* truth values are assigned but *how* this came to be in terms of the procedural mechanisms employed. Thus Quine's thesis-uniformitarianism comes to be seen as over-simple, and is advantageously replaced by a more highly differentiated approach which construes the justificatory process not just as one sweep "across the board" but as a complex interaction of differentiated stages or "moments."

Moreover, the thesis-uniformitarian approach of Quine's pragmatism is the source of yet a further crucial difference between his approach and that of the present theory. Quine's instrumentalism is developed in a manner that is strictly pragmatic across the entire board, repudiating the major traditional epistemological boundaries as untenable dualisms. This uniformitarian approach has it that if pragmatic considerations are to be operative *anywhere* they must be operative *everywhere*. One is driven to a one-track instrumentalism with a uniformly pragmatic teleology, and must thus envision the purposive aspects of factual knowledge in a light wholly akin to that of formal knowledge. The idea of different sorts of teleologies in the cognitive area collapses if everything must be viewed in the same dim light, as simply and solely a matter of assigning truth-values to propositions.

Clearly one of the strengths of the more highly differentiated teleology that becomes available on a *methodological* approach is its opening up the possibility of a pragmatic legitimation for a truth-criterion in the area of empirical fact, while yet espousing a more sophisticated instrumentalism on the side of our formal knowledge of logico-conceptual truths.

To summarize: the pragmatism of Quine's "Two Dogmas" differs from that of the present book in two crucial respects:

(1) Quine's pragmatism resembles its Jamesian predecessor in that it addresses itself directly to the allocation of truth-values to statements. It is, accordingly, a *propositional* pragmatism, rather than a *methodological* pragmatism like that of the present work—which applies the pragmatic standard to the validation of methods instead of the verification of propositions.

(2) Quine treats the process of pragmatic analysis as a comprehensive evaluation of the *totality* of knowledge claims within the scope of one single all-comprising assessment, and specifically one which refuses to admit any differential status to the formal and the empirical sciences. Our own theory envisages a multistage process, within each phase of which the logical and the factual sectors are kept separate and treated differently, although, to be sure, there can be feed-back effects going across sector boundaries as one moves from one stage to the next.

As this comparison between Quine's pragmatic approach and our own serves to show, two very different validation processes are at issue here, processes which—over-all conformity to the pragmatic/instrumentalistic strategy apart—have only a tenuous connection with one another.[5]

[5] This section draws upon Appendix I of the author's book, *The Coherence Theory of Truth* (Oxford, 1973).

Chapter XVI

LIMITS OF THE THEORY

I. THE FEASIBILITY OF "KNOWLEDGE FOR KNOWLEDGE'S SAKE"

The present theory of cognitive validation subsumes both *formal* and *factual* knowledge within the common framework of a conjointly instrumentalistic and evolutionistic approach. It views factual knowledge as *directly*, and formal knowledge as *obliquely* subject toward specifically pragmatic controls. Now one possible line of objection against this instrumentally evolutionist position is particularly interesting, because it is itself evolutionistic in structure. It runs as follows:

At the earlier and more primitive stages of the pursuit of knowledge, the cutting edge of the pragmatic efficacy of a practice can perhaps exercise a degree of effective control over our cognitive endeavors. Thus, the history of thought is laden with attempts to explain natural processes in terms of an animistic personification of things, or by a resort to magic, occult influences, etc., vestigial remnants of which remain in various pockets of present-day belief. No doubt, the impact of actual applicative practice can prove effective in countervailing against such crude devices. But as our knowledge becomes more sophisticated the link with everyday practice becomes attenuated and is eventually cut altogether. After all, think how little impact the abtruse theories of modern science make on the conduct of everyday affairs. Once man reaches a stage in the developmental process when knowledge is pursued for its own sake, rather than merely for that of its applications, the significance of the factor of survival-conduciveness is reduced, and the whole pragmatic element is pretty well left behind.

One flaw of this objection lies in its too narrow conception of practice. The *praxis* at issue in our discussion is clearly *not* limited in its purview to the everyday conduct of common life affairs. As knowledge becomes more sophisticated, so does the correlative technique and technology involved in its pursuit—electronic engineering, space-rocketry, computers, radio-telescopes, high-energy accelerators, complex experimental apparatus of all sorts, etc. It is crucial to our view of practical efficacy as the test of cognitive adequacy that the sort of highly sophisticated and contrived "practice" involved in the use of the investigative technology of experimentation and the acquisition and utilization of data should *also* be taken to lie within the domain relevant to cognitive justification.

But even more importantly, the objection draws the wrong conclusion from correct premisses. Nobody wants to deny that factual knowledge can be—and often is—pursued for practice-transcending ends, and that such a cultivation of knowledge simply for its own sake is a real and indeed, an admirable enterprise. What *is* being maintained here is merely that *the adequacy-tests of the thesis-substantiative methods by which this pursuit is carried on will lie in the practical sphere*—that pragmatic considerations provide the requisite *controls*, the proper standards of operative efficacy for our cognitive methodologies.

But does giving so prominent a role to pragmatic considerations in the legitimation of our cognitive mechanisms not degrade the standing of the search for knowledge itself? The Italian philosopher Giovanni Papini, a critical student of pragmatism, put the point in this way: "The true greatness of man," he wrote, "lies in his doing the useless precisely because it is useless," and he suggested that in proportion as our knowledge is actually *useful* we ought to despise it and turn our attention in other, more disinterested directions.[1] Now knowledge is surely one of the highest objects of human aspiration and the *disinterested* quest for it among the most splendid of human enterprises. Does the stress we have placed on the primacy of the practical not block the project of acquiring knowledge for knowledge's sake and pull the rigorously disinterested pursuit of knowledge off its pedestal as one of the noblest of human activities?

[1] Quoted in R. B. Perry, *The Thought and Character of William James*, abbreviated version (Cambridge, Mass., 1935), pp. 315–16. Scientists are not notably sympathetic towards those tendencies of material progress scorned by George Orwell as "making the world safe for little fat men."

Not at all! It cannot be too emphatically stated that a practice-oriented approach need not do violence to the *l'art pour l'art* aspect of knowledge for its own sake. Failure to realize this would involve a profound misreading of the implications of our discussions. We have argued, in effect, that the *criterion of validity* of factual knowledge is to be rationalized with reference to the sector of practical purpose. But there is no earthly reason why cognitive instruments whose *validation* lies in the crass domain of *praxis* cannot be employed in the context of practice-transcending purposes. Methodological pragmatism has to do with the *legitimation* of cognitive methods—the rational control of their claims as actually *knowledge*-producing—and it is this issue of validation alone that is held to operate through the pragmatic connection. Nothing is said to confine the *application* of such methods within the limits of practical issues.

A distinction must be drawn: With regard to a purely *theoretical* problem, one seeks the answer to a question simply out of a wish to have this answer—a desire for information. With a strictly *practical* problem, one seeks the answer to a question because one needs to have it, since this is required to guide action in an appropriate way. Our methodological pragmatism has indeed insisted that the adequacy-tests which provide quality-control over cognitive methods largely operate in the practical area. But this fact that cognitive methodology is to be *tested and validated* in practical contexts should cerainly *not* be construed to mean that it cannot be *used* in theoretical contexts.

It is thus crucial to distinguish between (1) the *objectives for which* inquiry is carried on (which may as readily be strictly theoretical as appliedly practical), and (2) the *validating considerations invoked* to support the methods of inquiry (which we have held to be ultimately practical in bearing). One can make use of cognitive methods validated on pragmatic grounds to extend knowledge simply for knowledge's sake, exactly as one can (say) use woodworking instruments that have proven their effectiveness in the humble context of furniture-making for the creation of more exalted woodcrafted artworks. The acceptance of practice as an arbiter over the adequacy of man's cognitive methods does not preclude them from serving the utility-transcending objectives of pure inquiry and knowledge for its own sake. It is *not* being maintained that *praxis* to the exclusion of *theoria* is the only purposive area relevant to cognitive methodology, but just that the methods used in the theoretical as well as the practical side have an ultimately practical/affective rationale of cognitive legitimation.

Accordingly, the fact that our cognitive *methods* are controlled and validated by pragmatic considerations does not entail that there need be anything crass or unworthy about our cognitive *endeavors*. Even if the legitimative grounding of our truth-criterion is pragmatic—and thus welfare-related—this certainly does not mean that there need be anything mean or unworthily self-interested about the pursuit of truth as such. As C. S. Peirce insisted so emphatically, a committal to knowledge of the truth is a *moral* commitment of the highest order, and should be seen as a matter not of self-interest but of dedication to an ideal. The present theory in no way conflicts with this stance. The primacy of practice and of the practical/affective sector of human purpose is maintained simply in the order of *legitimation*, not in that of *aspiration*.

The pragmatic aspect of the quality-control of cognition consequently imposes no limits whatever upon the cognitive purists' vision of knowledge for knowledge's sake. Nor is there anything to our evolutionary approach to epistemology that confines the effective range of the cognitive quest within the humdrum region of survival-conducive interests. Nothing in the present theory blocks the feasibility of a concern for intellectual fulfillment and a cognitive creativity reaching far beyond the issues of man's survival and the satisfaction of his practical needs. Even as the contender in an Olympic decathlon employs for impractical and strictly "sportive" ends highly developed physical skills whose basis is wholly evolutionary and survival-conducive, so the scientist employs for practice-abstractive and strictly intellectual ends cognitive methods whose basic *raison d'être* is pragmatic and evolutionary.

2. A PURPORTED DANGER IN STRESSING "PRAXIS"

The factor of "control over nature" represents a pivotal aspect of any theory of cognitive validation with reference to *praxis* and pragmatic efficacy. Like intelligence itself, this is a basic human capacity: other animals on this planet predominantly adjust to their environment, man drastically and diversely (and at times foolishly) readjusts his environment to suit himself. But any stress on this aspect of man as manipulator of nature must recognize the implicit dangers of this process—the technological triumphs that (according to the present theory) establish the adequacy of our knowledge may well represent a merely Pyrrhic victory. (As Frederick Engels shrewdly observed in the *Dialectics of Nature*,[2] nature always exacts her revenge for each of man's so-called "conquests of nature." Far from proving ultimately "successful," our Promethean penchant for the science-guided modification of the natural environment may so disturb the balance of nature as to bring to an end the continued habitability of the planet by *homo sapiens*. (The pertinent supporting arguments will be familiar to the reader.) Now, does all this not undermine one's confidence in the adequacy-credentials of a route to "knowledge" geared to a control of which human *hubris* can all too readily make mockery?

Surely not. For though all of this is perfectly true, it in no way detracts from the status of practical control as a mark of capacity and competence. Our pragmatic theory that control is the arbiter of cognition nowise conflicts with the sad truth that this control may well open the door to unforeseen, unwarranted, and unpleasant consequences. Knowledge is power, but a power indifferently serviceable for good or for evil—and, moreover, limited knowledge is imperfect power. Our knowledge is a two-edged sword—one that may prove in the absence of *wisdom* to be "a dangerous thing" (as the proverb has it). After all, the instrumental approach we have taken here views knowledge as just that—an instrument. And instruments are in general ambivalent from the normative or evaluative point of view: A hammer can serve to build houses or to smash heads; a drug can be administered to cure or to kill. Control of all sorts is in itself indeterminate between its justifiable use or illegitimate abuse. The issue of cognitive adequacy and the legitimation of the instrumentalities of knowledge-acquisition leaves wholly untouched the question of the inherent rationality of our *uses* of knowledge.

---

2 Tr. C. Dutt (New York, 1940), pp. 291–2.

L

3. LIMITS OF THE PRAGMATIC APPROACH

The present discussion has maintained the primacy of *praxis* as an arbiter over methods in the cognitive realm. It has argued that strictly pragmatic efficacy is directly crucial for the quality-control of our cognitive methodology in the factual sphere, and obliquely operative with respect to the legitimation of our formal knowledge as well. But what (if anything) about this account prevents its cognition-transcending generalization—what features of it preclude taking pragmatic efficacy also as operative standard in the *normative* as well as the *cognitive* realm? Can the procedures of the present démarche in epistemology be carried over into the value-oriented domains of ethics, aesthetics, etc.?

The answer is negative and its justification is simple. The pivotal point of the present approach was a "metaphysical deduction" which established a linkage between the truth-potential of an inquiry-method and the pragmatic success of actions based upon its deliverances. Just this crucial link between success and adequacy is absent in essentially normative and evaluative fields like ethics, aesthetics, and natural theology. Indeed the deepest thinkers of these fields have always insisted that *there is and can be no such connection*. This fact—if correct —would at once destroy any hope of carrying our pragmatic legitimation over from the sphere of cognition to the normative area. But is it correct? There is substantial reason to think so, though it is rather complicated to set out the needed substantiation.

Human purposes fall into two groups, somewhat along the lines of the classical distinction between necessities and luxuries. The one category relates to the essentials of human welfare: to the strictly *practical goals* relating to the material interests of man, and concerned not just with the biomedical aspect of what makes life *possible*, but also with the economic aspect of what makes life *pleasant* in terms of the availability of a wide range of goods and services. The governing concept in this area of basic needs comprises those that relate to man's *welfare*.

The second category of purpose relates to the transcendent concerns of man in matters that lie outside the range of his material requirements for food, shelter, clothing, goods, services, etc., and so go beyond the economic area and the whole sphere of man's pleasures. A few obvious examples—education, culture, and solicitude for one's fellow—will hopefully suffice to indicate the kind of thing at issue. Here we have to do not with man's needs for the basic requisites of a satisfactory life but with his enhanced desires for a life that is rewarding and meaningful. Not only happy but good people, and not only enjoyable or satisfying but commendable or even admirable lives are important in the evaluative scheme of things.

We may thus class the factors that augment the quality of human life into two principal groups: the excellence-conducive and the welfare-conducive. The latter relates to objectives in the traditionally *pragmatic* range; the former are extra-pragmatic, or, as we shall call them, *ideal* in nature, and relate to man's "higher" aspirations rather than to pleasure or satisfaction or happiness *per se*. Thus there are, or at any rate should be, important goals for people beyond welfare, goals whose attainment —or even whose mere pusuit—makes for a better, even if not necessarily a happier person. Such goals all revolve about the theme of self-development and fulfillment, a capitalizing upon the opportunities for the realization of a man's potential for appreciating and contributing to the creative impetus of the human spirit. The pursuit of such goals lays the basis for a legitimate view of oneself as a unit of worth—a *person* in the fullest sense. Accordingly, in assessing the quality of a life, one operates with an essentially two-factor criterion in which both welfare and human excellence play significant parts. And the *aristically* oriented notion that there are some things that make us *better* people stands on equal footing with the *hedonically* oriented notion that there are some things that make us *happier* people.

The central concept of this excellence-connected, trans-welfare domain is *quality*, particularly in the realization of human potentialities: in actual creativity, in the appreciation thereof, and in the forging of rewarding human interrelationships. Excellence, dignity, and the sense of worth are the leading themes throughout. Here we have left behind the domain of the minima at issue with welfare to enter another sphere—that of human ideals relating to man's higher and nobler aspirations.

It is important to recognize that the issue of a man's welfare— despite its diversified and multi-faceted character—has a certain *minimality* about it. The conception of the good life represents a comprehensive whole whose range extends far beyond the core issue of welfare. Welfare in all its dimensions deals only with the basic essentials. The man whose cultural horizons are narrow, whose physical environment is unattractive, or whose government is despotic, may not actually suffer privation in any of the dimensions of his *welfare*—indeed, he personally may conceivably even be every bit as happy as otherwise. Nevertheless, we could not view his condition in point of well-being with unqualified favor and esteem his as "the good life." Welfare is only the *foundation* of such a life, not the edifice itself. Its components—physical health, adequacy of resources, and mental and emotional well-being, etc.—are enormous and doubtless even indispensible aids toward a meaningful and satisfying life, but they are not in themselves sufficient for this purpose.

No matter how we shape in its details our overarching vision of the good life for man, welfare will thus play only a partial and subsidiary role, because a satisfactory condition of affairs as to welfare is compatible with a substantial impoverishment outside the region of welfare minima. A person—or a society—amply endowed with the requisites of welfare may but yet lack all those resources of personality, intellect, and character which, like cultivation of mind and fostering of human congeniality, make life rewarding as well as pleasant. Toward people or nations who have—even to abundance—the constituents of welfare, we may well feel envy, but our *admiration* and *respect* could never be won on this ground alone.

The upshot of this line of thought is that the domain of our strictly *practical* purposes cannot validly be regarded as exhausting the entire range of worthwhile human purposes. An extra-pragmatic, welfare-transcending dimension of legitimate human purpose must be admitted, one which is broader than the range of the specifically practical purposes that relate to human welfare in that it encompasses the ideal sector as well. Accordingly, the range of purposive justification will be broader than its specifically pragmatic subdomain.

The tenor of our whole theory goes to indicate that recourse to a specifically *pragmatic* mode of instrumental justification will be apposite only in a sphere in which the precondition is satisfied that the *practical sector of purpose* (relating to the specifically welfare-oriented interests of man) is exclusively or predominantly relevant to the issue of rational controls. Now this is indeed the case in the epistemology of factual knowledge, because the purposes of the only remaining category germane to this sphere (viz., the *theoretical* ones) are in principle inoperative as regards justificatory reasoning here (for reasons inherent in the Wheel Argument or *diallelus*). In consequence, we went on to develop a metaphysical rationale to link pragmatic success with cognitive adequacy. This metaphysical stagesetting is crucial for the validation of the specifically pragmatic line of legitimation adopted here regarding the epistemic methodology of factual knowledge. However, it now becomes clear that the conditions which establish a determinative role for practical considerations in the *cognitive* sphere are certainly *not* appropriate in much of the *normative* sphere. The probative force of pragmatic success is lost here precisely because the needed metaphysical rationale is not, and cannot be forthcoming. Thus when dealing with the assessment of human actions from the *moral* point of view, the *whole range* of human purpose must be clearly taken into account including those outside the characteristically practical sphere. Success in navigating amidst the reefs and shoals of our natural and man-made environment is the key test of cognitive adequacy, but other and larger issues are at stake in the normative domain. Accordingly, one could not properly use a specifically pragmatic line of methodological validation of an approach in ethics: one could not validly argue that some method for validating ethical precepts is (*qua* method) suitable on grounds of its success in exclusively practical terms.

It is consequently worth stressing that the specifically pragmatic mode of legitimation operative throughout most of this book cannot properly be extended across the board. The pragmatic approach is valid only where the range of specifically practical purposes is the controlling factor—as we have argued to be the case with respect to the epistemology of factual knowledge. But where—as in ethics and other normative areas—the relevant range of human purposes transcends the sphere of the practical considerations that relate to our material welfare pure and simple, a specifically pragmatic analysis is not appropriate. (From the present standpoint, a fundamental reason why ethics is in some measure autonomous of the realm of facts lies precisely in this, that the limited considerations determinative with respect to the latter are only one among other factors of which the former must take appropriate account.)

Recognition of the fragmentary and restricted scope of considerations of welfare and well-being in the over-all sphere of human teleology indicates why a pragmatically oriented validation of specifically *cognitive* methodology cannot be carried over as a principle of legitimation in the further reaches of the *normative* domain. The pragmatic method is a powerful instrument, but its power inheres in its very nature as a special-purpose device and is confined within the definite boundaries delimiting its range of effective operation.[3]

[3] Some of the considerations of this section are set out in fuller detail in the final two chapters of the author's *The Primacy of Practice* (Oxford, 1973), and its themes are also touched upon in his book on *Welfare* (Pittsburgh, 1972).

Chapter XVII

HISTORICAL PERSPECTIVES ON PRAGMATIST THOUGHT

Pragmatism is often seen as a characteristically American philosophy, sprung full-blown from the head of Peirce (on the basis of some suggestive remarks in Kant). This view is quite mistaken. Pragmatism has more complex and ancient antecedents, and its genealogy runs along a more elongated and more circuitous course. William James was quite right to speak of it as "a new name for ancient ways of thought."

The theory doubtless has its ultimate roots in the teachings of Protagoras (b. ca. 481 B.C.[1]) and the Sophists. But in the form in which we can distinctly recognize it, it arises out of the Platonic distinction between the realm of true knowledge (*espistēmē*) and that of mere opinion (*doxa*).[2] Plato held that cognitions of the inferior, merely opinionate grade—concerned with the sensed objects of our common-life world—are all very well for the conduct of practical workaday affairs attuned to the needs of those who (in the language of the Allegory of the Cave of Book VII of the *Republic*) are chained as prisoners to the exigencies of man's everyday corporeal life. But they will not begin to satisfy the intellectual demands of the philosopher in search for theoretically adequate knowledge. This Platonic contrast between philosophically genuine Knowledge (with capital K) and the philosophical insufficiency of the pseudo-"knowledge" of man's commonplace life provided grist for the mill not only to the Greek Sceptics who came to view the entire quest for capital-K Knowledge as quixotic, but also to those few ancient proto-pragmatists who urged that knowledge attuned to the needs of life is in fact quite good enough—indeed is all we have any right to ask for.

[1] See David Glidden, "Protagorean Relativism and the Cyrenaics" in N. Rescher (ed.), *Studies in Epistemology* (Oxford, 1975; *American Philosopical Quarterly* Monograph No. 9), pp. 113–40.

[2] Think especially of the incalculably influential model of the "divided line" classification of knowledge in the *Republic*, VI, 509d6–511e5.

The actual development of this form of theory began with the founder of the Sceptical school, Pyrrho (365–257 B.C.). He was profoundly impressed with the contradictory deliverances of the senses and the various cognitively negative implications of sensory illusions. On this (essentially Platonic) foundation he based, not the Platonic conclusion that, since genuine (certain) knowledge cannot be based on a sensory foundation, true knowledge of the world is to be had by reason alone, but rather the radical conclusion that any true knowledge of the world is altogether and totally unattainable. However, since we exist *in medias res* within a world-setting and must *act* on this basis, the rational (or "wise") man will guide his action not by what he *knows* of the world (for he knows nothing!), but rather by following the most *plausible-or-probable* appearances, constantly realizing that his action does not rest on any certainty regarding the real nature of things. For Pyrrho, such reliance on the plausible or probable is clearly a philosophically regrettable second-best, *faute de mieux* procedure that is unavoidable, given the unattainability of real knowledge. An action-facilitating acquiescence in the merely plausible or probable is—as seen by Pyrrho and his followers—a poor, albeit inevitable compromise forced by the unavailability of *real* knowledge owing to the inaccessibility of theoretical truth.[3]

The Pyrrhonian Archesilaus (315–241 B.C.) injected a heavy infusion of such sceptical ideas and arguments into the teachings of the Platonic Academy, of which he become the head. His main target was the Stoic foundationalist doctrine that man's empirical knowledge of the world rests on decisive impressions (*phantasia kataleptikē*).[4] Since genuine knowledge is unavailable, the rational man must, at the theoretical level at any rate, maintain a suspension of judgement (*epochē*). But this agnosticism need not paralyze action. For rational action need not rest on certain knowledge: given the unavailability of genuine *epistēmē*, it is quite proper to rely on the merely *eulogon* (reasonable), which one can support with good reasons agreeing with and supporting

---

[3] This brief sketch in the main follows E. Zeller, *The Stoics, Epicureaus and Sceptics* (tr. O. J. Reichel), revised ed. (New York, 1962), pp. 518–527; see especially p. 526.

[4] A useful recent discussion of the Stoic doctrine is F. H. Sandbach, "*Phantasia Kataleptikē*" in A. A. Long (ed.), *Problems in Stoicism* (London, 1971), pp. 9–21.

each other (even as a rope of suitably intertwined but individually weak strands can support a heavy burden). Accordingly, Archesilaus espoused what is, in effect, a criteriological coherence theory of *presumptive*—rather than certain—*truth*. Such *eulogon*-validating reasons are not theoretically conclusive, but are sufficient to provide effective guidance for our practical action (*praxis*). It is a crucial consideration here that *certain* knowledge is simply not required for rationally appropriate *praxis*, because plausibility and supportive consonance are perfectly sufficient.[5] To Archesilaus belongs the undying merit of having fathered a coherence theory of (presumptive) truth oriented towards the needs of the practical domain.

Carneades (213–129 B.C.) who also headed the Academy in his day, gave the theory of his eminent predecessor a decisively positive twist. Not only Pyrrho but even Archesilaus had accentuated the negative, stressing the inaccessibility of theoretically decisive knowledge as sought by the Stoics. Carneades in effect took the view that it is futile to hanker after the impossible. He taught that, if *certain* factual capital-K Knowledge is indeed theoretically impossible—because factual knowledge must always ultimately rest on inherently fallible sense-experience— then we must focus our attention on the question of the best sort of knowledge we can possibly hope actually to get. For Carneades, the idea—operative throughout the Sceptical tradition—that there are judgments on which (whatever their theoretical imperfection) the rational man can act with assured confidence was no longer a reluctant concession, but rather a crucially important fact. Carneades thus was the first and virtually the only Greek thinker to accord imperfect and defeasible knowledge a place of central importance and deserved dignity in the epistemic scheme of things. Viewing absolute truth as an unrealizable chimera, he undertook a detailed analysis of the nature of attainable because *apparent* truth (*alēthē phainesthai*) in the empirical sphere. He analyzed in depth its operative criteria, viz., being plausible (*pithanē*), and uncontroverted (*aperispastos*), and coherent (*periōdeumenē*). Each of these three factors corresponds to conditions whose workings were analyzed in considerable detail by Carneades who in this way developed—alone among the ancients —a sophisticated theory of the degrees of verisimilitude of man's

[5] This summary is based on Zeller, *op. cit.*, pp. 523–4.

putative knowledge. Judgments that meet the various fundamental criteria—though still not certain and irrefutable—represent seeming-truths of the strongest available kind. The rational man is warranted not only in acting on them with assured confidence, but in accepting them as satisfying all reasonable demands for knowledge.[6] With his eyes constantly directed towards the demands of rational *praxis*, Carneades developed along subtle and sophisticated lines the more schematic conception of Archesilaus of a coherence criterion of truth—not *absolute* truth, to be sure, but rather of what is *true-for-all-reasonable-purposes*, reasonable theoretical purposes included.

Thus in summary retropsect, six ideas are paramount in the thought of the Academic Sceptics:

(1) That the Stoic quest for certain foundations for factual knowledge is fruitless.

(2) That *certain knowledge* in the sense of the Stoics cannot be attained in the factual area.

(3) That the Stoic foundationalism must consequently be abandoned as representing a bankrupt epistemic program.

(4) That accordingly a shift in preoccupation is indicated in moving from the quest for certain and theoretically unimpeachable knowledge, to a search for *presumptive truth*.

(5) That such truth will not *and need not* be adequate to any hyperbolic demands of abstract theory; it suffices for presumptive truth to answer to the needs of the rational guidance of action (*praxis*).

(6) That a Coherence Theory of (presumptive) truth based on the tests of plausibility and coherence can provide the necessary mechanism for this purpose.

Throughout this tradition runs the idea that the "knowledge" attainable by man is good enough for practice (initially conceived of as *mere* practice—but ultimately broadened to comprise cognitive practice as well). To be sure, it cannot achieve rigorously theoretical validity. Still, our "knowledge"—albeit not absolutely true and flawless from a hyperbolically theoretical point of view—can indeed attain to *presumptive* truth. The pivotal idea of this tradition is represented by the view that: *If a thesis is presumptively*

[6] See E. Zeller, *op. cit.*, pp. 553–6.

true, then it will serve the rational man with an adequate basis for practice. Accordingly, the merely presumptively true (*eulogon*) is such that the rational man is warranted in basing his action upon it with every reasonable expectation of success.

The teachings of the Academic Sceptics were taken up and revitalized by the "Mitigated Sceptics" of the 17th Century. Marin Mersenne (1588–1648) stands out as the prime figure here. He taught that even if we grant the sceptics that theoretically failproof knowledge of the world is inaccessible, still the destructive force of an extreme Pyrrhonism is deflected by the crucial consideration that man can obtain information about the world adequate to the whole range of his practical purposes:

> Mersenne's contention was that, epistemologically, there was no solution to the sceptical crisis. But this did not deny the fact that in practice we do have knowledge, that is, reliable information about the world around us. We may not be able to establish [with demonstrative certainty] that there really is a world, or that it actually has the properties we experience, but we can develop sciences of appearances which have pragmatic value, and whose laws and findings are not doubtful except in a fundamental epistemological sense.[7]

This "mitigated" or constructive scepticism of Mersenne— adopted and extended by his fellow priests Pierre Gassendi (1592–1655; his best friend), Simon Foucher (1644–1696), and others in what might be called the French school of 17th century scepticism—faithfully reflects and restores the leading idea of the Academic Sceptics of a fundamental duality between theoretical and practical certainty and the epistemic sufficiency of the latter despite the inaccessibility of the former. The position of this French school was taken over *in toto* by David Hume and became in his hands a central theme of the subequent tradition.

Hume's own scepticism is indeed cast in the classical mould of the ancient Academics:

> The great subverter of Pyrrhonism, or the excessive principles of skepticism, is action, and employment, and the occupations

[7] R. H. Popkin, *The History of Scepticism from Erasmus to Descartes* (Assen, 1964), p. 142.

of common life. These principles may flourish and triumph in the schools, where it is indeed difficult, if not impossible, to refute them. . . . The skeptic, therefore, had better keep within his proper sphere and display those *philosophical* objections which arise from more profound researches. . . . For here is the chief and most confounding objection to *excessive* skepticism, that no durable good can ever result from it while it remains in its full force and vigor. . . . But a *Pyrrhonian* cannot expect that his philosophy will have any constant influence on the mind or, if it had, that its influence would be beneficial to society. On the contrary, he must acknowledge, if he will acknowledge anything, that all human life must perish were his principles universally and steadily to prevail. All discourse, all action would immediately cease, and men remain in a total lethargy till the necessities of nature, unsatisfied, put an end to their miserable existence. It is true, so fatal an event is very little to be dreaded. Nature is always too strong for principle. (*Inquiry*, Sect. XII, Pt. ii.)

The sobering winds of demands of practical life are not only permitted but required by Hume to blow across the hotbed plains of sceptical theorizing. For him, the reach of reason is emphatically limited, creating a need to let "our nature" and the practical demands of life predominate where issues of credence are concerned, so that rational belief "is more properly an act of the sensitive than of the cogitative part of our natures" (*Treatise*, Bk. I Pt. IV, Sect. 2). Note, however, that Hume and the moderns generally do not go so far as to manifest any interest in developing—as Carneades had done—the detailed structure of a theory of knowledge (or quasi-knowledge) as attuned to and justified in terms of reference to practice.

Hume's contrast between on the one hand an all-out, doctrinnaire, *Pyrrhonic* scepticism (as he termed it)—a scepticism which, unlike his own, is total and absolute—and on the other hand a mitigated, *Academic* scepticism, one that stops at the borders of practice, is based on setting up a straw man. Certainly *all* of the ancient Sceptics, Pyrrho included, and even the recent quasi-sceptics such as Descartes, were—like Hume himself—perfectly prepared to insulate the issues of ordinary-life activities against interference from the side of sceptical theorizing.

The Humean form of scepticism had a long and distinguished history in the British tradition in philosophy—indeed it can still be found, virtually intact, playing a limited but clearly discernible role in the philosophy of F. H. Bradley.[8] (Its influence was not confined to British philosophy alone, but was present in its American transplantation as well: Benjamin Franklin, for example, viewed utility as a mark of truth.) Throughout these later manifestations we have a continuation of the central doctrine of the Academic Sceptics: that while theoretically adequate Knowledge—secure against all possibility of criticism—is found unattainable, there is a mode of attenuated (or at any rate less than theoretically adequate) "knowledge" which suffices for the guidance of human action within the purposive framework of common-life *praxis*.

To be sure, this sceptical doctrine—which operates from the antiquity of Plato and the Academic Sceptics to the time of Bradley—stops well short of an actual pragmatism. It goes little further than to maintain the principle: *If a thesis is presumptively true, then it will serve for practice.* For the transition to pragmatism proper we need a Kant-reminiscent Copernican *inversion* of this principle into the form: *If a thesis serves efficiently for practice, then it deserves to be acknowledged as presumptively true.* With this inversion one effectively recognizes success (or practical efficacy

[8] Bradley is in essentials a Pyrrhonist on the issue of knowledge. He contrasts our ordinary, everyday, common life "knowledge" with true or genuine, theoretically satisfactory and philosophically adequate knowledge. The latter is in fact unattainable for us (for all our vaunted knowledge is enmeshed in incoherence), the former is sufficient to guide our action and to govern effectively the pratice of common life:

> This [full explicitness and express intelligibility of formulation] I take to be the way of philosophy, of any philosophy which seeks to be consistent. It is not the way of life or of common knowledge....Outside of philosophy there is no consistent course but to accept the unintelligible, and to use in its service whatever ideas seem, however inconsistently to work best. And against this position, while it is true to itself, I have nothing to say....(*Essays on Truth and Reality* [Oxford, 1914], p. 235.)

Authentic Knowledge is what the philosopher seeks for. Everyday "knowledge" is by its standard inadequate and imperfect. But this sort of "knowledge" is all we can attain in practice, and it suffices (all its imperfections notwithstanding) for the guidance of the practical affairs of life. In all these respects Bradley is at one with Pyrrho.

or utility) as a *criterion* of validity. Utility is now elevated from the status of a mere *consequence* that results from being true to that of the testing-standard of correctness, its very *arbiter* and hall-mark. Only with this inversion do we arrive at a full-fledged pragmatism. This step was taken by C. S. Peirce with respect to concepts and by William James with respect to beliefs.

Such an inversion required a step of great nerve and daring. For it accords to considerations of praxis and human action a status coordinate with if not predominant over considerations of theory: it elevates *praxis* to the status of an arbiter over *theoria* and *epistēmē*.

The way towards this crucial step was paved by Immanuel Kant. In the *Critique of Pure Reason*, Kant stressed the limits of theoretical reason and carved out a role for practical reason that transgressed these limits. He accorded to characteristically practical and, from the angle of theory, *imperfect* considerations a central role in the guidance of human action:

> In the transcendental employment of reason, on the other hand, while *opining* is doubtless too weak a term . . . the term *knowing* is too strong. . . . For the subjective grounds upon which we may hold something to be true, such as those which are able to produce belief, are not permissible in speculative questions, inasmuch as they do not hold independently of all empirical support. . . . But it is only from a *practical point of view* that the theoretically insufficient holding of a thing to be true can be termed *believing*. . . . The physician must do something for a patient in danger, but does not know the nature of his illness. He observes the symptoms, and if he can find no more likely alternative, judges it to be a case of phthisis. Now even in his own estimation his belief is contingent only; another observer might perhaps come to a sounder conclusion. Such contingent belief which [notwithstanding its imperfect basis] yet forms the ground for the actual employment of means to certain actions, I entitle *pragmatic belief*. (CPR, A 824=B 852; tr. N. Kemp Smith.)

In this passage—approvingly cited by Peirce and significantly influential upon him—Kant clearly stresses the action-guiding role of certain theoretically underdetermined beliefs. But, of course, larger issues loom in the background. The whole aim of Kant's second Critique is, after all, to establish that in the sphere of human agency and action the practical purposes and needs of men can play a determinative role with respect to cognitive issues.

For Kant, the primacy of practical considerations is thus established over a large and important area. Nevertheless, despite its scope and significance, this area is still confined within definite limits, limits from which the domain of pure and theoretical reason itself is definitely excluded. Though Kant maintained the primacy of practical over theoretical reason, he restricted this primacy to the sphere of human action and interaction, the domain of reason in the service of man's practical concerns in the domain of *praxis*. Kant expressly exempted theoretical reason itself from any impingement by practical considerations. The further aggrandizement of practical reason into the area of theoretical reason—a step crucial to the development of a full-blown pragmatism—had to await the efforts of post-Kantian thinkers, Arthur Schopenhauer in particular.

Schopenhauer's leading thesis in the relevant regards was that the analysis of the most general concepts in whose terms we contemplate and discuss the contents of our experience (concepts which Schopenhauer characterized as "ideas of reflection" or "ideas of ideas" [*Vorstellungen von Vorstellungen*]) shows these ideas to afford a comprehensive thought-framework which systematizes our characterization of reality. And further analysis reveals the crucial point that this framework has an essentially practical *ratio essendi*. By enabling us to perceive intelligently, record, generalize, theorize, learn from experience, etc., our intellectual tools serve the interests of the practical necessities of life. To "understand" what goes on in the world is to grasp it in terms of its generic interrelations as causes and effects and so to see them in terms of their potential uses by or implications for our agency—in short as possible means for the gratification of the will. Schopenhauer thus maintained a generally instrumentalist view of human thinking, and taught that the intellect is altogether the servant of the will.

This approach received substantial reinforcement in the teachings of Friedrich Nietzsche, who stressed the evolutionary dimension of cognitive effort. Opposing the quest for comfortable certainties, Nietzsche attacked all claims to theoretical adequacy or finality by an intellect evolved on the service of man's biological needs.

The Schopenhauerian thesis that the intellect is universally subordinate to the will—not just in the sphere of action, as for Kant, but in the intellectual sphere as well—was elaborated by R. H. Lotze[9] and Christoph Sigwart.[10] From these writers the doctrine of the centrality of practice moves on the German side to those neo-Kantian thinkers—such as Hans Vaihinger[11] and Georg Simmel[12]—who stressed the dominance of practical over theoretical reason, and on the American side through Peirce and James to the later pragmatists.[13]

One final observation seems worth making. Historians of philosophy have tended to ignore the profound similarity between the basic conception of utilitarian ethics (the "act utilitarian" contention that an action is right if its consequences redound to "the greatest good of the greatest number") and the fundamental idea of the thesis-oriented version of the pragmatic theory of truth (that an empirical claim is correct if its acceptance is maximally benefit-producing). Both theories envisage just the same utility-maximization model. Indeed, when "acceptance as true" is viewed as an *action*, the pragmatic theory of truth in its Jamesian version simply passes over into a special application of act-utilitarianism, once one adds the deeply Jamesian idea that one has a *right* to espouse as true what one morally "ought" (now understood in essentially utilitarian terms) to accept. That this confluence with utilitarian ideas exercised any influence upon the his-

---

[9] In the 1880's James considered Lotze the "deepest philosopher" of the day. See R. B. Perry, *The Thought and Character of William James*, Briefer Version (Cambridge, Mass., 1948), p. 329.

[10] See Pt. III of his *Logic*, tr. by H. Dendy (London, 1895; orig. German ed. Leipzig, 1878).

[11] Vaihinger was not a one-track Kantian, but drank deep at the font of Schopenhauer, whose work he greatly admired. Nor can Vaihinger be assimilated to pragmatism straightforwardly, because in stressing the utility of expressly false fictions he expressly barred the way to construing utility as a token of truth. Cf. *The Philosophy of "As If,"* tr. C. K. Ogden (London, 1924), p. viii.

[12] See especially his important paper "Ueber eine Beziehung der Selectionslehre zur Erkenntnistheorie," *Archiv für systematische Philosophie und Soziologie*, vol. 1 (1895), pp. 34–45.

[13] James explicitly mentions Sigwart with approval.

torical development of pragmatism in the thought, at any rate, of William James seems to me more than likely, given his early flirtations with this doctrine and his ongoing admiration for the work of J. S. Mill. (In an early letter James spoke of being "poisoned with Utilitarian venom.") At any rate, it seems not far from doctrinal accuracy to characterize pragmatism, in its Jamesian version, at least, as tantamount to cognitive utilitarianism.

This invocation of utilitarianism is useful as a reminder that the pragmatists' basic conception of *practical consequences* (i.e., *their* version of "utility") itself posed a problem—for, like their utilitarian confrères, the pragmatists never came to agreement on the interpretation of their basic concept. By the "practical consequences" of the acceptance of an idea, Peirce meant (except perhaps in some parts of his later work) the consequences for *experimental* practice: "experimental effects" or "observational results." For Peirce, the meaning of a proposition is determined by the essentially positivist criterion of its experimentally experiential consequences in strictly *observational* terms. For William James, however (in most passages outside some late papers), the meaning of a thesis is determined in terms of its experiential consequences in a far wider sense, namely in essentially *affective* terms.[14]

The Peircean condition looks to *cognitive* results in terms of *observation* (and has effective implications only via the coordinative principle that pleasure and dismay result from the meeting or frustration of our observational expectations); the Jamesian condition expressly looks to the actual *affective* results in terms of the over-all *experiences* that ensue on implementing action (and thus has cognitive implications only by way of this selfsame coordinative principle). Thus these two major pragmatists never reached a meeting of minds regarding the import of their stress on "practical consequences." This indecisiveness, of course, has a crucial bearing on the very nature of the doctrine at issue, for it makes a decisive difference whether the satisfactory consequences at issue are cognitive and wholly theory-oriented, or also affective and oriented to the ramifications of action.

Throughout the preceding discussion, our dealings have been with that tradition of pragmatism which stresses the relationship

[14] On this issue cf. Charles Madden, *Chauncey Wright and the Foundations of Pragmatism* (Seattle, 1963), p. 79.

between the practical *utility* of beliefs and their *truth*, ranging from the Platonic/Sceptical distinction between theoretical certainty and experiental adequacy to the Jamesian view of successful practice as test-criterion of factual truth. Amongst the strands of this tradition there runs yet another which, though beside the mainstream of present purpose must yet be mentioned, the idea of "effective practice" as *a standard of meaningfulness and a test of meaning* (rather than of truth). This line of thought—revolving about the implications of a thesis for *praxis* as a measure of its meaning—runs from Glanvill, Hume, 19th Century Positivism, and Peirce, through to the Logical Positivists and Operationalists of the inter-war period of the present century. It represents an intrinsically interesting and important tradition, but one that is somewhat beside the main point of present concern with the pragmatic theory of *truth*.

It would, however, be a serious fault to omit mention of another relevant tradition of pragmatic thinking. In his *Theses on Feuerbach* (1845), Karl Marx flatly maintained that *his* materialism (unlike previous materialisms) proposed to stress the active side of human cognition: "The question whether objective truth characterizes human thinking is not a question of theory, but a practical question. The truth, i.e., reality and power, of thought must be demonstrated in practice." And this perspective indicates the cognitive decisiveness of the factor of control: "Philosophers have only *interpreted* the world in various ways, but the real task is to *change* it."[15] Throughout his writings, Marx clearly insists on taking *praxis*, and in particular the sector of its social and

---

[15] In the *Dialectics of Nature*, Engels develops this point somewhat more fully:

> Natural science and philosophy have up to now quite ignored the influence of man's activity on his thought. They know only nature on the one side, ideas on the other. But it is precisely the alteration of *nature by men*, not nature as such in isolation, which is the most essential and immediate basis of human thought. Man's intelligence has increased proportionately as he has learned to transform nature. (Tr. by C. Dutt [New York, 1940], p. 172.)

For a discussion of Marx's theory see F. Chatelet, *Logos et praxis: Recherches sur la signification théoretique du Marxisme* (Paris, 1962), as well as Alfred Schmidt, *The Concept of Nature in Marx* (London, 1971).

economic applications, as the appropriate touchstone of theoretical cognition.

Marx's ideas regarding the role of practice and its relation to theory have had a vast subsequent influence (some of it upon otherwise emphatically non-Marxist thinkers such as Max Scheler). A good survey of the historical issues from a Marxist perspective is given in Nicholas Lobkowicz's *Theory and Practice* (Notre Dame, 1967). And the historical situation is also dealt with interestingly in Richard Bernstein's *Praxis and Action* (Philadelphia, 1971).

Important recent developments of praxis-oriented philosophy within a neo-Marxist frame of reference are represented by Tadeusz Kotarbinski in Poland and Jürgen Habermas in Germany. Kotarbinski has endeavoured to put the theory of *praxis* on a systematic basis within a special discipline he designates as *praxiology*.[16] Habermas has pursued the concept of *praxis* deeply into the domain of the sociological implications of technology.[17]

Whether this Marx-originating tendency of praxis-oriented thinking has exerted any significant influence upon the pragmatic tradition of Peirce and James (at any rate before Dewey) is not really to the point of present purpose. What has concerned us throughout this discussion is, after all, the history not of a particular "school," but of a doctrine or tendency of thought—the idea of the controlling role of the demands of practical life as the ultimate arbiter of cognitive adequacy. And if we wish to avoid undue parochialism, we must admit that the claim of the European Marxists upon this fundamental idea is every bit as good as that of the American pragmatists. Abstractly speaking, it seems to be an approach particularly congenial to those in whose thinking *economic* ideas are particularly prominent, be these ideas of capitalistic or of communistic provenience.

[16] See his *Praxiology: An Introduction to the Sciences of Efficient Action* (Oxford, 1965). See also K. Alsleben and H. Wehrstedt (eds), *Praxeologie* (Quickborn, 1966).
[17] See his books *Theorie und Praxis* (Berlin, 1963), *Technik und Wissenschaft als "Ideologie"* (Frankfurt, 1968), and also "Knowledge and Interest," *Inquiry*, vol. 9 (1966), pp. 285–300.

NAME INDEX

SUBJECT INDEX